NICKERSON'S
FOUR-STAR
MANAGEMENT
WORKSHOP

S0-ACJ-849

NICKERSON'S
FOUR-STAR MANAGEMENT WORKSHOP

PAT NICKERSON

PRENTICE HALL
Englewood Cliffs, New Jersey 07632

Prentice-Hall International (UK) Limited, *London*
Prentice-Hall of Australia Pty. Limited, *Sydney*
Prentice-Hall Canada, Inc., *Toronto*
Prentice-Hall Hispanoamericana, S.A., *Mexico*
Prentice-Hall of India Private Limited, *New Delhi*
Prentice-Hall of Japan, Inc., *Tokyo*
Simon & Schuster Asia Pte. Ltd., *Singapore*
Editora Prentice-Hall do Brasil, Ltda., *Rio de Janeiro*

10 9 8 7 6 5 4 3 2 1

Library of Congress Cataloging-in-Publication Data

Nickerson, Pat.
[Four-star management workshop]
Nickerson's four-star management workshop / by Pat Nickerson.

p. cm.
Includes index.
ISBN 0-13-622309-5
1. Management—Miscellanea. I. Title. II. Title: Four star management workshop.
HD38.N48 1988
658—dc19 88-28615
CIP

ISBN 0-13-622309-5

ISBN 0-13-622341-9 PBK

To Ken

Here's a book you don't just *read*, you interact with it and use it whenever you need it. The *Four-Star Management Workshop* gives you hundreds of management questions asked and answered by business people from many nations and all walks of business, industry, and government.

You're invited to evaluate the answers they gave each other at my management seminars, or to chip in better ideas of your own. In fact, if you've ever overheard a spirited management conversation, and itched to interject your own ideas, you already know how to use this book.

You're encouraged to rate people's answers on the familiar four-star rating system used in movie and theatre reviews. You'll award:

★★★★ To the most astute approach. Shrewd, politically aware, fast, or practical.

★★★ For workable answers even if they're somewhat pedestrian.

★★ For replies that sound better in theory than in practice, with obvious risks left uncovered.

★ For ill-advised or dangerous ideas, even if they are often repeated in management circles.

Use this book to gauge your management maturity against the ideas of other managers from Jacksonville to Geneva, Seattle to Sydney, L.A. to London.

HOW TO USE THE BOOK

You'll find the questions listed in the table of contents, and indexed at the back of the text for easy reference. Whatever your specialty—small or big business, finance, distribution, transportation, public service, health care, education, or the military—you'll find items of interest in every chapter.

Other features of the book include:

Nickerson's Recommendations
Wherever audience response fails to turn up a four-star answer, I've constructed a solution for astute managers, or pushed a three-star answer a step further.

Comments
Wherever discussion or research produces a special proviso or an offshoot issue, I've included these in comments throughout the text.

Fine Tuning
Following each set of questions and answers on a topic, I offer consolidated suggestions for further refining your approach, or for firming up principles to use when the classic problems keep arising. *Fine Tuning* also contains techniques to install in your everyday operation. Consult the index for a list of the many techniques outlined in the book.

Checklists
Each chapter closes with one or more quick-reference checklists giving the high-points of the chapter in short form and getting you answers when you need them in a hurry.

LOOK WHO'S TALKING

The book is meant to be kept handy as you face new problems in dealing with people, projects, or internal politics. If you're relatively new to business you'll gain quickly what others took years to learn. If you're an old hand, but find you are repeating yourself, you'll see some new arguments and ideas that may reignite your passion for management.

The people who took part in these seminar Q & A sessions came from every level of management: manufacturing, sales, finance, research, administration, personnel, teaching, engineering, computers, distribution, transport, medicine, government, military, agriculture, communications, and property management. Some were relatively inexperienced; others were old pros. You'll find your counterparts on many pages.

MEASURE YOUR MANAGEMENT WISDOM AGAINST THEIRS

Business people attending a seminar are often anxious at first. They've left a big day's work back at the office and they worry that their time will be wasted in too general a day. Managers from small companies don't think they have much in common with those from industrial giants. The profitmakers and nonprofit outfits think they have little to gain from one another. I want to prove the opposite. So I set them to writing down their most pressing problems—getting everyone to reply to three or four questions, anonymously and under pressure. In this high-speed "contest" atmosphere, everyone wakes up, gets to play expert, and everyone learns, as much from disagreeing, as from seeing eye-to-eye with others. My job is then to referee—using my own 25-years'-plus experience in business here and abroad—and to gain consensus on important issues.

When I go into companies for "on-site" seminars, I usually offer this technique. Co-workers learn how smart and supportive they can be. They get insights about each other's strengths that can work magic in team-building.

If you've felt isolated lately—if you're feeling some career "blahs" coming on, you may like what you read, and learn again that common sense is not common, and that there are choices beyond the customary.

THE PAYOFF FOR YOU

From the first questions onward, you'll find you are not alone. You'll get sensitive answers from people who've lived through the same problems that bother you. You'll recognize some new options. You'll get some practical pencil-and-paper or group *techniques* to work out answers for yourself. You'll revive your sense of humor and get a laugh or two, along the way.

The book is meant to help you find, not fight, your best management instincts. To help you achieve or regain the mastery, fluidity, and excitement that come from working in a job or profession that really suits your talents and lets you make a difference. In the right job, your work can be near play. My hope is that your involvement with this book will help put the joy back in your job.

Working with these lively seminar groups, and sharing their ideas and mine with you has put extra joy into the years spent writing this book.

Pat Nickerson
San Diego

ABOUT THE AUTHOR

Pat Nickerson is president of EBI, *Education for Business and Industry*, a management training company. She and her staff lecture daily for *Dun & Bradstreet* in America, and have given frequent lecture tours throughout Europe, the Mid-East, and Australia for EBI.

More than 100,000 managers have been through her seminars, including the currently popular Managing Multiple Priorities.^{sm} The press has called her "a gifted teacher . . . street smart, fast-paced, and funny."

With a bachelor's in English and a master's degree in Public Communications from Emmanuel College and Boston University, she spent her early career in management for a major retailer, produced television programs for WGBH-TV, and managed a London training company before she and her husband formed their own company, *EBI Limited*, in London in 1971, to import American know-how to Europe.

She began lecturing on management in 1976 and moved her company back to the United States in 1980.

Pat has written for *BIZ* magazine, has appeared on PBS business shows, speaks at major conventions, and numbers among her many client organizations American Airlines, AT&T, Boston City Hospital, Hershey Foods, IBM, Los Angeles County, New York State, Rochester Institute of Technology, Sheraton Hotels, Sovran Bank, Supermarkets General, as well as the U.S. Army, Air Force, Navy, NASA, EPA, Federal Reserve Bank, Dept. of Labor, U.S. Treasury, and many not-for-profit organizations: school systems, churches, and associations.

ACKNOWLEDGMENTS

Heartfelt thanks to consultant/lecturer Curtiss Bacon and writer/editor Dorothy Squier for their friendship, support, and advice over the past twenty-five years, and for their devoted help on this book. To Evangeline McLaughlin small-business owner and confidante for her detailed attention to the text, and to my sanity while writing it.

I'm indebted to old bosses of mine for the wisdom and freedom they shared so unstintingly: to Sidney R. Rabb (now deceased) and Irving W. Rabb of Stop & Shop Inc., for opening their minds to me as a young manager during a period of unparallelled growth, mergers, and acquisitions. To David M. Davis of PBS for the autonomy and guidance he deftly offered when I was a producer for WGBH-TV in Boston in its early days.

To business associates and friends: Mary North, director of our London company EBI for showing me how great managers lead with strength and follow with spirit. To Ernie and Elke Roberts of Bay Business Center, Cape Cod, for showing me how family businesses survive and thrive on courage; to Bill Frohlich of Dun & Bradstreet's Business Education Division for providing a platform and for gathering those big, beautiful audiences for my seminars. To Barbara Koval for lecturing so brilliantly on so many of my seminars to buy me the time to work on this book.

To attorney Steve Howe of Dane Howe & Brown for teaching me more about coolness under fire than any other executive.

To Anne Traynor of American Airlines, Dr. Robert Pearse of Rochester Institute of Technology, and Dr. Jane Zacek of New York State's Governor's Office of Employee Relations for bringing me back again and again to work with their people.

To Prentice Hall's acquisitions editor Bette Schwartzberg for her warm encouragement and firm editing which greatly strengthened this book.

Finally, and primarily, to my husband and partner Ken Nickerson, for twenty-five years of steadying savvy and heartening humor at home, in the office, and on the road.

CONTENTS

SESSION THREE

HOW SHREWD MANAGERS IMPRESS THE BOSS *113*

SESSION FOUR

NEGOTIATE: How to get all you need if you can't get all you want *161*

SESSION SIX

NO-GUILT DELEGATION 265

SESSION SEVEN

HOW ENLIGHTENED BOSSES APPRAISE PERFORMANCE 309

SESSION EIGHT

HOW POWERFUL MANAGERS STAY PROMOTABLE *361*

NICKERSON'S FOUR-STAR MANAGEMENT WORKSHOP

HOW ASTUTE MANAGERS DEAL WITH ANGER: WHEN TO CHOOSE IT, HOW TO USE IT

SESSION

ONE

HOW ASTUTE MANAGERS DEAL WITH ANGER: WHEN TO CHOOSE IT, HOW TO USE IT

INTRODUCTION

Why start a positive-minded management book with the subject of anger? Because business is about the power to get important things done, and anger is the most common emotion you feel each time that power is diminished or threatened. It's the emotion you're asked to control when it arises. But learning to channel it so that it energizes rather than drains you is a key skill that astute managers have developed.

From the podium, I can see them. Impassioned people whose frustrations glow hotly in their faces as they pose questions. I'm relieved when these firebrands "open up" in the relative safety of a seminar; many are at the flashpoint when they arrive. Often, they've been sent by a baffled boss for "renewal." Some stop by at the end of the day to tell me they were ready to throw in the towel until comments by fellow attendees showed them they were not unique. Some come for the courage to quit their jobs, but find options they'd overlooked or choices they'd barely explored. The best of them get the insight that they'd blindly expected the other guy to do all the changing.

Anger is the emotion most visible from the platform, and most obvious, too, in people's written questions and answers. Facing it, helping people with it, keeps every day exciting for me and my colleagues. Of course, lots of happy people attend seminars too. More about them later.

ANGER AT THE BOSS

The most likely target for your anger is the boss. Your expectations may be so high, your boss's veto power so great, your access to the boss so limited that your attempts to get your share of the boss's approval are often thwarted.

If you're like me, you may also wrestle with your own rebelliousness. When I was a young manager, I took part in a companywide personality test designed to match the right people with the right tasks and bosses in our large retailing company. My results showed that I was "authority defiant" at heart, while displaying docile compliance on the surface. This finding jolted me at first, but I came to accept the insights.

An authority-defiant manager stays on permanent alert in the boss's presence, demanding approval, keeping score, judging harshly any shortcomings of character in the senior person. Naturally, this behavior, even when submerged, cannot endear you to the chief and keeps your "vibes" twanging almost audibly. Your tinder is always stacking up, waiting for a spark; the slightest abrasion may start a blaze. (The remedy, for me, was to open my own company. People who have known me in both roles say I make a better boss than a subordinate.)

If you don't want to be an entrepreneur, you can deliberately reduce your sensitivity to boss behavior, silence your stress alarms, and increase your chances of getting all you need (but not all you want) from your bosses. But these mysteries had not penetrated for the four managers who speak now:

1. PUT DOWN

I'm sick of continual putdowns from a powerful VP who has no respect for me as a person and will not support my programs.

A

AUDIENCE RESPONSES

YOUR RATING

________ **a.** *Transfer away from this person's jurisdiction.*

________ **b.** *Get support from your peers. Speak to this manager as his peer, not his subordinate.*

________ **c.** *Ask why his or her way is better.*

________ **d.** *People who resort to personal criticism may lack confidence in their own abilities—they lack self-esteem. Factor this into your acceptance of their remarks. Write out and circulate your proposals before the ogre sees them, to get advance support.*

________ **e.** *Does this person need* your *cooperation and support too? Make a deal.*

	★	★★	★★★	★★★★
RATING	*NO!*	*RISKY*	*BETTER*	*BEST!*

★ **a. Transfer away**

No. If that were easy, you'd have done it. Instead, it's more likely that your specialty puts you correctly in this department; here you must succeed if you are to be judged promotable.

★ **b. Get peer support; sound equal.**

No. Pressure won't help you with the senior executive and will appear suicidal to your peers. Why should they defend you against this powerful senior? They have their own fish to fry.

Don't address VPs as if you were a peer. Instead, face the music. Your most important test now is to meet your boss's requirements.

> *Is this VP your direct boss*? If so, you must express your determination to meet his or her requirements. Make an appointment; sit down and earnestly ask for direction.
>
> *If this VP is someone parallel to or above your boss*, go to your own immediate boss now. Admit you have drawn a VP's fire and ask your boss how you can regroup. Remember, you may have increased your boss's risks and caused embarrassment by your behavior toward a powerful VP. Overcome your fear; get your boss's instructions.

c. Ask why his way better.

No. Asking an adversary "why" would be incendiary. Instead, say: "I want to use the method you prefer. I'd like to know more about its advantages so I can pursue them fully." This is the time to adopt a "learning attitude."

d. People may lack self-esteem. Circulate your ideas.

It's an assumption that people lack self-esteem when they criticize you personally. Why do we focus on the other guy's shortcomings to comfort us when we are in trouble?

Don't waste time trying to fathom this VP's motives. Instead, aim your energies at discovering what he or she wants and deliver it.

Sure, circulate your proposals; this may force you to write out and clarify your ideas. Getting a critique may improve your objectivity before submitting final drafts.

An important point: You can still be productive while "in the doghouse" if you are humble enough to submit your ideas *through* a person in favor. Your immediate boss or a lateral manager who has this VP's approval may be the right person to whom to address your ideas until you are rehabilitated. It hurts to sacrifice credit and keep a low profile. But you learn whether your ideas will fly when detached from you. Once your ideas get approval, your boss or ally can begin giving you credit (or including you). It will take patience to win back acceptance by easy stages, but frontal attacks may only draw more flak.

e. If they need you, make a deal.

If this VP regarded you as one whose support were *needed*, you would not be in the doghouse. Your bartering power is low. Don't remind disgruntled VPs that they *need* you. Instead, show you are eager and able to do things their way. Not a tasty dish—humble pie—but it fends off starvation until you can get back in the chow line. Don't yearn for the head table just now.

Nickerson's Recommendations

For a four-star answer,

- Succeed where you are.
- Sit down with your boss and get direction.
- Ask a mentor to check out your ideas before you submit them higher, until you're on the right track.

2. PASSED OVER

I've been passed over. My boss has broken implied promises. This really was my turn and I'm outraged.

AUDIENCE RESPONSES

YOUR RATING

________ **a.** *Get your anger out, alone.*

________ **b.** *Realize the other person may be better fitted; this need not be a criticism of you. Politically, this is not your turn; the matter is out of your control.*

________ **c.** *Ask why you are not being recognized. Find out your weaknesses and make plans to overcome them.*

________ **d.** *Ask your boss how you can improve your performance.*

________ **e.** *In private, create a new agenda with your boss. What will the boss need next? What does the department need? How can you be matched up with the next available promotion?*

	★	★★	★★★	★★★★
RATING	*NO!*	*RISKY*	*BETTER*	*BEST!*

★★

a. Get your anger out, alone.

It's natural that you're angry; being passed over is a hot trigger for most managers. Ventilating alone is better than doing it before peers. But if it helps to talk to someone, do it in safety. Call a friend—from home—not a company insider but a business-savvy friend who will let you blow off steam and help you brainstorm options. Once calm, you can decide what message you want to give your boss. In any case, now or later, say *nothing* designed to make your boss feel guilty. You don't want to make yourself a *corpus delicti* and force the boss to give you a hasty funeral.

★★★

b. Not your turn, it's too late now.

This is a lower-stress stance. This realist knows your chances of *reversing* this decision are zero. The *next* move up may be yours, however, if you communicate well now.

To feel better quickly, consider this: Even if you feel your technical merit and longevity outstrip the winner's, you may have been outclassed in the political skill department. A frontal attack now won't win you political points, so take *b*'s advice and walk away from this . . . and *toward* the next move.

c. Ask why . . . discover your weaknesses.

No. This would be blaming the victim—yourself. Don't ask "why" on *faits accomplis* . . . this will irritate your boss. Focusing on your weaknesses may demoralize you just now. Instead, focus on future chances. You'll be promoted many more times in your career—just not this time.

d. Discuss improvement plans with your boss.

Like answer *c*, this implies you've failed. Take a "no-fault" stance for the moment (unless you have something *big* to feel guilty about). No point in talking about it, just fix it. Instead, move to answer *e*—which takes you into the future with hope.

 **e. Create a new agenda.**

If you combine this answer with *a* and *b*, in a three-step process, you'll emerge healed and motivated. Here's how you might approach your boss:

> You've been looking at my qualifications recently, and I'd like the benefit of your advice as I prepare for the next quarter (half year, or whatever). I'd like to beef up any areas where I'll need more experience, and I'd like to contribute at full throttle to any projects that are really important. Before you move on to other matters, can I make an appointment for a "directional performance chat"?

Comment: This would also be a good time to add that you will give your full support to the "winner" (especially if you will now be expected to assist or report to that person). Should you be expected to report directly to the "winner" from now on, this will probably be your last chat with the old boss—otherwise, you'll be "end running" your new boss. So be fairly quick about this conversation, or, in a highly structured organization, it will be improper even to begin it.

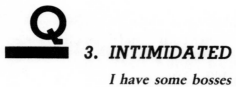

3. *INTIMIDATED*

I have some bosses who are hard, cold, and unpleasant to work for.

AUDIENCE RESPONSES

YOUR RATING

________ **a.** *Avoid them on prickly subjects.*

________ **b.** *Show them your stuff.*

________ **c.** *Don't give them the satisfaction of seeing you ruffled.*

________ **d.** *They may be short on healthy experiences. Look for and magnify their virtues. Live and let live.*

	★	★★	★★★	★★★★
RATING	*NO!*	*RISKY*	*BETTER*	*BEST!*

a. Avoid them on prickly subjects.

No. Learn their views on prickly subjects, especially if these subjects will continue to be important in your work. Avoidance would put you in constant stress and prolong your ignorance.

b. Show your stuff.

Only if you mean giving your best performance, showing enthusiasm, tooting your horn when you triumph, and thanking these bosses for giving you challenging assignments. *No* if you mean showing them you can dish out as good as you get.

c. Don't let them see you ruffled.

This would be stressful, too, if it meant just "stifling yourself." If, on the other hand, you control upset reactions through choice, for your own peace of mind—then yes. "I'm not going to let them see me upset" is not nearly as therapeutic as "I'm not going to make myself vulnerable to upsets."

d. They may be underprivileged. Live and let live.

They may or may *not* be short on good experiences. Avoid speculating on your boss's character flaws. Even if you had evidence, this would not help you deal with these bosses. Instead, spend your energy working on yourself, discovering why you feel so vulnerable.

The *second* part of *d*'s answer is the best: seeing and magnifying the virtues of your bosses is always good advice, particularly when you feel like a fish out of water. You may be in a business where toughness is required. (A competitive, profit-making business facing a downturn cannot be run by Pollyannas. Similarly, a nonprofit business when funding is denied must make sacrifices and painful cuts.) If you can fathom good reasons for the toughness you see, you may learn what it takes to stay the course at your company. "Live and let live" is healthy too. What are you doing about *living* on your job? What are you learning? If you come from a sheltered background, it may be valuable to live through tough times in your organization. It builds strength for the years ahead when you will be in leadership positions.

Comment: If none of the extenuators mentioned in the Analysis apply to your situation, and you still find their style repellent, shop around for a better organization. Leave only when your new nest is feathered. Observe impeccable etiquette in giving notice and taking your leave, especially if you work in a narrow specialty and you are likely to encounter these people again. Take care: In interviews or exit ceremonies, do not bad mouth these people. That's how you live and let live in unpleasant work situations.

4. NOT RESPECTED

How do I respond to executives who treat all workers under age 30 as if they were entry-level nobodies?

AUDIENCE RESPONSES

YOUR RATING

_________ **a.** *Some behaviors have to be ignored. Be sure your wardrobe is professional. Delegate jobs no longer appropriate to your level. If recently promoted, let your boss know you have delegated certain work; this is a test.*

_________ **b.** *Maintain a professional attitude. When* told *to do something inappropriate, gently decline; suggest they take it to an appropriate clerk.*

_________ **c.** *Find supporters among managers; ask them to back you on important issues. Be deaf to insults.*

_________ **d.** *Have a management meeting; convey these feelings openly. Explain you are contributing importantly to the business.*

_________ **e.** *Kill them with kindness. Smile. Win them over.*

	★	★★	★★★	★★★★
RATING	*NO!*	*RISKY*	*BETTER*	*BEST!*

★★★★

a. Ignore it. Delegate. Let management know.

A low-stress solution. If you once were "entry level" at this company, take the gentle view that old habits die hard. They "knew you when."

Issue new job descriptions and phone-contact sheets so managers know who handles what now. Also, realize that managers may be following the rules by coming to you with work that you will, of course, delegate to subordinates reporting to you. In many companies, it breaks the chain of command to go straight to clerks without first seeing their boss (you). When they come to you, accept the work and say crisply: "I'll see that one of my people handles this for you." You pass the "chain of command" test.

b. Gently decline.

Yes, but only if the work requested is outside your area. Otherwise, follow solution *a*.

c. Find supporters.

Although you need to build peer support all through your career, do not ask peers to join you in a fight against management on such a subtle issue. You waste your ammo and may need help on operating matters of more immediate moment. Frontal assaults about "principles" won't win you many allies. Be more circumspect about this.

d. Call a management meeting to ventilate.

No. Unless you call management meetings every day, don't call your first "big one" on an issue as volatile and unwinnable as this one.

e. Kill them with kindness, smile.

No. Insincere kindness and smiles through gritted teeth will give you maximum stress and will push your opponents toward sarcastic replies. Your mixed messages will elicit mixed responses.

Comment: Respondents *a* and *b* mentioned professional image. This includes wardrobe, voice, carriage, and official communications—all expressing your political savvy. If you rate high, you may be accepted by the level of management, clients, and contacts whose approval you want. John Molloy's *Live for Success*[1] and Jo Foxworth's *Wising Up*[2] may give you valuable insights into the many critical issues in gaining respect. You'll be able to form your own four-star solution in this case.

[1]John T. Molloy, MOLLOY'S LIVE FOR SUCCESS (New York: Bantam/Perigord Press, 1982).

[2]Jo Foxworth, WISING UP (New York: Delacorte Press, 1980).

ANGER AT PEERS AND CLIENTS

When peers must compete for scarce resources—power, perquisites, attention and approval, budgets, staff, projects, equipment, territories, space, raises, and promotions—each day offers fresh incitements to envy, anger, resentments. Sibling rivalry is alive in each ambiguous situation where no one's power clearly dominates.

It's a tribute to the genuine decency of humans that we get along so happily despite these tensions. Keeping expectations in check seems to be the secret. *Expectations*, learned in the nursery, schools, and early business years must mellow with maturity, or you'll be trapped in anger as circumstances fluctuate.

If you came from a department where work was shared and friends helped friends, you may bring altruistic notions to a department where it's "everyone for himself." You could become a patsy in a unit where self-interest and cynicism have taken root.

If you came from a profit-making company where your deeds distinguished you, you'll be puzzled in a bureaucracy where people compete passionately for titles, carpets, and larger desks. Differences in corporate values can retard the trust-building process that cements good teams together.

Since a peer lacks the clout to punish or reward, you may find it difficult to sue for peace first in a conflict. If you value harmony more than appearances, you may avoid some of the problems expressed in Part Two.

Healthy self-esteem is a prerequisite to empathetic and trustful peer relations.

5. *BADGERED*

I cannot seem to control my hairtrigger responses to co-worker badgering. They start—I escalate.

A

AUDIENCE RESPONSES

YOUR RATING

_________ **a.** *Recognize their differences as being part of the human condition.*

_________ **b.** *Some folks have ego problems. Pretend they don't bother you. Fake it.*

_________ **c.** *Accept some problems as theirs, not yours. When pushed, be assertive.*

	★	★★	★★★	★★★★
RATING	*NO!*	*RISKY*	*BETTER*	*BEST!*

★★ **a. Recognize human differences.**

You should, but it doesn't go far enough. Recognizing is not the same as accepting. This person's problem is not that others goad, but that he or she cannot gain control of inner responses. It is not so important to understand the other person, as to understand yourself. Ask yourself

- Why does badgering bug me more than others?
- Is this badgering reserved for me, or does everyone put up with it?
- What alternative responses have I tried? What would cost less? Laughing along with the badgerer? Saying "Let me write that down"?
- What do they badger me about? Why am I sensitive on that subject?
- Have I tried asking the person, "Tell me what you need exactly"? That might change the pattern just enough to stop the cycle.

Find a response that does not ignite your emotions—treat this more as an experiment in discovery than a conflict.

b. Pretend they don't bother you.

No. Try not to pretend with *yourself*. Work on yourself until they *really* don't bother you. Your short fuse ignites because of your own ego needs. Take care of these needs.

c. Accept some problems as theirs; assert when pushed.

Here's an answer that works. Once you've achieved *b*, you can go on to *c* comfortably. You can accept some problems as *theirs*, as long as you've taken care of the problems that are *yours*. There are low-stress ways to assert in this instance; for example; you might say

> I am interested in any legitimate needs of yours and am willing to listen. What is it you need?

Then, fall silent. Relax and listen as they respond. No hurry to reply: "I'll give that some thought" might be sufficient.

Comment: Because of our egos, we are in a hurry to *settle and win* disputes. If we can give up this pressure which we generate for ourselves, other people's badgering won't damage us. If you exhibit Type A behavior—perfectionism, hurrying, impatience with other people's shortcomings—you may be a target for other people's badgering. In their book *Type A Behavior and Your Heart*, Drs. Friedman and Rosenman recommend that Type A people do exercises to break themselves of "hurry sickness." For example, if you tend to run amber traffic lights, they suggest that you go fully around the block, approach the light again, and *wait*, this time. Tell yourself you are doing something good for your health in learning to ignore "hurry" messages.[3]

When you are calmer, less easily triggered, you are a less tempting target for game players. Try small simple exercises to break yourself of unwarranted perfectionism. Ease off even *one* temper tantrum, for your own sake, and you begin to break the habit. Give yourself a small reward for each provocation you divert—use the energy saved for something that makes you feel accomplished or tranquil.

---

[3]Copyright, © 1975, Meyer Friedman and Ray H. Rosenman, TYPE A BEHAVIOR AND YOUR HEART (New York: Alfred A. Knopf, 1975), p. 264.

6. *PROVOKED BY PANDEMONIUM*

How can I stay calm when everyone around me is going bananas?

A

AUDIENCE RESPONSES

YOUR RATING

_______ **a.** *Say a prayer.*

_______ **b.** *Help people understand that their problems are solvable.*

_______ **c.** *Control your temper. It takes time to learn how.*

_______ **d.** *Call everyone together. Ask everyone to sit still and consider the issues calmly. Get them to map them out on paper. If you have the authority, listen to their views and make a decision in the interest of all.*

	★	★★	★★★	★★★★
RATING	*NO!*	*RISKY*	*BETTER*	*BEST!*

★★★ **a. Pray.**

This suggestion is neither facetious nor wishful. For people with strong religious faith, prayer is an extremely effective calmative. Others simply close their eyes and count to ten. Some perform slow, regular breathing exercises while thinking "I am calm . . . I am calm . . ." on each exhale. Such *centering exercises* help to remove you from the maelstrom until you regain inner quiet. Once calmer, you can begin working on the problem around you if it is your responsibility to do so.

b. Help people see that their problems are solvable.

If not solvable, at least survivable. Often, people get into an uproar because they can see that their expected or most desired solution will elude their grasp. No sense telling them the problem is *solvable* if it is clear their preferred solution is unavailable. Your chore is to convince them that an acceptable or compromise solution may do the job *almost* as well and that *they*, rather than you, can reconstruct the situation for an almost-as-good solution.

c. Control your temper.

I'd like this better if it said "for your own sake."

d. Call everyone together, map out problem, make decision in the interest of all.

This sounds like it ought to calm people down. Some psychologists suggest using a *time-out*; a five-minute break in which everyone returns to base, sits down solo, takes a drink of water, meditates—and then writes down a list of pros and cons, possible options, and so on. As the group leader, you might divide the work load on options: some group members might tackle technical options, some financial, some communication—whatever is needed, so that no member is overwhelmed in the search for solutions. It is easier to start the work after a short time-out.

NICKERSON'S RECOMMENDATION

For a four-star solution, use *d*, with one proviso: The leader need not *decide* in the interest of all. The *group* can actually do this—and will feel more committed to implementing the solution if *they* do it. The leader need only facilitate, gather data from individual lists, summarize, keep the group on track, and take a vote. If people experience strong-fears or anxieties, *accept* these feelings as real: Help people channel their energies into making the best outcome possible for themselves.

7. INSULTED BY CLIENTS

How can I be expected to deal calmly with completely unreasonable, insulting clients in my service-oriented job?

AUDIENCE RESPONSES

YOUR RATING

_________ **a.** *Take the person aside and get the facts.*

_________ **b.** *Invite the person to sit, relax until he or she feels calmer. Then, discuss the problem in private.*

_________ **c.** *Separate the people involved if several are out of control. Emotion feeds on emotion, so don't let too much gather in one space.*

_________ **d.** *Keep in mind that their emotions are not directed at you personally. View the person as "needing to vent fear or frustration." Let the person get it all out. Then work together to define and solve problems or seek options that give relief.*

	★	★★	★★★	★★★★
RATING	*NO!*	*RISKY*	*BETTER*	*BEST!*

7. *INSULTED BY CLIENTS* ANALYSIS

a. Get the facts, in private.

This is prescribed but may be hard to get in certain settings. Especially if the client *wants* to make a scene. You can at least control escalation: Keep your own voice low; keep your body language still. If you say something *accepting*, such as: "This needs our attention" or "We need to sit down and work this out in detail with you" the person may be more willing to accept your offer of privacy or make an appointment for later, when information and options can be researched. Never say: "Calm down!"

b. Sit them down; talk in private.

As in *a*, once you have shown genuine concern, it is easier to get the complainer seated. I've watched health care and social work professionals do this masterfully. Once the party is seated, the "helping professional" offers to go get a glass of water or cup of tea or perhaps a required file. In your *brief* absence, distressed persons are often able to regain composure. By now, they want to. Then, problem solving can begin.

★★★

c. Separate the people.

This is difficult to do if the clients are members of a family or other group. They insist on staying together. If violent or abusive behavior breaks out, you may need the help of security officers to break it up. Usually, though, it is sufficient to assure each person: "You will be heard, and I'd like to begin by interviewing X, and then Y." If you draw a line down the center of a paper, give each person a column, people can see they will get—or are getting—their chance to be heard and that you are taking notes, equitably.

d. Don't take it personally. Let the person vent. Seek options.

Good service in a nutshell. One suggestion: Don't let them "get it *all* out" . . . but do let them get *enough* out to be clear about what they need. Sometimes, if you let angry clients continue their recital of grievances until they are sputtering or repeating, they relive too much of their pain and cannot move forward to solutions. When you judge that they've said enough to make their needs clear, you can often curtail the recital by saying

> Thank you, (name) . . . I can see how serious this is, and we want to get started right away to solve the problems. What do you think is your number one need from among the things you've mentioned?

Comment: Many service-job professionals recognize, among the signs of burnout, a form of paranoia where all clients begin to look abusive. Astute service-job professionals may need to use a *four-step strategy* for maintaining professionalism:

- *Bolster your self-worth*

  Some keep a "Good for Me!" file on past achievements and review it from time to time.

  Others consciously think or write out

  "I am trained to help."

  "I have tools, authority, support."

  "I am going to be all right."

  when they find themselves losing altitude.

- *Enhance empathy*

  Astute professionals look past a person's behavior and see a frustrated human who needs help.

- *Set limits*

  Through training and experience, astute professionals develop a list of unacceptable behaviors and warn clients of the rules.

- *Pursue joint problem solving*

  Professionals don't have to know all the answers. Clients can contribute 50 percent or more to the problem-solving process when told, "We are *both* intelligent and motivated. We will find acceptable solutions *together*."

That's a message as comforting to the speaker as it is to the hearer. I've met public service professionals who create their own self-help tools. One telephone counselor has a sign on his phone cradle: "That's my bread and butter calling." Another has a small sign where only she can see it:

> COMPASSIONATE DETACHMENT
> This problem is *not* about me personally

One seasoned professional, working in the office of CEO at a large service company, gets the "red hot" calls that Client Service has been unable to handle. When her "red phone" rings, she picks it up and says

> Chairman's office. This is Mrs. Scott. I'm *glad* you've called me because I can help you.

She means it. And her words start both parties off feeling calmer and more confident.

PART
THREE

ANGER WITH SUBORDINATES

Despite the powers vested in you, you will find it challenging to lead today's subordinates. Educated and propagandized to high personal aspirations, they've been told they can and should have it all . . . now.

If they have current technical skills, they want to sell them to the company offering the best deal. They're in a hurry, and they know they can become obsolete quickly. Sadly, many recent graduates view companies as a mere continuation of schooling, a place to learn new skills and enhance one's marketability—but not necessarily a place where one must contribute or commit oneself. Except in places of high unemployment, today's workers relish transferability. Platitudes about loyalty to company are largely wasted on today's workers. They must be shown how pursuit of corporate goals will help them to achieve their own. That's healthy.

The newer factor for today's bosses is the higher proportion of workers of all ages using drugs and alcohol. You may be trying to train and lead people who are in a chemical fog. In high-risk industries, regular physicals are finding and forcing some abusers into rehabilitation. On more ordinary jobs, where safety is not a paramount factor, employees may suffer consistent performance drag, sickness, absenteeism, inattention, and scrap, due to chemical abuse.

Nonetheless, you must behave (in the absence of evidence) as if you were leading rational people. Following are a few of the questions that baffled seminar participants.

8. COLD SHOULDERED

I have an employee who shrugs off my help in an offensive manner.

A

AUDIENCE RESPONSES

YOUR RATING

_______ **a.** *Tell him or her how this reaction makes you feel.*

_______ **b.** *Let someone else help him or her.*

_______ **c.** *Present the problem behavior as if it were someone else's. Ask how he or she would solve the problem of dealing with an unreceptive subordinate. Hear the employee out; you may learn about his or her attitudes.*

_______ **d.** *Cite your minimum acceptable performance standards.*

_______ **e.** *Explain that your interest in him is not altruistic. You are trying to save yourself and your company from risk. You insist on having your minimum standards met and are willing to help him do this. There will be negative consequences for failure to meet your standards. Be clear.*

	★	★★	★★★	★★★★
RATING	*NO!*	*RISKY*	*BETTER*	*BEST!*

8. COLD SHOULDERED ANALYSIS

★★ **a. Tell the employee how he or she makes you feel.**
No. Not yet. First, examine how *you* make yourself feel when rejected. Psychologists Ernst Beier and Evans Valens assert that no one can make you feel a certain way; you do it yourself.[4] Face *your* feelings squarely. Are they the feelings of a rejected parent? friend? child? supervisor? You may discover that your feelings toward this worker are not detached enough. You may expect the behavior and response of a family member or a close mentoree, instead of an employee. When you do not seek to influence this person's attitudes and feelings toward you, but only his or her behavior toward the organization, you are in a more detached stance and can ask for the performance you require.

★★★ **b. Let someone else help the employee.**
Yes. You can delegate the training and development of some employees to your lieutenants. There is no obligation to take every single employee under your personal tutelage.

★ **c. Present the employee's problem as if . . . .**
No. Who has time for parables? It isn't important for you to probe attitudes, but you must direct him or her to upgrade job performance.

★★★ **d. Cite your minimum standards.**
Good! Start here.

★★★★ **e. Insist on standards, offer help, show consequences.**
Best answer yet. A complete short course in basic supervision. I would only add: Get up a set of benchmarks with reasonable goals jointly agreed upon, and follow through with this employee. Option *b*: Doing all this through one of your lieutenants is also practical.

[4]Ernst G. Beier and E. G. Valens, Jr., PEOPLE READING: HOW WE CONTROL OTHERS, HOW THEY CONTROL US. (New York: Stein & Day, 1987), Paper.

9. *IRRITATED BY A "KNOW-IT-ALL"*

I have a smart alec employee whose smugness irritates me.

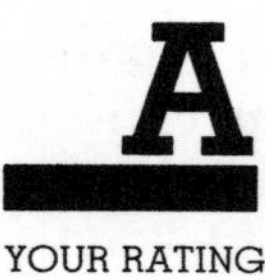

AUDIENCE RESPONSES

YOUR RATING

_________ **a.** *Acknowledge his "wonderfulness" and ask his advice in solving problems. Have him write out his ideas and check them out before submitting them to you.*

_________ **b.** *Counsel this employee. He may be unaware how he comes across.*

_________ **c.** *If you cannot cure this, subtly incorporate this person into a team, and define his role narrowly. The team will elbow him when he's out of line.*

_________ **d.** *Hold regular meetings with all staff members. Emphasize the contributions of each to the common goal. Help him see his niche—that he's not a one-man band.*

	★	★★	★★★	★★★★
RATING	*NO!*	*RISKY*	*BETTER*	*BEST!*

9. *IRRITATED BY A "KNOW-IT-ALL"* ANALYSIS

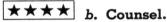

★★ *a.* **Get his "wonderful" advice, in writing, checked out.**

Although the answer is sarcastic in tone, I think it is therapeutic to acknowledge whatever virtues this employee does have. Many "smart alecs" crave the approval you withhold. Give him his due.

No, don't *ask* for his advice. But when he offers it, do insist that his ideas be accompanied by substantive research, risk/benefit data, and comparisons with other options. Learning to document his ideas will upgrade the quality of this employee's creative suggestions.

b. **Counsel.**

Yes. If an employee's manner is offensive, you would cover this in your regular performance reviews by citing specific examples of actions and words (not mere attitudes) that give offense. Ask the employee to suggest which kinds of actions and words would accomplish his ends effectively and compliment him when you see a difference in performance.

c. **Subtly let the team fix it.**

No. While the group may well clobber him for you, this is not their responsibility, and it may waste the group's energy needed for project work. You can delegate training and development to others, but *not* discipline.

d. **Use meetings to show him his niche.**

I'm against using public means to solve private problems. While I am all for regular staff meetings, and they do show people their collaborative roles, they are not the primary means for curing an employee of abrasive behavior. Do this directly. As a rule, keep hidden agendas out of your meetings; they reduce group productivity.

10. DISGUSTED WITH McSWINE

How can I get an employee to respect the job when she doesn't even respect herself?

AUDIENCE RESPONSES

YOUR RATING

______ **a.** *Develop an informal relationship and help this person to develop self-esteem.*

______ **b.** *Make task assignments specific and measurable. Establish goals. Build a sense of accomplishment on the job.*

______ **c.** *You sound baffled. Seek advice from a third party. Is your assessment of this worker shared by others? If there are serious personal problems here, you may be wise to ask your boss or employee relations department about your dilemma.*

	★	★★	★★★	★★★★
RATING	*NO!*	*RISKY*	*BETTER*	*BEST!*

★

a. Develop informal relationship. Help build self-esteem.

No. Here's the "good savior" complex at work. You are not this person's missionary, parent, or psychiatrist.

★★

b. Specific assignments, goals, to build accomplishment.

Yes. You owe specifics to all employees. But to *expect* that these will build a sense of accomplishment is overly optimistic. David McClelland has pointed out in several books that about 10 percent of employees are "indifferent"[5] and will not respond to goals. However, if you set up and document your goal-setting sessions, you can also document this worker's failure to meet them, and move toward discipline or dismissal if required.

★★★★

c. Get advice on your observations, consult boss or employee relations department.

Right. Document performance shortfalls in your formal reviews with this employee. If this person was once a good performer and is now declining, she is not one of McClelland's 10 percenters, but she is experiencing some other problem. Offer your help with any work/technology problems this worker faces, but do not venture into her personal life. Offer her a list of assistance options (inside or outside the company) that address personal, financial, legal, emotional, and family problems. Strongly recommend that she come to you for help with work issues—and that she pursue other required assistance without delay. Follow up to observe any performance improvements. Give encouragement, not advice.

Comment: Many large companies have EAPs (Employee Assistance Programs) to help employees with personal, health, and family issues that may interfere with job per-

[5]David C. McClelland, ASSESSING HUMAN MOTIVATION (New York: General Learning Press, 1971).

formance. If you work in a small company, or an organization with no such help, don't take on this role yourself. Instead, in one of your regular staff meetings—at a time when people are feeling stable (don't pick the week when someone is bereaved or is taking his or her foes to court—that will put pressure on the individual's privacy) ask all group members to bring in data collected in the community about various *non*profit referral services. You can post the collected data without endorsing any particular helpers. This raises the group's consciousness that *any* group of adults will experience the inevitable human problems: financial, family, marital, health, legal, emotional—and that help should be sought from professionals rather than from one's co-workers or supervisors.

11. DEFIED

How should I react to deliberate acts of defiance done in front of other employees?

AUDIENCE RESPONSES

YOUR RATING

________ **a.** *Make your authority clear. Tell him or her there is no need to challenge your authority; it is undisputed. Say that you will listen to problems and proposals if put with human courtesy.*

________ **b.** *Take this employee behind closed doors. Ask if he or she wants to stay here and improve. If so, you are willing to help solve problems within your authority and company policy. Ask for the person's response to that.*

________ **c.** *Ask this employee what he or she wants. Say that the person is damaging staff morale and is testing your patience. Tell him or her to make you a proposal you can accept about his or her future behavior, or you will have to fire the employee for insubordination.*

	★	★★	★★★	★★★★
RATING	*NO!*	*RISKY*	*BETTER*	*BEST!*

★★ **a. Make your authority clear.**

This is a high-stress, authoritarian message more for your own benefit than the employee's. If done on the spot, in the open, it may make you seem threatened, and your opponent more formidable. If authoritarianism is your style, you might do better with

> I'll discuss this matter with you in my office in fifteen minutes. Be there, please.

Then turn and move out of range. I much prefer answers *b* and *c*, because they give more chance of success and serenity for you.

★★★★ **b. Behind closed doors, ask what the person wants; remind person of your authority and company policy; let him or her speak.**

Right. Let the employee do 80 percent of the talking in this "behind closed doors" encounter. Don't hurry with your response. Say that you will think about what has been said and that, meanwhile, you want to see an end to provocative behavior. (Give some examples.)

★★★ **c. Ask what employee wants. Say that he or she is in trouble. Ask for proposal, threaten to fire.**

Also good, except for moving to threats at the end.

> Don't vocalize about firing unless you are preparing to carry that out, with low cost to your operation.
>
> Do get across the point that such behavior will have consequences in other areas that matter to this employee: assignments, compensation, promotion. Assure this person that you want to see him or her succeed. Put the focus on getting fresh commitment from the employee; let the employee do the talking.

12. FRUSTRATED BY INDIFFERENCE

One apathetic employee evades tasks, never does anything right the first time, never reacts to warnings and complaints.

AUDIENCE RESPONSES

YOUR RATING

_________ a. *Counsel. Direct this employee so the person develops good feelings about the project before starting.*

_________ b. *Give smaller, more measurable/attainable goals that give this person a sense of worth and confidence.*

_________ c. *Explain the person's role and impact. Remind him or her that it takes less time to do it right, and more time to fix it when wrong.*

	★	★★	★★★	★★★★
RATING	*NO!*	*RISKY*	*BETTER*	*BEST!*

12. FRUSTRATED BY INDIFFERENCE ANALYSIS

Alas! For the first time, all three respondents miss the mark, opining that all burdens belong to the boss.

a. Counsel; develop good feelings.
Habitual apathy requires firm confrontation. The use of the word "never" throughout the problem makes it clear that this employee will not respond to mild approaches.

b Set smaller, measurable goals.
Good for an inexperienced, learner/employee, not for an indifferent one. If you ease the goals for this employee, you are unfair to others who perform the work properly at this level of difficulty. If this employee cannot or will not perform at the level proven achievable by others, he or she cannot be retained in the slot. Your organization is paying for performance to a fair standard, and must get it.

c. Explain person's role, impact, and so on.
This is a sermonette. Turn it around. Ask the employee to tell *you* how he or she sees his or her role/impact. Ask him or her to tell you the advantages in an apathetic performance. (Short term, there *are* some . . . the employee can relax, let others do his or her job, and so on.) You must not cushion an indifferent employee with chats in which you carry the burden.

Nickerson's Recommendation

For a *four-star* answer, this employee must be shown your disapproval. Here's a format you might follow in your encounter:

"I am not satisfied with the quantity and/or quality of your work." (Cite recent examples.)

"You have been warned in the past." (Cite written warnings.)

"You are now entering your final test period when your performance must improve to *X* standard." (Cite cutoff date.)

"Failure to meet this standard at the deadline will result in your discharge or demotion for failure to perform your job description."

"What are your comments? I need specific commitment from you on what you will do to meet these standards. Give me your written plan by (deadline)."

13. DAMAGED BY DESTRUCTIVE WORKERS

How tough can I get with destructive employees who are not inspired to do a decent job? Their carelessness costs money and hurts production.

A

AUDIENCE RESPONSES

YOUR RATING

________ **a.** *If you can't change them, fire them.*

________ **b.** *Put them on probation. If no improvement by deadline, FIRE.*

________ **c.** *Terminate after thorough evaluation/documentation.*

________ **d.** *Experiment with various approaches since there is more than one individual involved. As a minimum,*

State regulations on waste, scrap, breakage.

Set deadlines and benchmarks for improvement.

If no improvement, impose probation.

Terminate when ready.

Document as you go.

________ **e.** *With destructive individuals, I like to find out the underlying causes. They may be due to personal problems that can be dealt with. Meet individually on a regular basis until improvement is clear.*

	★	★★	★★★	★★★★
RATING	*NO!*	*RISKY*	*BETTER*	*BEST!*

13. DAMAGED BY DESTRUCTIVE WORKERS ANALYSIS

★★ **a. Fire, forthwith.**
Do this only if you have documented previous remedial/disciplinary steps. In large companies or union shops, you would be called to task for precipitate action.

★★★ **b. Put them on probation, then fire.**
Because it implies investigation and previous warnings, this works better.

★★★ **c. Terminate after proper steps.**
Ditto.

d. Try various approaches: Minimum regulations, deadlines, probation, and so on.
Here are the steps spelled out. To clarify this respondent's suggestion that you deal with each person individually, you might investigate with an employee by asking the following questions—which would show you his or her attitudes without your "leading the witness":

> "Give me your estimate of the cost of your scrap for a typical week." (The person's reply may show ignorance rather than malice.)
>
> "Can you describe what happens farther down the line if your scrap level is high? Where are the effects the worst?" (Let him or her talk.)
>
> "What do you think causes your high scrap levels?" (Be quiet; let him or her answer.)
>
> "What can I tell *my* boss when he asks me if there's a chance of your improving? How could you improve? I need specifics from you." (Let him or her talk.)

These open questions will elicit a lot of information from the employee about problems he or she faces and information he or she may lack. If the employee reveals that *retaliation* is the cause of the destruction, you must counsel and apply disciplines as necessary. The employee must be shown that asking for what he or she needs, not taking action against the company, will get the desired results. You are always teaching your group that *penalties follow attacks*, while *advantages follow negotiation*. Follow up with this employee.

e. Probe causes, discover personal problems, see regularly

However well-intentioned, unlicensed psychiatry is off limits for managers, despite the many encouragements you may have had to try it. The only "causes" you are qualified to handle are *work-related causes*. Even if you suspect or know about personal/psychological or family upsets in a worker's life, you are not authorized or educated to deal with those. They must be handled by professionals; you can only suggest that the employee consult such help.

14. BAFFLED BY THE GRAPEVINE

Office gossip has me buffaloed. When I show my disapproval, the talk continues underground worse than ever.

AUDIENCE RESPONSES

YOUR RATING

________ **a.** *When a situation arises that would tend to trigger gossip, sit the group down and candidly relay the facts. This dissipates the power of gossip.*

________ **b.** *Inform the group at your staff meeting that you have seen gossip disrupt the peace, damage reputations. Invite them to bring their worries to you.*

________ **c.** *Gather the group quickly and try to persuade them to stop. You must control this.*

________ **d.** *Regular staff meetings clear the air and prevent doubts from building up too long.*

	★	★★	★★★	★★★★
RATING	*NO!*	*RISKY*	*BETTER*	*BEST!*

14. BAFFLED BY THE GRAPEVINE ANALYSIS

★★★ **a. Sit them down, relay facts.**

Don't always sit them down; formality glamorizes the subject matter. But, yes, make yourself the source of fast facts when worrisome situations arise. The grapevine operates in the absence of clear information from management. *Regular* informal sharing with the group takes the heat off your communications about difficult issues.

★ **b. Discuss the evils of gossip.**

No. Preaching by managers has not raised resistance to "sin" in consenting adults. Chide subordinates privately for character assassination if you see it. You can give good example by nipping personal gossip in the bud when it is brought to you. But contain your expectations. Slander is an enticing temptation for many.

If the gossip concerns people's job security, on the other hand, you should not attempt to outlaw this. People have a basic need for job security and legitimate claims to information concerning their job security. They have a right to get this information from a credible authority (you) and should not be impelled to go to the grapevine for reassurance. If you don't want an active grapevine, get there first, yourself, with timely, relevant information.

★ **c. Quick, persuade them to stop.**

This action will stimulate further talk.

★★★★ **d. Hold regular staff meetings to clear the air.**

Right. *Regular* is the key word. If people know you will answer their pertinent questions, or get them answered quickly—once a week, in a group—they do not need the grapevine. You will be their preferred credibility source if you are available and open, once a week.

Comment: A few years ago, a seminar delegate described a process used in her company to keep people informed. She called it a "Living Agenda," and here's how it worked:

> If the manager planned a regular meeting for, say, Friday, she posted a chart in an accessible place on Monday. Down one side, she listed the subjects she needed to cover, with time allotments required. On the other side, staff members were free to list subjects they needed to cover, with suggested time limits. Staff suggestions could be initialed or anonymous. People got the idea that staff meetings were a group responsibility. Fears and concerns had a legitimate forum. Managers got advance warning that certain items needed coverage.
>
> One important rule: NO CENSORSHIP ALLOWED. If a requested item seemed premature, or too hot to handle, the manager could exercise two options:
>
> -*Postpone it* (but state renewal date).
>
> -*Assign it* to the person who made the request or to an expert in the subject, so that members could bring suggestions, and the assignee could investigate further, with management blessings. A renewal date was also announced.
>
> On the eve of each week's meeting—agenda items were reshuffled, renumbered, to be handled at the meeting, in the order of their impact. (I have had letters from managers at Rochester Institute, American Airlines, and other companies attesting to the simplicity and effectiveness of this "instant improvement" idea.)

What if senior management won't let you tell the truth? With this decision, senior management elects to pay the price of reducing your credibility and their own—and enhancing the credibility and power of the grapevine. Some seniors value secrecy more highly than credibility. In this case, you might go to top management with the rumor you are trying to address. Supply a short memo outlining various replies you have considered. (All may be true, but variable as to details offered.) Then, ask top management to focus on which reply to authorize rather than on whether to communicate at all. If you do your homework rather than going in empty-handed and expecting seniors to construct a reply, they may be less inclined to dismiss you. Managers often find it simpler and more comfortable to select a reply rather than create one from scratch.

Of course, there will be times when competitive threats force top management to maintain silence even at the cost of losing credibility with insiders. If they insist that they've calculated the costs accurately, you will have to acquiesce, for now.

15. ANNOYED BY BLAMERS

My staff is great at identifying and griping about problems, but they are unwilling to work on solutions.

AUDIENCE RESPONSES

YOUR RATING

________ **a.** *Observe the problem closely with them. Ask questions to draw your people out so that they can see causes and think through solutions. Don't be so quick with answers yourself.*

________ **b.** *Give acceptance to their complaints and fears. This builds their self-worth. Then ask them to think about and submit solutions. Don't be in a hurry. Their confidence will build.*

________ **c.** *Ask for their ideas. Try some "what ifs" to help them see the more sophisticated issues. This helps them to develop judgment. Ask them to outline their problems in writing and always to jot down several possible solutions before coming to you.*

	★	★★	★★★	★★★★
RATING	*NO!*	*RISKY*	*BETTER*	*BEST!*

15. ANNOYED BY BLAMERS ANALYSIS

All answers, *a*, *b*, and *c* would rate four stars if the employees were deemed *unable* rather than *unwilling* to find their own solutions. (All three respondents took the view that these employees needed to build confidence.) The tone of the question indicates, however, that these employees were willing to work only on problem-free tasks and that they saw the boss as the problem solver.

Nickerson's Recommendations

To get a four-star answer, you need to include "Problem Solving" in the job description of each employee. With this step built into job descriptions and performance reviews, you can then invite employees to submit ideas; ask them to try the "what ifs" suggested by respondents *a*, *b*, and *c*. Employees will learn that problem solving is a joint effort in which they play half the parts and enjoy much of the satisfaction.

Comment: Since Adam blamed Eve, human beings have clung to the practice even though it destroys relationships and impedes problem solving. As Robert Bramson says in his book *Coping with Difficult People*: "Blaming is not Changing."[6]

Blaming is a negative instinct that slows down progress. Knowing that *you* want something different and setting out to work for it—that's a better strategy.

[6]Robert M. Bramson, COPING WITH DIFFICULT PEOPLE (New York: Ballantine, 1982), p. 136.

16. ELUDED BY TROUBLEMAKERS

I have some trouble makers in my office, but I never can catch them with the smoking gun.

A

AUDIENCE RESPONSES

YOUR RATING

________ **a.** *They'll cut their own throats in time.*

________ **b.** *Find out what their problems are and go about joint problem solving. They need counseling.*

________ **c.** *Share with them the fact that they are developing a reputation with you different from what they might wish for themselves. Warn them.*

	★	★★	★★★	★★★★
RATING	*NO!*	*RISKY*	*BETTER*	*BEST!*

★★

a. They'll cut their throats.

Wishful thinking. Some bad guys escape retribution their whole careers. (They move around a lot, of course.) Don't rely on fate.

★★★

b. Find out the problems, counsel.

Yes. If the "smoking gun" issues are minor "trick or treat stuff." Keep it light and simple; don't make a big thing of it, or game players get more fascinated with the game.

★★

Less useful if the damage is major. It may be too late for simple counseling. Instead, you must use the "cite . . . document . . . set deadlines . . . discipline . . . put on probation . . ." process already covered in this session. If you cannot catch them with the smoking gun, who can? Do you have a lieutenant or supervisor who is covering the department when you are not? You may need help in surveillance.

★★★

c. "Share" with them the effect they are having . . .

This felicitous phrase-turner sounds like Edward VIII giving his abdication speech. Go ahead and "warn" but accept that such warnings may only add spice to the game with these employees. Are they singling you out for "teasing" or have their previous supervisors suspected them too? How good is their work production while they are playing their games? Can you begin disciplinary procedures on that basis, so you obviate the need to find the smoking gun? Don't pursue or fall in with games.

Here's a situation that illustrates: A production manager got caught in a cat and mouse game with an employee who liked to loaf on the job but who always "looked busy" when management walked by. When the subordinate was assigned to a night shift, the manager warned the night supervisor, fearing the behavior would worsen. Soon the night supervisor confessed that this employee had been caught napping on the job and sought the chance to discharge her on a second and third offense.

Our hero decided to go in one night to see if he could catch her, himself. (This is obsession.) When she ran into the boss in the hall, and asked what had brought him visiting at night, the manager replied tartly that he'd come to catch her napping on the job, and was surprised to see her "up."

"If you ever catch me," she answered with a grin, "I'll simply write you a list of all the others, including supervisors, who sleep in the same room I use when things get slow around here."

These plots do tend to thicken.

Nickerson's Recommendation

For a four-star answer; scrutinize job performance. Insist that specific standards be met. Be blind to minor "teases." If matters get serious, however, and you become the butt of employee games, avoid dramatic pursuit which might damage your dignity, and maintain patient, discreet surveillance. Once you get the goods, you apply discipline firmly.

17. OUTWITTED BY A "GODCHILD"

How do I manage a tough, cantankerous, resentful employee who is a favorite of my boss?

AUDIENCE RESPONSES

YOUR RATING

________ **a.** *Take it easy. Say, "I like your potential, but I don't like (specific behavior.) What are your reactions and suggestions?"*

________ **b.** *Find out why he is unhappy, what causes this resentful behavior.*

________ **c.** *Ask what he needs from you. Cite the behavior you find objectionable. Ask if the job, your behavior as a boss—or personal matters are the cause. Let the employee know you want to help and are authorized to do so . . . on job matters.*

	★	★★	★★★	★★★★
RATING	*NO!*	*RISKY*	*BETTER*	*BEST!*

17. OUTWITTED BY A "GODCHILD" ANALYSIS

a. "I like your potential; I don't like your behavior."
Best done in the performance review where your supervisory status is most clear to your subordinates. (One option: If you suspect that the big boss is grooming this employee for better things, you may want to go over this review "upstairs" while it is still in the planning stages. Some companies routinely ask their managers to review planned negative reviews one stage higher, to keep things objective. The big boss's reactions may clue you if there is a special status for this employee. If you're lucky, you may find that the big boss values your data and wants to cool this person down, too. Ask for guidance; be tactful with the boss.)

b. Find out why he is unhappy, what causes resentment.
No. Cite *your* unhappiness with resentful behavior. If the employee has a legitimate *why*, you'll hear about it; you won't have to ask. Confront firmly on unacceptable behavior.

c. Lay it out. Ask what he needs. Offer help.
An excellent recipe for a detached approach to this employee. If you were more sure about what the big boss intends, you could be firmer here.

Comment: If you need to get clarity about what the big boss intends . . . if you have reason to believe this person is being groomed for high places, you should still attempt to form a healthy supervisor/supervisee relationship where you are. Be fairly patient about this. Remember, it's natural for employees to seek the company of the kingpin, especially when the kingpin encourages this. In a small informal company, you could choose to relax about the matter.

In a larger, more formal company with a rigid chain

of command, you could *not* afford to stay so relaxed. You might inquire of the chief,

> Is there something special I should know about employee X? If you want this person to receive special coaching or privileges, do let me know. Otherwise, I have no option but to exact the same performance standards as for our other people, and I am not getting good performance now.

The boss's reply will alert you if caution is required. You may be pleasantly surprised to hear that this person is no godchild, or you may be told that special plans *are* being laid for this person, yet the kingpin wants full performance from the godchild. Use tact at all stages by concentrating on your responsibilities as a supervisor, not on the kingpin's behavior.

PART

FOUR

FINE TUNING: MAKING DECISIONS ABOUT ANGER

Recall the way our questioners phrased their problems: "put down" . . . "passed over" . . . "damaged" . . . "baffled" . . . "outwitted" . . . . They were feeling "acted upon" by others and were puzzled or reluctant about taking actions themselves.

ANGER IS A CHOICE WE MAKE WHEN WE FEEL CHOICELESS

Choicelessness—feeling thwarted and threatened at the same time—is one of life's circumstances that ignites anger in most of us. Just watch a red-faced executive being bumped off the last flight out or denied a hotel room at a convention. You'll see fireworks learned in the nursery, updated for business use, and delivered in booming baritone. Depending on the cut of his coat and the clout of his corporation, you may see this complainer calmed, cossetted, and compensated. A seat is found in first class, lodgings are located in the director's suite. If anger succeeds this time, it will be trotted out next time too, on flimsier provocation.

ANGER IS A HABIT

Made comfortable through repetition, it undermines effectiveness as it drains energy. Bosses may come to label the anger addict as moody, unreliable. Peers may tire of your outbursts and strike back with a vengeance; subordinates may turn off, taking their resentments underground and giving you grudging cooperation. The anger habit costs you.

ANGER CAN BE APPROPRIATE

Yes. There are reasons for feeling and expressing anger: You can express your anger, immediately and firmly, over a deliberate attack, gross carelessness, rampant injustice. Say that you are angry; ask for what you want. Anger can be an energizer when used appropriately.

Use the energy your anger generates to work for improvements to your own situation and that of people you care about. Anger can fuel a sincere effort. It's all right to get angry, but it is health-threatening to sit with your anger, doing nothing.

AVENUES FOR AVOIDING ANGER

If useless anger is wearing you down, try these two self-caring routes to getting control:

1. ***Reduce your sensitivity to natural events*** If certain factors are natural to your business (such as red tape in government, noise at airports, crying babies in nurseries), you can learn to tolerate them or make a different choice for your life's work. This sounds like the commonest sense, yet I counsel managers all over the country who have chosen a line of work perfectly suited to produce ulcers, given their personal sensitivities.

2. ***Limit your expectations of yourself and others based on needs, not preferences*** In her book *Anger, the Misunderstood Emotion*, Carol Tavris makes fresh observations about those of us who have been convinced we should *have it all* and *have it now*.

> When desires of the self come first, the needs of others are annoying. When we think we deserve it all, reaping only a portion can enrage.[7]

No one is suggesting that you reduce your aspirations to ground level or settle for second best. But if your expectations are so high that you curse when your coffee spills, or seethe at someone's stupidity even when it's none of your business, you are depleting your anger energy wantonly. You might benefit by keeping an "anger diary" noting what triggers set you off— and then making conscious efforts to avoid or ignore that trigger next time, especially if there's nothing you can do about it. Then, repeat the process until that trigger no longer controls you.

[7]Copyright © 1982 by Carol Tavris, ANGER, THE MISUNDERSTOOD EMOTION (New York: Simon & Schuster, Inc.), p. 65.

A PROGRAM FOR PERSONAL SERENITY

Chronic anger addicts may benefit by adopting, gently and gradually, some of the following behaviors:

1. ***Practice courtesy as a first instinct in a crisis*** Apply it like a lotion when you get up in the morning, and use it like a balm for the bruises life deals out. Courtesy buys you time for choosing actions that help *you* while you maintain your dignity.

2. ***Practice patience as some people practice piano*** Not because you *must*, but because you like the calming music. Replace a *tantrum* with tranquility just once. Then repeat it.

3. ***Expect less, negotiate more*** Management psychologist Thomas Gordon drives directly to the heart of healthy work relationships when he advises[8]

   - Expect that others will act in their own interests.
   - People behave in ways that get their needs met.
   - People follow managers who help them get their needs met.

   What a relief. You are released from expecting others to act in your interests. You need not expect them to follow you unless you help them get their legitimate needs met. Disagreements become more manageable when we give up presuming that others will bow to our unilateral demands. Instead, Gordon shows us that if we discover

   - *You* cannot bow to *my* solution
   - I cannot bow to *yours*

   Then we may both invest time in a third solution that satisfies us both, without struggling over the first two. The work takes longer, but the load is divided and the power shared.

4. ***Empower yourself: take your time*** There may not be ample time, but there is *some*. I have to be reminded of this often. A very successful friend of mine, well into her eighties, responds to my howls over urgent business frustrations by asking, "Is it life-threatening, dear?" After the laughter, I can see that some issues can be renegotiated—others abandoned altogether for some better opportunity. Self-will is the piston that drives my frustration and wastes my fuel.

[8]Copyright © 1977 by Thomas Gordon, LEADER EFFECTIVENESS TRAINING, L.E.T. (Ridgefield, Conn.: Wyden Books), p. 17.

5. ***Ventilate with caution*** When a series of frustrations or conflicts develops, you may lose your perspective and need advice and consolation from a trusted colleague. Proceed judiciously. Your confidences may be betrayed, your friends may be quizzed, indeed grilled, about what's bothering you. Or your retelling of unhappy events may reopen old wounds. If you need to ventilate, choose the right person and use the right method. The person should be one who will neither betray you nor feel burdened by your tale; consult a fellow professional who does not work inside your organization. Your method should concern *your* reactions, *your* anxieties, *your* options, *your* plans. Avoid recitals about the "villain" of the piece ("Blaming is not *changing*," *Bramson*). Concentrate on yourself.

   You are talking to test your sanity before proceeding with decisions.

6. ***Go after what you need, not what you want*** Save your passions for the noble and/or winnable battles. In the end, for those issues you deem "life or death" you will almost always have to negotiate. Dr. Hans Selye put it elegantly:

   > "Whatever situation you meet in life, consider first whether it is really worth fighting for. . . . Try to keep your mind constantly on the pleasant aspects of life and on actions which can improve your situation."[9]

And remember one more thing: You may need, not merely want, the solace of forgiving those who have aroused your anger in the past. Reaching out to reconcile can help you, even if the other party turns away. You can relax and let go of resentment, knowing you've done all you can. Peace of mind replaces anger. The tug-of-war ends because you have let go of the rope.

Anger will always be a choice, but you choose it least, and last.

[9]Copyright © by Hans Selye, M.D., STRESS WITHOUT DISTRESS (New York: Harper & Row, Publishers, Inc. 1974), p. 134.

PART FIVE

CHECKLIST FOR MANAGING NEGATIVE EMOTIONS

1. Remember, other people's behavior is about them.
2. Don't try to fathom other people's motives; fathom your own.
3. Gradually limit the number/nature of events that can trigger your angry feelings.
4. Budget your energy for the good things.
5. Express your needs openly without fear that you'll be at your opponent's mercy.
6. People can't mind read.
7. Discipline is one responsibility you cannot delegate.
8. Your employees are often stronger and smarter than they let on. Add problem solving to their job descriptions. When they ask your opinion, get theirs first.
9. The grapevine is not more powerful or more credible than you.
10. Accept people's strong emotions when they first pitch them. Otherwise, they keep on pitching, and the game is hardball.

HOW SECURE MANAGERS HANDLE PEER CONFLICTS

SESSION TWO

HOW SECURE MANAGERS HANDLE PEER CONFLICTS

INTRODUCTION

Ever since Abel had that trouble with Cain, corporate siblings have been stewing over territorial rights and competing for the chief's attention and esteem. The questions you'll read in this chapter hint at the jealousies, insecurities, and frustrations that fester beneath many a professional veneer. The answers, those from productive and secure managers, remind us that competitive drives are better channeled into the service of public needs, the pursuit of new opportunities, and the defense against common enemies, whether rival companies or economic threats. Instead of draining or destroying team cohesiveness, competitive urges can be harnessed and directed toward mutual goals.

A common theme among the replies is that we must learn to trust one another. Surprisingly, many respondents espouse getting to know each other informally, outside work, as a primary basis for trust. I take the opposite view. Coming to know each other in our *working roles* seems to me the basis for building sound working relationships. We need to see consistent, honest, forthright, effective performance in our peers; we need to witness determined fulfillment of commitments, above-ground discussion when disagreements arise, willingness to compromise, and eagerness to help and be helped, in order for trust to build.

It takes patience and experience as collaborators before peers can form bonds strong yet flexible enough to withstand our inevitable jostlings for scarce spaces in the corporate sunshine.

PART

ONE

FACING OPEN AGGRESSION

You may be surprised at the degree of egalitarian thinking among the businesspeople in our supposedly pluralistic society. As you'll see in the first part of this session, many of the questioners (and many responders, too) seem to think that "well-brought-up" businesspeople ought to work peacefully side by side, sharing equally in the burdens, tasks, rewards, and glories of the enterprise. They want to slot executives into parental roles, handing out assignments, promotions, and raises in benignly equal portions, whether to the swift or to the slow.

In government, nonprofit agencies, and huge bureaucratic corporations, you may uncover the entrenched view that each job description should contain an equitable share of glory and garbage and that no elite jobs should be allotted to elite performers without public scrutiny.

This nonsense causes enough grief when it arises between subordinate and boss. At least bosses can lay down the law and correct such attitudes fairly abruptly. But when this set of ideas rises between peers, it becomes a source of endless wrangling and hand-wringing about fairness.

When naive workers notice aggression from stronger peers, they often react as children do to playground bullies. They hit back from weaker positions and get a "bloody nose." They go complaining to the monitor/boss—to be stung again if they are labeled "cry babies." They don't see that business life is about survival—survival of customers, clients, patients, and companies. They forget that business and professions deal with vital issues to which we and our peers commit ourselves—therefore actions and reactions will be strong. They don't see that business is about the apportionment of scarce resources—money, manpower, equipment, authorizations—and that our peers will fight very hard for a share, fair or not.

Because they will always be with us, our peers will be our biggest challenge throughout our careers. To hope they will be bland and noncompetitive when we challenge them for power—and to run to the boss for solace and protection when they outmatch us—will guarantee us a draining of our energies. As you move up the organizational ladder and grow stronger yourself, you'll meet a new hierarchy of peers as strong as or stronger than you. Coming to relish the contest, to learn from one another, cooperate and coalesce—there's where peace and progress will develop. But the questioners in the first section don't know that yet.

1. STUNG BY POISONOUS POINTERS

A colleague likes to critique several of us in front of others. We feel angry and embarrassed.

A

AUDIENCE RESPONSES

YOUR RATING

_______ **a.** *Be patient with this person. Praise him when he deserves it. Perhaps he'll return the favor.*

_______ **b.** *Respond with positive comments. Look for the good.*

_______ **c.** *Take initiative for yourself. Talk with him privately. Be sincere but protect yourself. If the situation feels potentially explosive for the group, involve the boss.*

_______ **d.** *Listen for what is meant between the lines. Does this really have to do with you, or could it be a lifelong hangup for this person to be a know-it-all. Shrug it off.*

	★	★★	★★★	★★★★
RATING	*NO!*	*RISKY*	*BETTER*	*BEST!*

1. *STUNG BY POISONOUS POINTERS* ANALYSIS

★★ **a. Be patient. Praise him. Perhaps he'll return it.**

Beware. Behavior you notice will be repeated. If you praise your critic, you'll encourage further criticism. If, on the other hand, you follow the dictum "When in doubt, give positive strokes," you *can* elect this path *provided you have no expectations* of improved behavior in the other person. Many people give positive strokes convinced that this "sugar" will sooth the critic better than vinegar would. Then, they endure hours, days, or weeks of stress, waiting for the other person to sweeten up.

★★★ **b. Respond positively; look for the good.**

Yes, you can respond with real sincerity and detachment: "Thanks for your suggestion. I know it was motivated by a sincere desire to help, I'll think it over." You may then be able to go about your business without engaging in a long-winded defense or argument. Buying time this way can allow you to find the positives (if any) in peace and quiet and without scrutiny or pressure. It forces the "critic" to wait for satisfaction. Some critics *do* get their satisfaction from the argument or embarrassment that follows the critique. When you deprive them of this instant gratification by your detached response, they may abandon you and seek more excitable victims.

★★★ **c. Talk privately; protect yourself. If explosive for a group, involve the boss.**

Yes. Since this behavior seems habitual, you might say on the next critique, "I'd like to talk to you about this. Let's adjourn . . . or set a time to talk." Then, when you have privacy, you can be straightforward. Say "I feel annoyed (embarrassed, angry—whatever is true) when I am criticized or prompted continually before others. I'd like to ask that you reserve your opinions when others are around." How you proceed after that depends very much of this colleague's relationship to you.

Has this person been appointed by the boss as a senior coach? If so, the critiques are appropriate . . . but the group setting is the problem. If not, the continual promptings are inappropriate in themselves, and you might say "I would prefer to get my corrections and critiques from the boss, unless my way of working interferes directly with your needs. In such a case I would prefer you to ask me for what you need, rather than to coach me without my requesting it."

Now, as to your second suggestion—that you involve the boss for the sake of the group—I recommend against this. Are you an official spokesperson for the group? If not, don't assume this role. Others in the group must fend for themselves. Involving the boss will escalate this issue's importance. Budget your trips to the boss. You may need the boss's help on other requests soon, and you don't want to squander your time with the boss on anything but matters that will benefit you in a major way.

d. **Listen between the lines. Shrug it off.**
I like the attitude, but not the behavior. During the actual criticism, to ignore or shrug it off may cause your critic to try harder and may get you the reputation of callousness with both the critic and other onlookers. While you are right to be slow to anger, you might try a peacemaking but directive response such as, "I hear your criticism, Mike. What is your request? I respond better to requests and proposals than I do to criticisms. Requests have a future." In this way, you show your practical orientation and willingness to listen to actual requests.

Nickerson's Recommendation

To upgrade responses *b* and *c* to four stars, admit that criticism is uncomfortable to most people, because it focuses on your past errors. Coaching/suggestions feel better if they are not intended to humiliate. Avoid imputing motives to your critic. Take your critic forward by asking for what you need: *privacy*, *suggestions*, *proposals* (and only when assigned by the boss, requested by yourself, or required by the critic's work related needs).

Comment: Despite your feelings of closeness to the group, do not act on their behalf unless you have been elected their spokesperson, or unless you are willing to compete for informal leadership of the group.

2. SHUNNED BY CHAUVINIST PEERS

I've been promoted, but cannot get acceptance and respect from the group I've now joined.

A

AUDIENCE REACTIONS

YOUR RATING

_________ **a.** *This is always difficult. Listen and observe how they interact and succeed. Fit in.*

_________ **b.** *Feel them out.*

_________ **c.** *Stand your ground when it matters. Show them the edge of your energy.*

_________ **d.** *When you encounter objectionable behavior, you let the other party know. Tell them how to get the best cooperation from you. (If they can hurt you, however, you play on their egos, get what you want, maintain professional courtesies, and ignore ignorance wherever you can.)*

	★	★★	★★★	★★★★
RATING	*NO!*	*RISKY*	*BETTER*	*BEST!*

2. *SHUNNED BY CHAUVINIST PEERS* ANALYSIS

★★★★ *a.* **Always difficult. Listen, observe, fit in.**

Brilliant brief response. All newcomers face some chauvinism, whether sexual, geographical, technical, or hierarchical. This "protectionism" is about the chauvinist, not about you. Therefore, *detach*, as the respondent suggests. Avoid frontal attacks on the barriers erected by the group; the abrasion wears *you* down. Observe the customs that help them get along. Adopt their customs until they feel comfortable with you as a useful fellow professional. This is not the time to dare to be different.

★★★ *b.* **Feel them out.**

Good, provided you do it by observing, listening, not by direct probing.

★★ *c.* **Stand your ground when it matters. Show them your energy.**

"When it matters" is the operative phrase. If you take their resistance as natural and temporary, you will reserve your direct fire and use your energy on tasks, not on confrontations. It is better that they see the edge of your humor rather than your anger.

★★ *d.* **Help peers see and use what motivates you. Flatter heavies; use courtesy and forbearance with them.**

A prickly approach to take when you are new to the group. From the Machiavellian tone of the response, I'd guess that this person enjoys manipulative games and may be expert at them. A possible four-star approach if you are expert at game playing—but not recommended for beginners. (You see, good game players enjoy the moves and strategies so much; they are not disappointed if the outcome goes against them. They always have a new "inning" around the corner.)

3. *SHAKING UP SHIRKERS*

How do I handle uncooperative peers who will not carry their fair share of a load we must shoulder together?

AUDIENCE RESPONSES

YOUR RATING

________ **a.** *Request disciplinary action.*

________ **b.** *Make them aware of your willingness to cooperate with them. It may be reciprocated.*

________ **c.** *Do it your way. Don't waste any more time waiting for them.*

________ **d.** *Patience, tact, kindness are eventually returned. They'll cooperate without realizing what they are doing.*

________ **e.** *Use diplomacy and flattery. Make them feel important and respected. Continue to press your point in a friendly way.*

	★	★★	★★★	★★★★
RATING	*NO!*	*RISKY*	*BETTER*	*BEST!*

3. SHAKING UP SHIRKERS ANALYSIS

★ **a. Request disciplinary action.**
This should be your final, not your first, recourse.

★ **b. Express cooperativeness; hope it will be returned.**
Don't leave work-sharing problems to hope.

★ **c. Do it your way. Don't wait for them.**
No. You may not be able to shoulder your own load plus theirs without endangering the job. Before taking on another's load, go ask shirkers for what *you* need. Only if they refuse you should you go to your boss, asking to be authorized to carry a double load (for double pay, of course.)

★★ **d. Patience, tact, kindness will eventually win cooperation.**
Not without a direct request, they won't! But patience, tact, and kindness combined with your direct request for fair assumption of the load make a good beginning.

★★ **e. Diplomacy and flattery; continue to press your point in a friendly way.**
I'm in favor of diplomacy but against flattery in this case. You have reason to be angry and frustrated at what you assume is noncooperation. To flatter your "shirker" under these circumstances will build your resentment and its accompanying stress. Examine how you have been pressing your point—and don't repeat pressure that has failed so far. Try a new tack.

Nickerson's Recommendation

For a four-star answer, consider work sharing for what it is, a vital negotiation issue. Don't leave it to hope, chance, flattery, or a repetition of previously ineffectual ploys. (I am assuming that the shirking here is actually increasing your burdens. If another employee's shirking is *not* affecting your own work load, you can safely ignore the issue since it is the boss's business and not yours at all. You are not your boss's monitor. The only person who should complain to the boss is the person whose work load is actually increased by the shirker's failures.)

Assuming that you are personally disadvantaged by the shirker's behavior, you should

1. Privately, tell your co-worker what you need as minimum cooperation. Describe the risks/consequences to you and the department, whenever this person fails to perform.
2. Ask the co-worker if there is any barrier to his handling the work. Assure him or her that you want to understand any problems before pressing your point further. Listen well.
3. If you can help remove the barrier (if you caused it inadvertently), *do so*. If the boss or others would have to remove the barrier, ask your co-worker to pursue this and state a deadline by which time you must have assurances and a new commitment. Remind yourself and your co-worker that problems are best solved at the level where they occur, without escalation.
4. Make a brief record of the conversation and deadline; you both keep a copy.
5. If a solution fails to materialize by deadline, or the co-worker refuses to commit to a new plan, then, and only then, take it up to your boss.
6. If you must go to a boss about a co-worker's recalcitrance, remember to ask only for what you *need*. Do not suggest what the boss should do about the other party; do not accuse the boss of unfairness, even by suggestion. Just ask the boss for *what you need* (time, access to data, extra manpower—whatever is required). You are going to the boss *for* you, not *against* another. This reduces the risk of your complaining, judging, or demanding. It keeps the boss's guilt to a minimum and helps the boss focus on the solution, not the complaint.

4. *PEER WITHHOLDS INFORMATION*

How do I deal with a coordinator who keeps data under wraps that I need to perform?

A

AUDIENCE RESPONSES

YOUR RATING

________ **a.** *Explain the problems that this causes.*

________ **b.** *Insist that he or she share the data.*

________ **c.** *Remind person of his or her responsibility to keep you informed of this material.*

________ **d.** *Suggest that management give the communication responsibility to another person.*

	★	★★	★★★	★★★★
RATING	*NO!*	*RISKY*	*BETTER*	*BEST!*

4. *PEER WITHHOLDS INFORMATION* ANALYSIS

★★★ **a. Explain the problem this causes you.**
The right way to start. Then, follow through. Listen carefully to the response. Ask what risks this manager would face by helping you. Listen again. Then ask what the manager would like changed to reduce these risks. Offer any options you can to reduce your peer's risks. Follow the method cited in the previous question.

★★ **b. Insist that the manager share this data.**
Only if you *supervise* this other manager can you insist. If the manager is a peer, he or she will react: you *in*sist, they *re*sist.

★ **c. Remind the person of the responsibility to keep you informed.**
The previous answer applies here.

★ **d. Suggest that management give the communication responsibility to a third party.**
No. Avoid suggesting which remedies your boss should take regarding another person (the withholder in this case). Merely speak about your own needs, and ask the boss to help you get the information at least risk and inconvenience to the boss. Make clear that you have tried the method you are empowered to take (as in *a*) and have come up empty.

Nickerson's Recommendation

For a four-star answer, I'd like to add one important concept to *a*'s response: *Between peers there is no power differential.* Hence no clout is available for forcing one person's will on the other. In such an instance, each peer must bring options to the table—in sufficient variety so that at least some options will appeal to the peer's self-interest. So, as reply *a* recommends,

1. Outline your risks to the withholding peer.
2. Invite the peer to outline his or her risks.
3. As each of you listens, you may see options for covering the other person's risks while getting what you need.
4. Then offer a list of options that will make cooperation easy.

Frankly, when a peer withholds information, we get so angry we often march in with demands designed to make it harder for them to cooperate. Wishing to punish them, we penalize ourselves. If you don't have a list of options before a debate starts, don't start.

5. *OUTFLANKED BY GLORY HOGS*

Certain colleagues hog all the glory jobs, take advantage of every opportunity, and elbow others out of the way. They are oblivious to my comments.

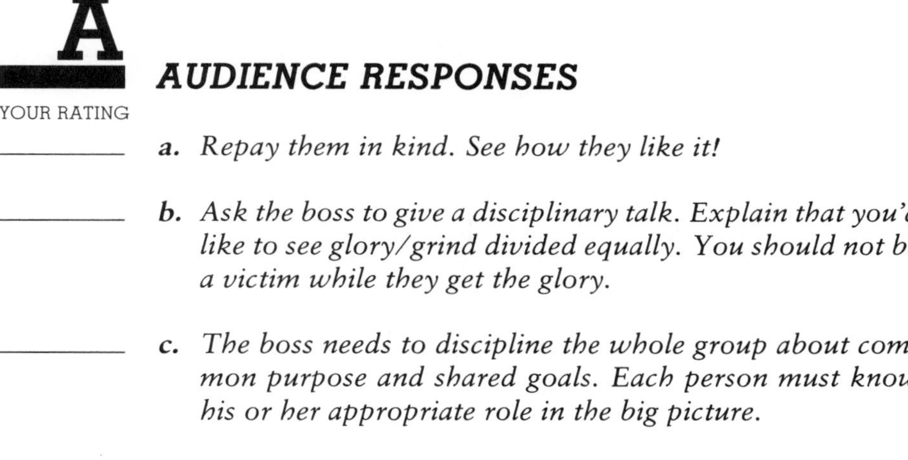

AUDIENCE RESPONSES

YOUR RATING

________ **a.** *Repay them in kind. See how they like it!*

________ **b.** *Ask the boss to give a disciplinary talk. Explain that you'd like to see glory/grind divided equally. You should not be a victim while they get the glory.*

________ **c.** *The boss needs to discipline the whole group about common purpose and shared goals. Each person must know his or her appropriate role in the big picture.*

________ **d.** *Ask the boss to call a meeting on teamwork.*

	★	★★	★★★	★★★★
RATING	*NO!*	*RISKY*	*BETTER*	*BEST!*

5. *OUTFLANKED BY GLORY HOGS* ANALYSIS

★

a. Repay in kind. See how they like it!
This will prove a high-stress approach. Your opponents are tough, unprincipled, and well practiced at spotting the tasks with potential and going after them. You need not do anything to your peers. Just look for hot projects for yourself. Be alert, be there early. Build muscles before you start flexing them.

★

b. Ask the boss to give a pep talk and share glory jobs equally.
Whatever made you think that meaningful jobs were life rafts that must be shared equally? Plum jobs are "yachts" that go to those deemed fittest to skipper them. Start practicing and demonstrating your superior yachtsmanship. Otherwise, you'll go on rowing the dory, and deservedly.

★★

c. Boss must discipline the whole group about common purpose and shared goals. Each person must know his or her role.
Certainly, morale and performance both rise when the group embraces shared goals. But this does not mean that all members share equally in the tasks, without regard to talent, experience, seniority, and track record. The boss needs to "inspirit" and encourage, not homogenize the team as it moves toward shared goals. Look again; it may be true that the elite members of the team *are* moving in the direction and at the speed that the boss wants.

It could be that you and others must hitch up your courage and follow the leaders at a faster pace. The boss has no obligation to slow down the regatta so you can catch up, but the boss may need to give you extra coaching to build your knowledge and stamina. Ask for this. The stronger members of the group may indeed know their appropriate roles in the big picture. Do you?

★ *d.* **Ask the boss to call a meeting on teamwork.**
No. Ask the boss to help you grow smarter and stronger yourself. Or talk things over with one or several mentors until you develop a taste for competitive "rough and tumble."

Nickerson's Recommendations

For a four-star answer,

- Review the goals set by the boss for the whole team. Is this going to be a rugged race?
- Admit that some team members are always stonger and smarter. They will get the plum jobs.
- Work on being stronger and smarter yourself, and assess your likely timetable for this.
- Be wonderful at your current assignment; it will be your passport to better ones.
- If your colleagues all start looking tougher and are rewarded for this—wear a life jacket at all times. A slower boat may have to fish you out of the water at the finish line.

PART TWO

COMPETING LIKE A CHAMPION

If you know what you want, and you use economy of means for getting it, you may be seen by your peers as ruthless, lucky, favored by someone in power, or all three.

If you are a baby-boomer (born between 1946 and 1965), you'll tend to compare yourself strongly against your peers since you are surrounded by more of them than any generation before or since. Yours is the group in which 60 million people competed for entry-level positions. If the entry-level jobs were scarce, the competition will be fierce again as you mature into competition for mid- and high-level slots.

You've seen some people rise like meteors to vice-presidencies while in their twenties and to presidencies of midsized firms while in their thirties. But ordinary mortals find themselves capped off at 35, competing with fellow M.B.A.s and Ph.D.s for jobs far below their potential.

Economists add further gloom by reminding us that the United States is turning into a service economy as our overseas competitors beat us to market with low-priced, high-quality goods. They're right, but they cannot see the future. Neither can we.

What these economists fail to admit, often, is that fellow baby-boomers who compete with you for upward mobility are also the biggest and richest consumer group ever known. We have developed needs for products and services that would have boggled our parents' minds. Airline travel is for everyone, video camcorders have adjoined the Polaroid on every second beach blanket this summer, while two or three cars crowd the driveways of many suburban homes. Yuppies discuss the merits of their time-share vacation villas and second-home condos while they crowd the speedboat marinas that line our beaches and lakes. It may all be done with plastic (instead of mirrors), but no one is holding back. Your career may be built on products or services we don't even know today.

If you are an optimist among the upwardly striving, you tend not to worry about what your peers are thinking until they surprise you with a sneak attack.

In the questions that follow, you'll see managers suddenly shocked by a display of jealousy from a peer, suddenly attacked by "backstabbers" who wanted the assignment, too, or manipulated by a manager even more single-minded than they! And you'll meet some managers who are uncomfortable with their own urgent strivings to get ahead as the musical chairs are drawn in closer.

Learning to accept that others will have anxieties; that the competition is visible, real, and frightening for some of your colleagues; that there is little you can do about it except to maintain your courtesy and equilibrium will be a worthwhile process to begin now. The higher you climb, the scarcer the slots will be, and the more your peers will protest as you conserve your energies and channel your efforts toward goals you have taken the trouble to clarify for yourself, and with your boss and team.

LEADING GROUPS OF UPWARD STRIVERS

If you lead groups of upwardly striving managers, you can reduce their anxiety by being precise about job descriptions, clear about assignments, generous about offering training and retraining to managers whose functions are declining. Reduce overlap and ambiguity in departments where the "fat" is being trimmed or funds are being cut. Courageous actions and communications on your part can spare your people from turning on one another.

While technology and marketing create jobs in the consumer goods field, we face even bigger challenges elsewhere—vast problems in pollution control; awesome health threats, AIDS and drug addiction among them; tremendous problems of poverty and social reform—and all will demand our best people working harder than ever for solutions.

The jobs will be there. The leaders will be needed. We'll require all our baby-boomers, all our M.B.A.s and Ph.D.s, all our experienced front-line workers to meet the stunning challenges of the next decade.

We'll be working with talent and dedication. But we'll also be laboring under our character flaws that continually distract us and draw off our energies. The questions that follow show how pervasive and insistent these human fears and flaws can be. If we cannot overcome these universal blocks to achievement, we may fail in meeting the challenges of the 1990s. How would you lay to rest, once and for all, the annoying questions which follow?

6. SIDESTEPPING SLANDER

We have some backstabbers in the office. If you get something they want, they slander you with higher-ups.

A

AUDIENCE RESPONSES

YOUR RATING

________ **a.** *Conduct a friendly investigation. Confront the backstabbers, or expose them if you can.*

________ **b.** *Detach from this backbiting. Be consistent in your dealings with others, but take little interest in what is said behind your back. Your virtues will be noted by fair-minded people.*

________ **c.** *Pick a neutral spot, like lunch, and confront them calmly. Ask if they can think of a way that* all *can win.*

________ **d.** *Be civil but not open with such people. Tell them nothing of your hopes and plans. Stick close to your boss; do a good job, toot your horn, and avoid these birds.*

	★	★★	★★★	★★★★
RATING	*NO!*	*RISKY*	*BETTER*	*BEST!*

6. SIDESTEPPING SLANDER ANALYSIS

★★ **a. Friendly investigation, confrontation, exposé.**
Do this only if you have time on your hands and crave excitement. If you shake this can of worms, it may explode. Investigations only give importance to matters beneath contempt. It's lucky we never hear most of the gossip leveled against us. Think of the energy we save!

★★★★ **b. Detach. Be consistent; your virtues are clear to the fairminded.**
Right on all counts. If someone fairminded should ask you about the accusation, of course you'll cite your amazement at the slander, but don't dignify it with more than a few words. Try two: "You're kidding!" And smile.

★ **c. Pick a neutral spot like lunch; confront, collaborate.**
Never invite a python to lunch.

★★★★ **d. Stay "civil and strange." Stick with your job and your boss.**
Yup.

Comment: Years later, people will tell you what they used to say about you back at XYZ Corporation. You'll be glad you never knew 'til now, and you'll laugh out loud. Practice early, practice often, until you can do it during a crisis as a reflex action. Laughter will relieve your tensions. Should explanations really be called for, you'll make them more easily, convincingly, . . . and *sparingly*, please.

7. PEER ENVY

My former peers are jealous of my success with a recent promotion.

A AUDIENCE REACTION

YOUR RATING

______ **a.** *Innocently ask what's bothering them.*

______ **b.** *Maintain a totally professional demeanor.*

______ **c.** *Help them feel less intimidated by dealing with them in ways that enhance their self-esteem. Stay friendly.*

______ **d.** *Don't make their problem your problem. They may eventually see that the way you work and interrelate is what made you successful.*

	★	★★	★★★	★★★★
RATING	*NO!*	*RISKY*	*BETTER*	*BEST!*

7. PEER ENVY ANALYSIS

★★ **a. Innocently ask what's bothering them.**
Do this only if you need it, that is, if you are not getting cooperation from them on vital tasks. Don't expect much of an answer.

★★★ **b. Maintain a total professional demeanor.**
Do this if you've always done it anyway. If you suddenly adopt an aloof manner, you'll add fuel to the fire *and* confuse other nonjealous peers.

★★★★ **c. Help them feel less intimidated. Enhance their self-esteem; stay friendly.**
This is a good way to live in any circumstances. Just don't labor at it. You have no obligation to deal with their jealousy.

★★★ **d. Don't make their problem your problem. They may see that your way of interrelating made you successful.**
Yes to the first part. Whether they *see* the second part or not is beyond your control and is not likely to happen soon if jealousy is at work.

Comment: Once you diagnose other people's behavior and motives ("They're jealous," "They're insecure"), you run the risk of changing *your* behavior to suit your diagnosis. Just rest with, "They're uncomfortable," and behave mildly and consistently yourself. You'll feel better, so will they. Time, not your actions, will ease discomfort on both sides.

8. *PEER COMPLAINS UPSTAIRS*

How can I deal with a woman who won't confront me directly with a problem but goes over my head to my boss?

AUDIENCE RESPONSES

YOUR RATING

_________ **a.** *See this person in private. Express your concern. Confront. If she stonewalls you, or denies it, hold your ground. Ask for a commitment to come to you first when there is a problem. Express willingness to help with future problems. Then wait, and listen while she replies.*

_________ **b.** *Suggest an informal out-of-work chat. Lunch, a drink after hours. Discuss some shared personal interests to gain the person's confidence. Then ask for what you want.*

_________ **c.** *Suggest regular meetings to anticipate and solve problems in advance.*

_________ **d.** *Don't clash over her personal shortcoming of "not confronting." Preaching won't work, but a good experience will. So give her a good experience with you. Sit her down; let her talk; and listen.*

	★	★★	★★★	★★★★
RATING	*NO!*	*RISKY*	*BETTER*	*BEST!*

8. PEER COMPLAINS UPSTAIRS ANALYSIS

★★★★ **a. Privately confront. Ask for commitment, cooperate, listen.**
Yes. This *is* important enough to warrant a confrontation. If this co-worker keeps going to your boss about work-related issues, your boss may doubt your effectiveness in your position. Yes, express your concern about your authority to handle your job without your boss being brought in. Yes, ask for a commitment. Yes, listen. If the problem continues, you will have to ask your boss for one simple change: Next time this person visits the boss about your work, the boss must ask, "Did you already check this out with (your name)? If not, do so before coming to me." That should nip the problem at both ends.

★★ **b. Lunch, informal chat, then ask for what you want.**
No. This is an "at-work" problem. Settle it there. Small talk and round-about methods are too kind here. You owe this person nothing.

★★★★ **c. Suggest regular meetings to anticipate and solve problems in advance.**
Once you do *a*, this suggestion is a fine follow-up.

★★★ **d. Give her a good experience; let her talk. LISTEN.**
If this translates to "Don't complain about the past, but show her a painless present and work toward a better future," I'm for it. But you need to emphasize that you look harshly on people going over your head to the boss. Offenders need to see what you are asking them to stop, as well as start, doing.

9. *MANIPULATIVE PARTNER*

How can I defeat a lazy, manipulative co-manager who shares half the staff, budget, and reponsibility but produces far less than I.

A

AUDIENCE RESPONSES

YOUR RATING

_________ **a.** *Confront. Tell this manager he or she is not getting away with anything.*

_________ **b.** *Ask to meet about more equitable sharing out of duties and output.*

_________ **c.** *What do you want? Sit down with this manager and make your needs clear. Map out a better (50/50) split and get an agreement.*

_________ **d.** *Watch out for your own methods. This manager may delegate better, while you do all the hard slog of your half by yourself. Often, the manager who delegates well wins the loyalty of his or her staffers, while the nondelegating manager isolates and fails to win staff cooperation, thus ending up buried.*

	★	★★	★★★	★★★★
RATING	*NO!*	*RISKY*	*BETTER*	*BEST!*

★

a. Confront. Tell this manager he or she is not getting away with anything.
But he or she *is* getting away with it, whatever it is. This stance would get you into a fight, with you, as the belligerent one. You don't sound as if you know what you want yet. You are still focusing on "defeating" the other party.

★★

b. Ask to meet on sharing of duties and output.
Give it a try, but don't expect to control the outcomes. This manager, if smart, may suggest you work out your own fortunes since he or she is satisfied with things as they are. Imagine several possible responses before issuing your invitation.

★★★

c. Make your needs clear; map out a better (50/50) split and get agreement.
Now you're talking. Know what you want, sketch out on paper the split you deem more equitable, and give your partner time to look it over and then talk it over.

★★★

d. Check your assumptions: Is this manager a better delegator?
Wisely said. When we start labeling another person as lazy and manipulative (or any other label), we need to check our own mental health and work habits. By contrast, we may be authoritarian or martyred (as this response suggests), or we may be lazy and manipulative too, but amateur in our results, compared to another. If you focus on a sibling rivalry with another manager, you allow your energy to drain away in this hopeless direction. If, on the other hand, you focus your energy on what you want or need, and match that to company objectives, you rechannel your energies in healthful directions. In most companies there is room for you and your opponent. Focus on making your own way, improving your own leadership style.

Nickerson's Recommendation

For a successful four-star approach, start with *d* and then move to *c*.

10. JOYLESS COMPETITOR

How can I control my own feelings of competitiveness against my peer managers?

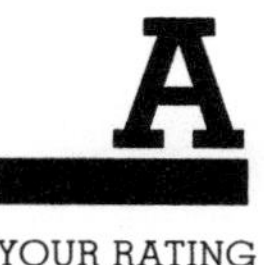

AUDIENCE RESPONSES

YOUR RATING

______ **a.** *Have self-respect and respect for your peers.*

______ **b.** *Approach one or another of these managers and confess your confusion in a friendly way, with humor. They may share your feelings.*

______ **c.** *Competition can be a healthy drive, as long as it is directed toward results, not downgrading of others.*

______ **d.** *Have an informal talk in which you reach agreement on dividing work loads so you do not waste or duplicate effort. Channel your competitive drives against your real competition in the marketplace. Be ready to learn, gain, and share cooperation with your in-house colleagues. Your different talents and abilities can complement one another. There are problems enough in any business to use up* all *our abilities.*

	★	★★	★★★	★★★★
RATING	*NO!*	*RISKY*	*BETTER*	*BEST!*

★★★★ **a. Have self-respect and respect for your peers.**
There's much wisdom in this brief reply. Respect is an excellent and traditional partner to competitiveness, shared by generals of opposing armies and athletes competing for a single crown. When our self-esteem is high, we don't feel obsessive about the other guy. We feel stimulated by racing against really worthy opponents.

★ **b. Confess your confusion with humor. They may share it.**
No. You may find yourself the only naive party to the conversation. This may have the same effect as confessing, "I used to hate and fear you but I don't anymore." Why bring it up? Accept competitiveness as natural (and even fostered by many senior managers) and save your confessions for your memoirs.

★★★★ **c. Competition is a healthy drive aimed at results.**
Right. Get comfortable with it.

★★★ **d. Agree on dividing work loads with no waste or duplication.**
A good idea, except in organizations where top management runs a subtle contest on each major new project or assignment. Often, commitment and results are both greater when worthy opponents throw their best energies and ideas into winning the assignment. New products and processes often arise out of these contests, doubling the company's potential successes. In such cases, the apparent duplication is fruitful, not wasteful.

Comment: It's okay to feel competitive. You are in competition. Your business, hospital, school, government department *is* in competition with other similar groups for limited funding, assignments, promotion, and glory. You must get comfortable about being a friendly competitor, using judgment and courtesy so you will know the moment when the opponents can best join forces and pull together against common threats. Competition is a spur, a spice, a stimulant.

11. AFRAID TO RECONCILE

How can I renew relations with a peer? I damaged our friendship by my behavior.

AUDIENCE RESPONSES

YOUR RATING

________ **a.** *Go and mend fences. Offer whatever recompense, emotional or material, is called for.*

________ **b.** *Tell this person: "I feel bad. Our situation is entirely my fault. What can I do to make it right with you?"*

________ **c.** *Request a peacemaking meeting. Ask for a new start.*

	★	★★	★★★	★★★★
RATING	*NO!*	*RISKY*	*BETTER*	*BEST!*

11. AFRAID TO RECONCILE ANALYSIS

★★★★

a. Mend fences. Offer the recompense called for.
Right. Your offense may require this. For example, if you embarrassed this person before others, you may have to make it right before others. If you slandered the person, for example, you will have to clear the person's name with the relevant people. This is hard, but it completes the transaction and clears the record. If you deprived this person of some material goods, you must work to restore these. Always bear in mind that the action you take should not reembarrass the victim, but don't use this notion to weasel out of your responsibilities.

★★★★

b. Accept responsibility. Ask what would make it right?
If, on considering *a*, you are baffled by how to make amends without further embarrassing the victim, you might try approach *b* and let the victim suggest a way. You are free to negotiate until a reasonable way is found.

★★

c. Request a peacemaking meeting; ask for a new start.
Too ambiguous. The other party may think you want *mutual* apologies when this duty is really yours. Apologize immediately. Accept your responsibility for the damage. Then, if you want to postpone discussion until a later time, if you need to allow time for the victim to think things over, do so. But apologize immediately. Reconciliation is so sweet, a clear conscience so comforting, that you should waste no time before apologizing. Control your expectations, however. If the other party is slow or reluctant to take your hand on it, you can be at peace for having extended a sincere apology.

12. "TOO GOOD" FOR THEM

I've had an advanced management education. The engineering managers around me know their technology, but lack even the rudiments of management knowledge. Yet they lord it over me.

AUDIENCE RESPONSES

YOUR RATING

_______ **a.** *Take control subtly. Learn what experience they needed to acquire their positions. Patiently gain such experience yourself. Keep your performance in tight control. You'll gain respect gradually.*

_______ **b.** *Engineers have a tendency to act as if they know all the answers. You must present all ideas logically and numerically to win their ear.*

_______ **c.** *Casually mention your own education, background, and experiences when discussing problems. Ask if you know any companies, people, or personalities in common. Inquire where they gained their excellent management lore. Be friendly.*

_______ **d.** *Let them lord it over you until they tire of it.*

_______ **e.** *Once you've been out of management school a few years—as they've been out of engineering school—you'll all be on a level with each other. Relax.*

	★	★★	★★★	★★★★
RATING	*NO!*	*RISKY*	*BETTER*	*BEST!*

★★ **a. Take control subtly; patiently gain experience. Perform.**
The only thing you can take control of is your set of responsibilities. Strive for acceptance as a peer, not control of the in-group's reactions to you. Patience is a key word here. Contempt for your fellow managers will bleed through your veneer and retard your acceptance.

★★ **b. Engineers are "know-it-alls". Present your ideas with logic and numbers.**
Say "no" to the first statement, "yes" to the second. Use the language the in-group finds comfortable. But don't accept labels of any kind attached to categories of managers. Engineers are as distinct from one another as any other type of manager.

★★★ **c. Look for common ground: Ask about common interests, ask where they got their experience.**
It always makes sense to explore common interests: mutual friends, geography, military, sports, and professional experiences are all possible shared grounds for getting acquainted. But beware of asking too many questions and making too many probes. Make admiring comments when truly warranted and sincerely meant. Flattery from a person who thinks he or she is "too good for them" will be seen as manipulative.

★★★★ **d. Let them lord it over you until they tire of it.**
If this says "relax," I'm for it.

★★★★ **e. After a few years out of school, you'll all be level.**
Another good reason to relax. Certainly, it makes sense to remember the prejudices that battle-hardened managers feel toward "ninety-day wonders" or recent graduates. You feel you're too good for them? They feel they're too good for you. So you're even already!

Comment: Assess what you do have to offer when you're fresh out of graduate school. You may have the latest research data, but do you have experience and a track record of leading, negotiating, and selling your ideas and the company's products? What you have are educational prerequisites. You don't yet have qualifications. Those you earn as you amass a track record of winning performances for your employer.

Your approach will work better if you convey by words and actions "Here's what I have to offer. How can I be most useful to you? In this engineering-oriented business, here's where a nonengineer like me can make a contribution." I think they'll hear you, with or without numbers.

PART
THREE

SOLVING POLITICAL PUZZLES

Simple person-to-person conflicts between you and another party can be baffling enough to give you sleepless nights.

When the plot thickens, however, when you are tackled by a group, pressured by several people, or asked for a judgment in a conflict involving other parties, you sense greater danger. Your decision, however sane or just, will be observed by onlookers, each with a complex set of opinions.

In a dialogue involving you and a single opponent, you may be able to control half the impact. In a test before onlookers, especially powerful onlookers, your ability to sway opinion, or even elicit reactions worthy of response, grows diffuse. The more the murkier.

Loyalties and friendships add joy to your life but complicate your decision making when friends foment a palace revolution. Do you maintain your independence, counsel caution, take sides? Are you your brother's keeper?

There are principles, but no easy answers as the next few questions point out.

13. VOLUNTEERED BY PEERS

My peers volunteer me for tasks brought up during meetings. This puts me in the embarrassing position of having to say "no."

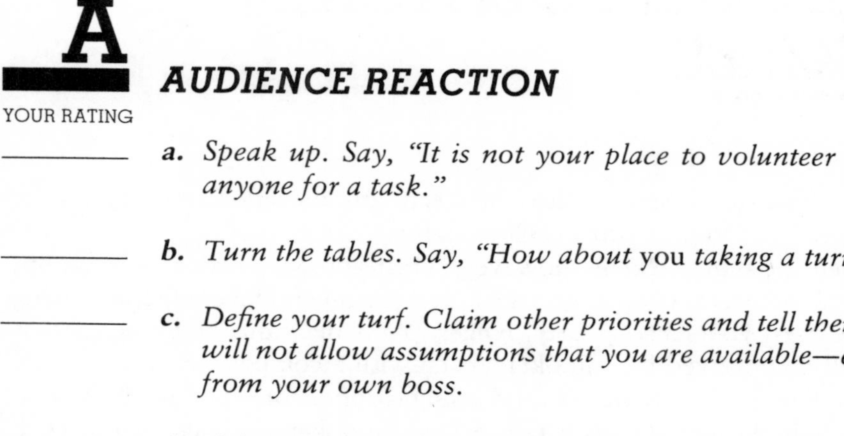

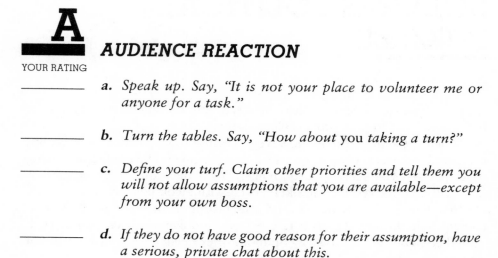

AUDIENCE REACTION

YOUR RATING

________ **a.** *Speak up. Say, "It is not your place to volunteer me or anyone for a task."*

________ **b.** *Turn the tables. Say, "How about* you *taking a turn?"*

________ **c.** *Define your turf. Claim other priorities and tell them you will not allow assumptions that you are available—except from your own boss.*

________ **d.** *If they do not have good reason for their assumption, have a serious, private chat about this.*

	★	★★	★★★	★★★★
RATING	*NO!*	*RISKY*	*BETTER*	*BEST!*

13. *VOLUNTEERED BY PEERS* ANALYSIS

★★ **a. Say, "It is not your place to volunteer me . . .".**
This is a negative approach. Try stating what you would prefer rather than what you forbid.

★★★ **b. Turn the tables: "How about *you* taking a turn?"**
Sure. If you can keep a gleam in your eye and a light bantering tone. Before they can press you, say, "I cannot take on that task just now, with the best will in the world." Offer no further explanations.

★★ **c. Define your turf. Claim other priorities. Say that only your boss can assign you.**
Right thinking, wrong timing. Better save this for a private word later. Right now, maintain your cool by saying: "I have to pass this time, folks. I'm overcommitted. Anyone else want to volunteer?"

★★★ **d. Unless there's a reason they volunteer you, have a serious private chat.**
Combine this with answer *b*, for a *four-star solution*. Get off the hook quickly and gracefully now. After the meeting, discuss your discomfort with their assumptions. Listen carefully; you may have said or done something to make them think of you as a "buck stopper"—or your boss may have made some remark authorizing them to dump on you. Listen up, find out.

14. FRIEND GOING DOWN IN FLAMES

How can I turn around a colleague who continually battles against corporate policy?

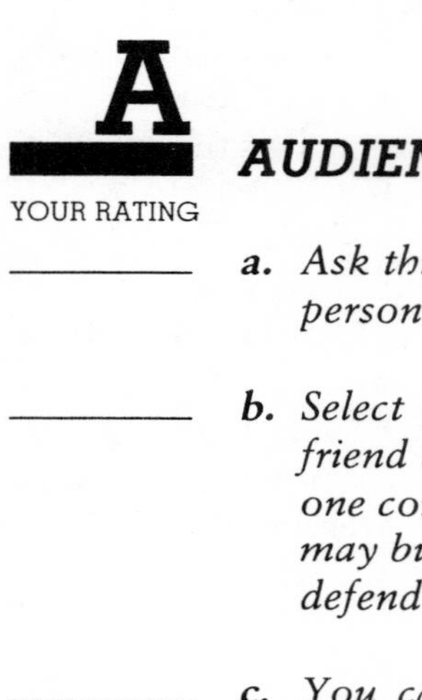

AUDIENCE REACTION

YOUR RATING

________ **a.** *Ask this friend's reasons. If they are weak, work with the person to help him make the change.*

________ **b.** *Select a short, closed-end issue and suggest that your friend develop two concise views of the policy. One pro, one con. Have him discuss and sell you on each view. He may buy into the view he's been opposing when he has to defend it.*

________ **c.** *You can try preaching about how this attitude wastes group time and frustrates those of you who want to move ahead on the issue. This is difficult. He may have a hidden agenda that makes him buck authority. Ask him to examine his inner mind about his motives and to accept the majority rule gracefully.*

________ **d.** *Mind your own business (MYOB) and distance yourself from rebellious friends. You may be seen as a co-rebel.*

	★	★★	★★★	★★★★
RATING	*NO!*	*RISKY*	*BETTER*	*BEST!*

14. *FRIEND GOING DOWN IN FLAMES* ANALYSIS

★★ **a. Ask his reasons. Coach the person.**
What a nice person you are! It may help your curiosity to know what motivates him. He may answer; he may not really know the truth himself. Counseling as a friend is best done when you are asked for it.

★★ **b. Have him sell you on pros and cons of a significant issue, opening up to both sides.**
This would be a superb approach for a boss to take with a subordinate whose other contributions (technical, not political) are so worthy that the person is worth saving, and even coddling. But for you as a peer to attempt it is the heart and soul of self-sacrificing friendship. If you're a self-sacrificing friend and get pleasure from such exercises, go ahead. But limit your expectations, and save enough time to get your work done.

★★★ **c. Preaching is difficult; suggest he examine his motives and accept the majority rule gracefully.**
This is a much better approach. Having done this much, you can do little more, other than suggesting he get some counseling from a wise, detached, experienced third party. Be prepared to sympathize when he gets bounced or exiled for this repetitive rebellion of his.

★★★★ **d. MYOB. Distance yourself.**
Having tried *c*, this is a good final choice.

PART

FOUR

FINE TUNING: DEVELOPING HEALTHY COMPETITIVE DRIVES

To my mind, there are three healthy avenues for developing your own drive for success while building strong and lasting peer support relationships.

1. ***Distinguish yourself*** Stand out from the crowd, not by being different but by making a difference.
2. ***Eliminate the term "personality conflicts" from your consciousness*** Explore only issues conflicts since these are within your power to solve.
3. ***Admit your interdependence with peers, superiors, and subordinates*** Relish it. Develop it.

DISTINGUISH YOURSELF

While nice little boys and girls are taught not to brag about themselves, smart businessmen and businesswomen know how great it feels to make a difference, and to let others know it.

How do *you* make a difference to your organization?

A Quiz on Your Contributions

- Define your special abilities:
  - A linguist?
  - A skilled negotiator?
  - An expert in contract law?
  - A breakthrough researcher?

A specialist in education?
A recognized authority on a vital subject?
An award-winning salesperson?

- What specific problems, vital to your boss's mission, have you solved this year?
- What specific contributions did you make to a team effort this year? To the launching of a new project? To the solving of a long-standing problem?
- What did you study and learn this year that will benefit your department?
- What special "political" connections do you use to the advantage of your department or company?
- What letters of commendation did you add to your personal file this year?
- How many dollars did your efforts add to profits, or subtract from costs?
- How many lives did you save, or persons did you return to health?

(Add your own questions. . .)

Once your mind starts operating along these lines, you will develop some questions of your own, and you'll write specific answers. You'll know how you have distinguished yourself in the eyes of your seniors.

You may discover that your own list is more impressive than you would have thought. In some cases, you'll realize that your peers could write an equally impressive list and that, together, you make outstanding contributions as a team. Feelings of cohesiveness, collaboration, and collateral merit replace feelings of competitiveness. You realize your gifts are unique but complementary—that together you can make two-plus-two equal five or six! When you take the trouble to outline and examine your own self-worth, you are more comfortable allowing others theirs, and rejoicing with them.

About once a month, write yourself a short list under the heading, "How I Made a Difference This Month." Every six months, give your boss an index card with the highlights. Distinguish yourself through your contributions. Make them known.

ELIMINATE THE TERM "PERSONALITY CONFLICT"

The saddest diagnosis in the whole personnel lexicon is "They are having a personality conflict." Sad, because it is so hopeless. Your personality, according to most psychologists, was almost fully formed by the age of 7.

If you take the depressing view that your fully formed personality is at odds with someone else's fully formed personality, what hope is there of reconciliation and accord?

It is much more fruitful to admit, instead, that you and your peer are having a temporary conflict over some issue. That is almost always true. The issue is usually power of some sort: The power to do something or to avoid doing something; the power to use money, equipment, or time as you see fit; the power to advance; the power to have access to people or facilities. Trace the events leading up to your so-called "personality conflict". Make a list of which powers you are conflicting over.

Often, you will discover that the supply of this power is not so limited that your having some will preclude the other person having any. It becomes a test of degree.

In any case, when you approach your peer for a negotiation, it helps greatly to focus on the issues outside yourselves rather than on the personality traits (or flaws) inside you both. You can attack the problems without attacking one another.

This simple change in focus can salvage relationships through many difficult conflicts.

ADMIT YOUR INTERDEPENDENCE

On one of those dark nights when you work too late, you may be heard to mutter, "I'd like to see them survive without me!" On one of those days when troubled colleagues queue up outside your door, you may be heard to seethe, "If only I could run this place by myself!" But when the pressure passes, you are ready to admit your dependence on one another.

When my London seminar company was young, my husband and I ran our little departments, hardly seeing one another from start to end of the day. But like many small companies, we depended on vendors to make the difference for us: printers, mailing houses, travel agents, freight forwarders, catering managers—all came to know our business needs so well, they would call to remind *us* when a deadline was getting dangerously close.

Admit your interdependence and relish it.

Build strong alliances by being an ally yourself. Do help a fellow manager out of a bind when your energy or expertise are called for—and ask for help when you need it. Review, consciously, the variety of talents and skills that stand out among individuals you work with. Who are the technicians, the politicians, the peacemakers, the "fixers," the high-energy people, the work horses? Let them know, with your thanks and reciprocation, that you value them.

Consciously seek to widen your circle of professional connections inside your company. If you've been having lunch with the same crowd month after month, don't dump them but begin to break away, one day a week or so, to meet new people whose fields you know less about. In a large company, your distinction will not become known unless you are willing to carry it beyond your own department doors.

Despite your heavy work load, make it your business to join a professional group or business network, so that your horizon of information and exposure is wider than before. When your boss comes to you with a problem, you may be able to say, "Let me call a few of my connections and see what their companies do about this." (I'm not recommending this just for newcomers to a business. If you've been around a long time, and people think they've got your number, move out to enlarge your professional network so your "number" gets to look more interesting. A stale, stalled career can take a quantum leap with the nourishment of new connections. One evening's conversation with a circle of new people can really point you in a new direction and give you new energy that's noticed at work.)

If you've been bothered by the petty behavior of some peer, with small arguments, games, double-crosses—if you're obsessive over which move to make next—make a move toward your networking acquaintances. Spend an evening talking with them about big problems and big accomplishments, and you'll see how minor your current skirmishes are. You'll save your energies for worthwhile efforts, and leave the games to those who need them.

IS BUSINESS A COMPETITION?

Certainly. At any moment in your company, each department is competing for a bigger share of the money, talent, manpower, time, authority, and attention that everyone seeks.

Even if you stand out as an individual, those who apportion the resources of your company will do so, department by department, and project by project.

While you will always work to distinguish yourself, you must contribute your efforts to the group you're in, so that the overall result produced by the group this year will justify even greater shares in the company's resources for next year. You can contribute, not control.

When a group of people takes this in, and works (despite individual differences) to maximize their impact for the company, they gain the power to go on excelling for another year.

CHECKLIST FOR ENJOYING YOUR CORPORATE CLIMB

1. Form alliances, not friendships. (The friendships will form all by themselves, as a bonus.)
2. Compete for elite assignments; they are not birthrights.
3. Behavior you notice will be repeated. Don't notice negative behavior. Say what you need, instead.
4. Budget your trips to the boss when peers offend. If you must "go up," go *for yourself*, not *against another*.
5. To negotiate with peers, you must cite options; you cannot use power differentials. (Your peer must do the same.)
6. Don't label peers' motives. You won't have time to do your work.
7. Pay your debts.
8. Reconciliation is sweet. Who should initiate it? The one who can.
9. Embrace interdependence. Contribute, don't control.
10. Relish the race. Competitiveness has raised some people's performance from good to glorious.

HOW SHREWD MANAGERS IMPRESS THE BOSS

PART FOUR

FINE TUNING: WISE OPTIONS FOR RELATING TO "THE CHIEF" *151*

PART FIVE

THREE RELATED CHECKLISTS: WHAT WE OWE ONE ANOTHER *159*

SESSION

THREE

HOW SHREWD MANAGERS IMPRESS THE BOSS

INTRODUCTION

Whether you love 'em or loath 'em, you're probably fascinated with the people you call "the boss." Questions about the boss outnumber all others two-to-one in my seminars. People want to know how to meet the boss's "unreasonable" demands, how to "manage" the boss, how to outsmart the boss, how to curry favor—the list is endless, the fantasies and frustrations are acute.

Subordinates judge their bosses narrowly, demanding unerring consistency, wisdom, fairness, and technical proficiency. Subordinates want plenty of protection from above when they err, but hands-off freedom when they're feeling their oats.

Among seminar attendees some chortle, "My boss is perfect compared to the others I heard about today," while others sneer, "My boss should have been here instead of me; the boss needs it more than I do." I take both viewpoints as feelings, not facts.

Small wonder, though, that managers agonize over their bosses' actions, motives, character flaws, and secrets. Whether you mourn or rejoice at your leader's career fortunes, you are hardly indifferent. If your boss moves up, you may be elevated yourself. Or you may face the task of impressing a new executive, sometimes from scratch.

In the multiboss milieu of today's big companies, you may need to impress very different types in a single day: demi-gods and drill sergeants, slave drivers and den mothers; all can complicate or clarify your work.

Ironies abound. Some CEOs maintain a mannerly, statesmanlike grace under all conditions. But a few levels below, midmanagers may rage like mad potentates, driving their departments without mercy and issuing non-negotiable decrees. Everyone wonders if those at the top see what's going on with the "galley slaves" below decks.

In other settings, middle management leads the way in humanism, practicing participative management, boosting subordinate self-worth, and shielding the troops from the disdainful scowls of those at the top. Often, these middle managers soldier on, while being deceived or excluded entirely from the planning process, themselves.

Bosses are always learning and growing if they're any good. I meet many reformed autocrats, struggling to master "walkaround management." They complain of the disorientation they feel while trying to open up communication with subordinates, yet protect trade secrets and their own right to decide for the corporation.

If battle-hardened "insiders" find the boss/subordinate link a continuing challenge, what surprises await the newly hired manager trying to accommodate to the corporate culture. Some of the newly arrived managers you'll meet next are bursting with ambition, eager to grab for glory, but stumbling incautiously on the toes of their seniors. Others are bogged down and bored, once the initial glamor of arrival has worn off. Most managers want more of the boss's time and trust than seniors can safely give. They want to take chances without counting consequences. The gaps between expectations and eventualities can be glaring and stressful.

The questions you'll read next were not singled out for their rarity. They came up again and again in public meetings and private seminars. See if you relate to them in your dual roles as boss and subordinate.

PART

ONE

GETTING THE BOSS'S EAR

"THE BOSS WON'T LISTEN!"

In some cases you're right. Some bosses *won't!* On principal! No one listened to them—now that they've made it, they won't listen to you! They practice and preach the sink or swim method. They rely on your ability to turn your peers into coaches.

Some bosses are kinder than that, but they're preoccupied, temporarily. They're busy saving their own skin or making their next move and won't take on extra risks. Some have lost their nerve. They want to daydream their way to retirement. New ideas are unsettling. It will go easier with you if you find another ear for now. No need to accuse or reform your boss. Help *yourself.*

Consider the possibility that some bosses can't listen. They are so busy learning new technologies, managing larger spans of control, relating to whole new categories of workers, coping with more sophisticated questions from consumers or the press—they are simply running on overload. They have turned off; they need help and support, not added problems from you. Sometimes, they simply do not understand the language you are speaking; they are generalists, you are a specialist, speaking your own vocabulary.

You have choices. Provide extra support and put your problems on hold until the timing is better. Find another adviser for the time being, or *make it easier for your boss to hear you.*

In fact, making it easier, more attractive, and more beneficial for your executives to hear you will have the desired effect whichever mental blocks may isolate your boss.

Make your proposals, your requests, and your messages to the boss as irresistible as you can:

- Keep your message brief.
- Keep it simple (one idea at a time).

- Focus *only* on what is still possible (the present and the future).
- Don't review the past; don't repeat yourself.
- Keep your eye on everything that will benefit the boss.

When you've got your message together, *make it graphic* so your executive can grasp your proposal in a single glance from five paces. If it's not that clear yet, you're not ready to communicate yet with a tired, harried, or unreceptive senior executive.

Shouldn't all bosses be good listeners? Not primarily. They must be good decision makers/risk takers. They may have more pressing or consequential messages than yours to listen to just now. In choosing to listen or not, they may be taking decisions that will satisfy *their* bosses. You will have to accept and respect that.

But it won't be easy, as the next few questioners testify.

1. BOSS WON'T LISTEN

My boss "turns off" every time I start talking and hurries away. I can't get what I need.

AUDIENCE RESPONSES

YOUR RATING

________ **a.** *Make an appointment; don't just hunt down your boss. Write a short outline on your vital issue; share your notes with the boss and stick to them. You'll be able to track your proposals later from your notes.*

________ **b.** *Keep quiet.*

________ **c.** *Listen to the way the others do it. Listen to the way the boss communicates with others. Follow their lead.*

________ **d.** *When talking with the boss, start and finish a single issue at a time. You may be confusing the boss by leaping from topic to topic.*

________ **e.** Do *more. Don't hang around waiting for permissions. If you need training, chase it yourself. Don't ask your boss to do your thinking for you.*

	★	★★	★★★	★★★★
RATING	*NO!*	*RISKY*	*BETTER*	*BEST!*

1. BOSS WON'T LISTEN ANALYSIS

a. Make an appointment. Use notes to limit talk.
Good advice even when your boss is receptive. When the boss is evasive, notice whether you are singled out or if this is the boss's way with others. If only *you* are shunned, check your communication style. Prepare. Jot your vital points on an index card. Rehearse how you plan to cover them; tape-record your presentation. Is your talk simple and direct? Do you wander? Do you complain about the past? Or suggest about the future? Are your recommendations easy or risky? Are you invading another manager's territory? Are you showing your boss a benefit?

b. Keep quiet.
Good. There's a rule of communication which some wise people follow: When your listeners show resistance, *don't try harder*. Be quiet. Let them talk. Break off and regroup. Your reticence is born of self-preservation, not sulking. You can get to the boss by other means. Memo with vital beneficial information. Or ask a colleague to put your questions to the boss if the colleague has the boss's ear. Experiment until you no longer offend the boss, and you're more likely to get what you need.

c. See how others do it; imitate them.
Yes . . . do this, but be sure you know what to look for. Talk to one or two peers whom you trust. Ask their advice: How do *they* go about communicating with this boss? Do they wait until asked? Does the boss prefer written outlines, numerical data? Does the boss have specific times of day when certain items are welcome? Staff "clinic sessions"? Does the boss have certain "hot" deadlines when all informal communications are seen as interruptive? Let a peer know you are having trouble and get some advice.

d. Stick to one issue at a time.
Yes. Often, your boss allows you a hearing on a single topic of interest—and "while you're at it," you get into

other subjects, imposing on the boss's time and decision-making energy. Let the boss's secretary know what you want to discuss. She'll fit you in at a logical point where your subject matter will be valued most and where she can prepare the boss's data to give you the best chance of a prepared hearing. When you've finished, thank the boss and leave. No extras!

e. Do more, talk less; seek what you need without involving the boss.
Yes. Then, take your lumps or laurels like a pro. Also, remember that the boss is not the sole source of information for you. Peers, subordinates, vendors, and other departments may help find pieces of any puzzle for you. If you are singled out for this treatment by the boss, response *e* may have identified your problem as dependency.

Nickerson's Recommendation

Consider all five responses, *a* though *e* to build yourself a four-star solution.

2. BOSS RESPONDS TOO SLOWLY

My boss delays getting back to me about urgent daily problems.

AUDIENCE RESPONSES

YOUR RATING

_________ **a.** *Discuss this with a senior colleague to work out solutions. If your boss has to make your daily decisions, you are not ready for your assignment.*

_________ **b.** *Leave a note on boss's desk with statement of your problem* and *your solution. Then go ahead.*

_________ **c.** *Act. Your boss has shown he or she is not concerned. When uncertain, check with a fellow manager at your level for a second opinion. If the boss objects to the route you took, remind him or her that you did try to consult, sought a second opinion, and took a chance. Agree on a modus operandi for future cases.*

_________ **d.** *Transfer to a new boss or company.*

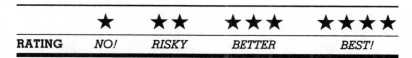

	★	★★	★★★	★★★★
RATING	*NO!*	*RISKY*	*BETTER*	*BEST!*

2. *BOSS RESPONDS TOO SLOWLY* ANALYSIS

a. Use senior colleague as mentor; if you need the boss so much, the boss doesn't need you.

If you are generally prepared for your job, and these urgent questions are arising from a new, unexpected set of situations, you may solve the problems by making appointments or "clinic sessions" and covering many issues at one sitting, until normalcy returns.

If, on the other hand, you took this job without realizing what you were getting into—if your questions are not due to new and unusual circumstances—you are indicating unreadiness for the job. You have two choices: get trained at least cost to your boss, or *get lost*.

How do you get trained? Ask if there is a training/orientation course or manual available from previous regimes. Study; ask questions on only those items you cannot understand from private study. If there is no orientation program, you must still limit the number of questions you ask. So do your legwork. Make notes on every answer provided to you so far. Check the files; talk to previous jobholders, vendors, and other knowledgeable people for details on the most often asked questions. Check the company's *Standard Operating Procedures* for answers that apply to your job. Organize this data into an indexed, orderly, simple *desk manual*. Consult this, always, before bothering your boss or senior colleagues. People have assumed you know your business, If you don't, make it easier to train you than replace you.

b. Leave a note on boss's desk with problem and solution—then go ahead.

Yes. For questions with unusual risks.

c. Act; cover risks with fellow manager; agree when risks arise on policy for future use.

Yes. Making occasional errors is safer than nagging your boss for every little thing. Keep a sense of proportion about getting reassurance from fellow managers, too. If they have to do your thinking for you, they'll soon want to get paid for it.

d. Transfer to a new boss/company.
Insecure managers will take the same insecurities to their next slot. Fix it here and now.

3. CAN'T GET PAST THE SECRETARY

I need time and advice from the boss, but I can't get an appointment. His secretary keeps putting me off, suggesting I leave messages in writing.

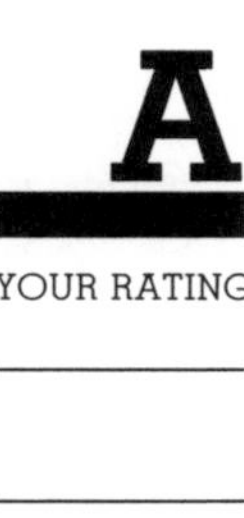

AUDIENCE RESPONSES

YOUR RATING

_________ **a.** *Keep harassing the secretary.*

_________ **b.** *The boss has choices of whom to see. Make it more appealing for the boss to* want *to spend time with you about your issues.*

_________ **c.** *Do as the secretary suggests. Write the boss a memo about direct impacts on business. Await an appointment or reply.*

_________ **d.** *If you've shown yourself as petty, manipulative, complaining, or critical of others, you may continue to be frustrated. Send clear messages: "I need X" or "I've noticed Y and want to suggest Z," and be sure the subjects go beyond "self-serving" and will benefit the boss and the department.*

	★	★★	★★★	★★★★
RATING	*NO!*	*RISKY*	*BETTER*	*BEST!*

3. *CAN'T GET PAST THE SECRETARY* ANALYSIS

★ *a.* **Keep harassing them.**
Why add persistence and insensitivity to your current unpopularity? While there are rare cases of secretaries overprotecting their bosses, most are doing their boss's bidding when they keep you out. Bosses must first take care of the largest risks on their agendas. Yours may not measure up.

★★★ *b.* **Bosses have choices. Make your issues more attractive.**
There's wisdom here. Work on solutions to your problems that will constitute an opportunity (to save time, money; to beat the competition; to create a new service, etc.). Present your ideas that way, and the boss may grant you a hearing, or scribble an okay on your memo.

★★★★ *c.* **Show the direct impact on the boss. Memo for appointment or await an answer.**
There's your answer.

★★★★ *d.* **Rehab your image; send direct, clear requests; settle for written questions and answers.**
Another practical approach.

Comment: Your boss's secretary knows the order of events in the boss's plan for any day. If you send your requests in writing and work through the secretary, you have a better chance of being slotted in favorably. Work with, not against, the secretary.

PART

TWO

BUILDING AND RESTORING TRUST

Some bosses have been burned by extending power to untried subordinates. When your bosses take you on, you are still a bundle of unfulfilled promises. Your bosses may have hope, even faith, but it takes time and consistent excellence from you in *this* role before they really trust you, however glowing your reputation from previous jobs. Meanwhile, these bosses have other subordinates, already "broken in," to whom they can hand off power. Trust is a process, slow and emotional, not an event, instant and rational.

Some subordinates have been burned, too, by biased, prejudiced, or manipulative bosses. They have languished under sluggish leadership while peers moved gloriously ahead under go-getters. Later, in a good situation, their old reservations and suspicions drag them down, making them appear wary, even cynical. This block brings out the worst in the boss, of course, who anoints other minions more willing to sign up with full commitment.

Even the best boss/subordinate relationships are volatile. Review the history of your best working partnerships. Weren't there errors on both sides? Omissions, rifts, bad feelings that took time to heal? We never quite learn about each other entirely. Pride gets in the way. See how quickly the next few questioners take offense at puzzling boss behavior.

4. BOSS HOVERS

My boss hovers, makes constant suggestions, oversupervises my every move. My staff notices this. Why is my boss so insecure?

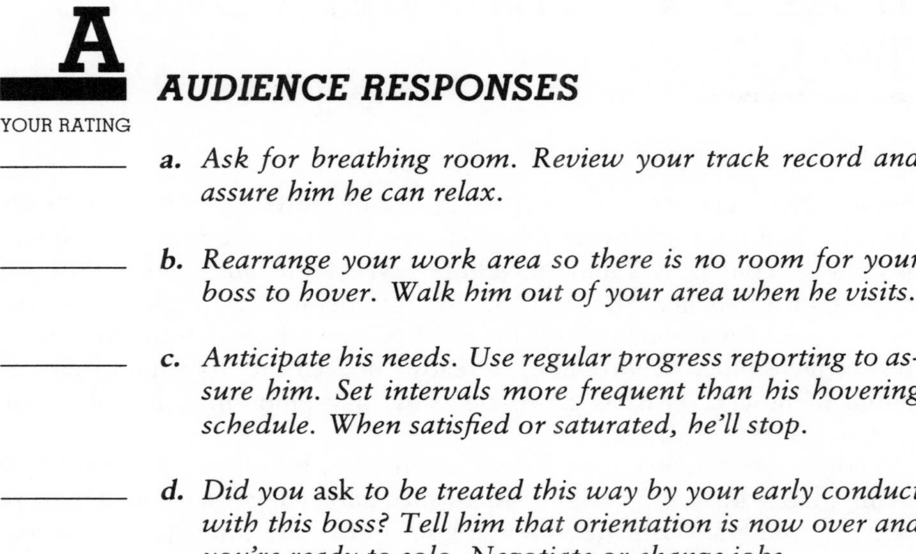

AUDIENCE RESPONSES

YOUR RATING

________ **a.** *Ask for breathing room. Review your track record and assure him he can relax.*

________ **b.** *Rearrange your work area so there is no room for your boss to hover. Walk him out of your area when he visits.*

________ **c.** *Anticipate his needs. Use regular progress reporting to assure him. Set intervals more frequent than his hovering schedule. When satisfied or saturated, he'll stop.*

________ **d.** *Did you* ask *to be treated this way by your early conduct with this boss? Tell him that orientation is now over and you're ready to solo. Negotiate or change jobs.*

	★	★★	★★★	★★★★
RATING	*NO!*	*RISKY*	*BETTER*	*BEST!*

★★

a. **Ask for breathing room; use track record to reassure boss.**
Could work. Could also offend the boss. Your past record got you promoted *to* this job; it does not guarantee your performance *in* this job. Rather than judging your boss's motives ("Why is the boss insecure?") make it easy on yourself and just accept that some bosses want to give and get extra protection with any new assignment. Ask what risks your boss particularly wants covered on each assignment. Show how your plan of operation and your reporting methods will cover these risks fully. Then follow through.

★

b. **Rearrange your work area so boss cannot hover; walk him out.**
Both will be seen as manipulative. "Walking people out" of your area is a ploy to use on nonentities, not bosses.

★★★★

c. **Anticipate his needs; report progress more frequently than his "hovering" schedule.**
Absolutely. Meet your boss's needs. It always pays. Work to satisfy, not saturate, your boss with information and risk coverage.

★★★

d. **Did you *ask* for this? Ask to solo, negotiate.**
No need for self-blaming. What's done is done. It's easier to accept that this manager, for now, is asking for safeguards. Don't ask to solo. Ask what risks the boss wants to see covered, and cover them, efficiently.

Try this technique: When moving through an orientation program with a new boss, you might create a simple index card system to assure that you know and cover large risks. For example:

Assignment: *NEW PIGGYBACK SHIPPING SYSTEM*

Procedure: Step 1.
2.
3.
4.
5.

Risks to avoid a.
b.

Safeguards to apply: a.
b.

Signal/report method and timetable a.
b.

Imagine using such a card while interviewing or being trained on the new procedure. Imagine using such a card when you are training your own subordinates in the future. *Every new assignment has risks.* Stop taking it personally; instead, get your boss and yourself covered.

5. *BOSS TRASHES MY ADVICE*

My boss asks my advice, then ignores it. If he's not going to use it, why bother me?

AUDIENCE RESPONSES

YOUR RATING

________ **a.** *Follow up; ask why.*

________ **b.** *Next time, remind boss what happened this time. Refuse an opinion next time.*

________ **c.** *If the subjects are critical, bone up more. Improve the quality of your advice. You may be failing your "oral exams."*

________ **d.** *Your input is only one of several your boss may request. There is no requirement that your boss take your advice in preference to others'. Be grateful you were polled at all.*

	★	★★	★★★	★★★★
RATING	*NO!*	*RISKY*	*BETTER*	*BEST!*

★★

a. **Follow up; ask why.**

No. Follow up and ask what ("why" demands justification and probes motives; "why" is a combative question). Instead, ask your boss what his final decision was, which factors influenced him most, what you can learn from the process. Show genuine interest in learning what not why, so you can contribute more effectively next time.

★

b. **Refuse an opinion next time.**

Your boss has no obligation to poll you. But you have an obligation to comment when polled, if you have any information or contribution to make. Don't rebuke your boss if you value your job.

★★★

c. **Bone up. Improve the quality of your advice.**

Yes. In fact, don't be sensitive about your advice being ignored. Perhaps parts of it *are* being used. Keep a record of the advice you give. Check the final solution: where does it diverge? *Which risks do the divergent elements cover?* Perhaps these risks are outside your area of expertise. (Perhaps you suggested technical solutions, whereas the remedy covers a legal or financial risk too.) By keeping such a "decision diary," you can ask questions that are specific, structured, and substantive, rather than carping.

★★★★

d. **Your input is one of several. Be grateful you were polled.**

Yes. Besides polling from several different disciplines, your boss may poll among people in the same discipline who take divergent views. This may help the boss anticipate consequences better, or it may help him or her enlist support later, from a wider base. Often, your boss will poll several views, then take an entirely new tack, embracing none of those polled. If you must ask a question, ask your boss: "How useful is my advice in general? Often, I cannot see my ideas in the solution you finally select. Should I be giving you something different?" The boss's reply may reassure and reignite you.

6. *MOODY BOSS*

Despite best efforts to ignore them, my boss's moods infuriate, depress, or frighten me.

AUDIENCE RESPONSES

YOUR RATING

_________ **a.** *Develop an automatic "nice and easy" response to your boss's varying moods. Ask if there is anything you can do to make the day go more smoothly. Avoid probes about the moods themselves. Moody people are irritated when you notice the moods.*

_________ **b.** *If the mood is tolerable and not aimed personally at you, you can just ignore it. Otherwise, if the moods are disruptive and out of control, take the problem to the next higher level of command.*

_________ **c.** *Concentrate on what is happening that's good in your own day. Try to stay positive and productive regardless of how another is feeling and acting around you.*

_________ **d.** *Reschedule your solo and contact times. When my boss is out of sorts, I stay clear.*

	★	★★	★★★	★★★★
RATING	*NO!*	*RISKY*	*BETTER*	*BEST!*

6. MOODY BOSS ANALYSIS

a. "Nice and easy" response.
Wonderful advice. The responder has learned that other people's moods come from inside them and are not caused by someone else. Offering anything you can do to make the day go more smoothly is courteous, caring, and professional. The other essential is detachment from any expectation that *your* calm demeanor will bring about a calm response. If it does, great. If not, at least you are calm.

b. Ignore the mild behavior; take the disruptive stuff up a level.
No. Don't ignore it. Accept it. There's a big difference. If the mood causes disruptive behavior, you can let your boss know this behavior is disruptive for you, without escalating to a level over your boss's head. You cannot expect to change how a person is, only how a person acts toward you. So, you would not say, "Don't be moody" to your boss (or to anyone.) But you could say, "When you slam doors and throw things in the office, I get upset. May I ask you, please, to try another less invasive way of dealing with your upsets when I am around?" I would never suggest going above your boss's head as a first resort. Instead, if your request for calmer behavior does not succeed, go to a peer of your boss's, for example, a professional from Personnel or Employee Assistance, and ask for help or advice. Complaining over your boss's head will have punitive results in many structured companies.

c. Concentrate on the good in your own day.
Another detached viewpoint. It will help you accept the other guy's pain as his own, without having to "stuff" your feelings (you won't have such strong feelings about it) and without having to fix or remedy his moods.

d. Reschedule your solo and contact times. Stay clear.
If you have control over your contact times, excellent. If the boss has control, however, and doesn't have the sense

to hide out, you can always offer to "come back another time if you're under pressure now."

Comment: If you have strong biases about bosses—if you think they should maintain a stiff upper lip at all times—your discomfort during an outburst will be coming from your expectations, not from your boss's behavior. Keep up your hopes, keep down your expectations, and you'll suffer less tension when others lose control.

In my travels, I've heard many horror stories from subordinate managers who watched bosses deteriorate into depressions, illnesses, or substance abuse. If you are feeling such strain, get help for yourself. Contact your personnel department or Employee Assistance Program about your own distress. If personnel or the EAP people judge it proper, they may pursue the issue with the sick person. Meanwhile you've taken care of you, which is your prime responsibility.

PART THREE

AVOIDING SELF-DEFEATING SUSPICIONS

The single most salient fact about your boss is that the boss always has more formal power than you. You may find this useful, encouraging, and a spur to your own ambitions, if you use your boss as a facilitator/role model.

On the other hand, you may have been brought up perversely. Power differentials may make you rebellious, resentful, judgmental, even envious of your boss if you cannot figure out why the boss, not you, should have all this power. (Lucifer, they tell us, had the same problem.)

THE COMPULSION TO CHALLENGE THE BOSS

If you bristle when you hear the words "office politics"—if you earned your reputation as a rebel in schools, neighborhoods, the military, and early jobs—you may be a prime candidate for corporate suicide and go down in flames that everyone will notice.

You may see other people's respect for bosses as "toadying," and you'll say so, loudly, and with loathing. You may get your thrills from flouting organizational taboos—and you'll flout all of them. You'll pester bosses for equal rights when their favored high-flyers get ahead. You'll badmouth your boss recklessly. You'll throw tantrums at regular intervals. You'll violate the chain of command blindly; you'll make official, written complaints if you are frustrated for longer than a week, on an operating problem.

If management can find cause to bounce you (summary execution), they will. But in these days of litigiousness, you'll more likely be isolated in some hopeless corporate warren where your ravings will be muffled. Eventually, you'll have to escalate, doing something silly—like quitting without references or a new job.

After a few episodes of righteous grandstanding, you may have to pull in your horns just to pay the rent. Your loose cannon gets locked away; your anger goes underground.

UNDERGROUND RESISTANCE TO BOSS POWER

If your early angers were penalized, you may choose a tight-lipped judgmental approach, sniffing at your boss's decisions, complaining of errors only after it's too late, comparing this boss odiously with earlier bosses (whom you vilified at the time). Your conversations will be largely in your head or with people who are powerless.

If you are technically proficient, your passive complaints may be tolerated or ignored. You may become a corporate mummy, upright in your chair, able to make slight movements and squeaky sounds through your wrappings, rendered daily more faded and impotent.

Suspecting your boss of heartlessness or stupidity, procrastination, or laziness—common temptations—can retard your career and sap your energy.

Don't suspect... ask for what you need. Don't complain... request. Don't seek sympathizers for your resistance... seek support for your proposals. That's my advice to the boss-resistant managers whose questions follow.

7. BOSS IS INCOMPETENT

Technically, financially, and managerially, each of us knows more than our boss. How does the boss hang on?

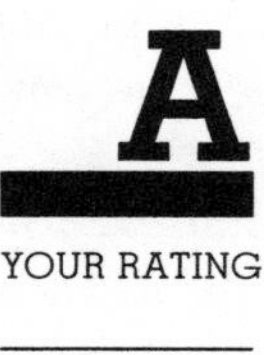

AUDIENCE RESPONSES

YOUR RATING

________ **a.** *Keep lines open to your boss's boss. Don't badmouth* your *boss. Just keep the big chief aware of your own abilities and willingness to contribute importantly.*

________ **b.** *Do nothing to rub your boss's nose in it.*

________ **c.** *Prop your boss up. Show him or her your loyalty and reliability.*

________ **d.** *On specific tasks beyond the boss's reach, volunteer to help, or perform them entirely yourself. Offer this service as a time saver to your boss. It keeps the boss from blocking your progress.*

	★	★★	★★★	★★★★
RATING	*NO!*	*RISKY*	*BETTER*	*BEST!*

7. BOSS IS INCOMPETENT ANALYSIS

★★

a. Keep lines open to your boss's boss. Show ability and willingness to contribute.

Be careful. If you are in a large, hierarchical organization, your efforts to end run your boss will be noticed by your boss, his or her boss, and fellow players. If your loyalty is questioned, you'll take the consequences.

b. Do nothing to rub your boss's nose in it.

Wise advice. While you may meet some incompetent bosses (misplaced, out of their depth, or ill), most are quite competent at what their bosses require of them. They may not be as good as you at your specialty, but they may be excellent at their own. Many are in place to facilitate work politically so that you "competent subordinates" can do your work well. Some are in place to make friends in high places, some are in transitional slots while waiting for their real jobs. You may be right, but don't be blunt about this with your boss or others.

On the other hand, do cover your operating risks. Memo this boss with recommendations, warnings, and deadlines for reply on risks you must cover at your level.

c. Prop your boss up. Show reliability/loyalty.

Yes. While the boss may not need as much "propping" as you think, it is always advisable to show reliability and loyalty in highly structured, hierarchical organizations. Smaller companies are also led by people who value loyalty and reliability. Develop these traits as a first resort. All bosses everywhere have the right to call on their subordinates for the best work—technical, financial, and managerial—of which the subordinate is capable. You did not sign a conditional agreement when you took your job, offering to do your best only for bosses you approve of wholeheartedly. The tacit agreement is: You'll do your best when you take that paycheck—and if you don't like it, you'll negotiate, or depart. Making the harsh judgment that your boss is incompetent puts you in a poor position to negotiate.

 ***d.* Volunteer for specific tasks to save time.**
Sure. Many a great career has been built on such volunteering.

Nickerson's Recommendation

For a four-star answer, combine *b*, *c*, and *d*.

8. BOSS VACILLATES

Important discounts, opportunities, and advantages vaporize while the boss vacillates. My work is wasted.

AUDIENCE RESPONSES

YOUR RATING

________ **a.** *Give deadlines. Clearly state consequences of delay. Cite opportunities and rewards for promptness, offer to help. Follow up.*

________ **b.** *Increase the pressure. Risk nagging.*

________ **c.** *Give better lead time. Ask for the decision slightly earlier than you need it.*

________ **d.** *Offer very clear lists of options so the boss can select rather than create answers. Let him or her check off the appropriate box on the form. Make it easier.*

	★	★★	★★★	★★★★
RATING	*NO!*	*RISKY*	*BETTER*	*BEST!*

★★★

a. Give deadlines with consequences and rewards. Offer help.
Good, if the problem is merely work overload on your boss's part. But the requester cites vacillation, not just delay. You must give data that reduces your boss's risks, in choosing one path over another. Add any other form of help to this essential form.

★

b. Increase the pressure; nag.
No. A boss under pressure does not make good decisions. Reduce the pressure. Reduce the risks; increase the boss's certitude about your preferred course of action.

★★

c. Give better lead time.
Again, it's good to give extra time, but you must really give extra certainty, extra evidence that the boss will win by taking a certain route, and taking it *early*. I think you need to stop pressing for individual deals and work out a low-risk modus operandi with this boss.

★★★★

d. Make it easier. Create a checklist of safe options and let the boss choose one.
Here's the astute idea. It reduces risk and saves time. Furthermore, a collection of such checklists would make the backbone of a procedures manual you could use as a precedent for the future, thus leaving your boss in peace while you get on with work approved, in principal, for yourself.

9. *HOW CAN I TELL THE BOSS OFF?*

How can I tell my boss how ridiculous his ideas are and what an embarrassment it is to work for him?

A

AUDIENCE RESPONSES

YOUR RATING

_______ **a.** *Don't.*

_______ **b.** *Forthrightly.*

_______ **c.** *Show alternatives to his ideas that will convince him to go that way. Welcome debate.*

_______ **d.** *Focus on what you need. Turn a blind eye to the rest of the boss's ideas. If they don't directly concern you, they are his business.*

	★	★★	★★★	★★★★
RATING	*NO!*	*RISKY*	*BETTER*	*BEST!*

2. HOW CAN I TELL THE BOSS OFF? ANALYSIS

★★★★ ***a.* Don't.**
Right! Even if you think the boss is a fool, never say so to the boss or anyone else. Remember the biblical injunction against calling your brother "fool." It applies double to bosses.

★ ***b.* Forthrightly.**
Here, both the question and the response come from people yearning to commit career suicide.

★★★ ***c.* Show attractive alternatives. Welcome debate.**
Yes, to the first part. No, to the second. You are not your boss's debating partner, but you are obligated to contribute ideas with distinct advantages when your boss proposes a plan of action. If you are a good politician, you'll discuss, not debate, with your boss. Take the junior stance. Ask your boss to teach you the advantages of his or her ideas. Listen and learn. Then, show how you differ, and offer the advantages of your ideas. Suggest a brief test or trial period, using the best of both. That's smart politics.

***d.* Focus on your needs. Be quiet about ideas that don't concern you.**
Yes. Combine this detached approach with suggestion *c* and you have a four-star answer.

10. BOSS AS BARRIER

The boss is prime resister to every change that is announced. We're all ready; she holds back, making the department look bad upstairs. Shall we expose her?

A

AUDIENCE RESPONSES

YOUR RATING

________ **a.** *Don't accuse the boss of being wrong or balky. Meet the boss and ask for changes you are willing to invest yourselves in.*

________ **b.** *The boss may have good reasons for caution yet be unwilling to engage you in debate.*

________ **c.** *Avoid criticizing your boss to others. Be patient. You are not being judged harshly for your boss's timidity. The people upstairs know who runs your department.*

________ **d.** *Keep your sense of humor. Then let your boss know what strengths, time, and energy you are willing to dedicate to the projects you espouse.*

	★	★★	★★★	★★★★
RATING	*NO!*	*RISKY*	*BETTER*	*BEST!*

10. BOSS AS BARRIER ANALYSIS

★★★ **a. Don't accuse the boss. Ask for change. Invest in it.**
Well said. If your proposal *guarantees* to cover your boss's risks, you may be able to sway the boss. Ask which risks are holding your boss back. Show in detail how you can control or contain those risks; which specific actions you'll take. If your boss is not satisfied, better luck next time.

★★★ **b. The boss may have good reasons she is unwilling to share.**
True. And if you've made a habit of pressuring the boss, that unwillingness will harden. I am not saying that your boss is right or always right. Indeed, a pattern of resistance from your boss can demoralize your department and cut you off from involvement in "hot" new projects. If the problem is really chronic, you might dare to gather a group of your boss's most trusted subordinates to encourage and hearten the boss about the next hot project. You would all need to follow the guarantee process outlined earlier. If you cannot give guarantees that convince, you are back at square one.

c. Avoid criticizing your boss. You aren't being judged here.
Right. It's politically wise never to disparage a boss. Speak only about yourself: what you need, what you propose, what you are willing to contribute to a project.

d. Keep your sense of humor. Make an offer.
Yes. One caution. Once you have offered, don't expect carte blanche acceptance from your boss. She may still shy away if the guarantee you produce is not thoroughly convincing. Be willing to invest again and again to build the boss's confidence in you, piecemeal. Expect steady progress, not dramatic victories.

Nickerson's Recommendation

For a four-star answer, combine *a*, *b*, *c*, and *d*. A further word about method. If the majority of people in your group join you in frustration over a pattern of blockage, you need to confront the boss in a constructive, nonaccusing way. In a formal meeting, show data on a pattern of inaction or noninvolvement. You must be able to demonstrate that other departments have gone along with prior proposals and have reaped successes. Then give the boss data that guarantees risk reduction on the next proposed item. Give the boss time to meet you again and give you an instructive response. Remember: You are subordinates. You cannot challenge the boss to defend her position, only to teach you or instruct you about risks you cannot see yet. This stance keeps you nonjudgmental. It prevents you from attacking your boss's courage or integrity. This approach may result in the boss opening up, rather than silencing you. From there, healthier negotiations can begin.

11. BOSS AS DICTATOR

My boss runs a totalitarian regime. There is only one way of doing things, no matter what it costs everyone else!

A

AUDIENCE RESPONSES

YOUR RATING

________ **a.** *Be diplomatic. This too shall pass.*

________ **b.** *Try to communicate feelings and concerns diplomatically.*

________ **c.** *If you support this person consistently, in time he or she will trust you enough to ask for and consider your views. On the other hand, if his or her way is effective, why should the boss change for you?*

________ **d.** *Change jobs.*

	★	★★	★★★	★★★★
RATING	*NO!*	*RISKY*	*BETTER*	*BEST!*

11. BOSS AS DICTATOR ANALYSIS

★★ **a. Be diplomatic. This too shall pass.**

Sure, diplomacy is required when dealing with tough people. But this too may *not* pass. (In some government and military posts, either the boss or you may be transferred in two to three years. You can wait it out.) But in commercial life, this dictator may continue to rule indefinitely. Limit needless clashes with this person. If you are heavily outgunned, actively seek a transfer and nourish outside contacts who may offer you a job.

★★ **b. Try to communicate your feelings and concerns diplomatically.**

"Try to" is a phrase used by potential victims. Your feelings and concerns may fall on deaf ears.

★★ **c. If you support this person consistently, you'll be trusted and your views sought. On the other hand, if the boss's way is effective, why should the boss change?**

Your consistent support will be demanded, not rewarded by such a tough guy. The second thought is more realistic. If the boss's way is working for the boss, it will continue. (We daydream that tough guys will reform or get chewed out by even tougher guys. But often, they are doing tough jobs, and they are applauded by their even tougher chiefs. You may be too meek for the strains inherent in this particular business.) You have choices. It may be wiser to leave than to dream of reforming the boss. Your departure may hardly be noticed.

★★★ **d. Change jobs.**

While I normally reserve this as a "last resort," I recommend it for people who have labeled the boss a villain. You may have started to burn your bridges already. Begin a methodical job hunt; seek a lower-stress climate than this one.

Nickerson's Recommendation

For a four-star answer, or for "next time around" this subordinate may need some pointers:

1. The tougher your boss, the more you need peer alliances and lateral mentors to help you keep perspective.
2. Timing is vital. Many of these tough guys have effective number 2 executives who know when to stay out of the way, when to announce views strongly, and when to work through others rather than down-face the chief directly. Observe and learn.
3. Try to see the virtues of tough bosses: decisiveness, insight, experience, ruthlessness. If you would not have been happy in the court of Caligula, you won't be happy in the corridors of certain corporations either. When the dictator's vices outweigh his or her virtues, your choices will be about you, not the boss.

FINE TUNING: WISE OPTIONS FOR RELATING TO "THE CHIEF"

As everyone knows who ever bought "the old school tie" or mentioned "mutual friends" in a job interview, it can help an ambitious manager to share backgrounds and sensibilities with the boss. But you need not immerse yourself in psychology to understand what your boss wants. Your bosses will always hire you for one reason: They think you can contribute significantly to department or corporate goals. It will be these goals, not your boss's background, beliefs, or motives that you must learn quickly and embrace fully if you are to make yourself valuable to your boss.

COMMIT YOUR BOSS'S GOALS TO PAPER

It can be difficult to specify your boss's goals if they change quickly. In volatile market conditions or turbulent times you must listen for goal directives every time your boss speaks, whether in a chat or a formal meeting. When you see the boss marching to a new tune, think about what you will have to do—what your group will have to do to keep up. Work up a chart today about your boss's goals. Understand it. Analyze it. Work with it until you can produce such a chart rapidly and accurately whenever you need to.

BOSS'S RISK VALUE CHART

BOSS'S GOALS FOR THE YEAR (Quarter or period)		
GOAL	RISK/VALUE RANK	HOW I COULD HELP
A ______	______	______
B ______	______	______
C ______	______	______
D ______	______	______
E ______	______	______
F ______	______	______
G ______	______	______
H ______	______	______

Start with the left-hand column. List what you know your boss's goals to be for the next quarter or year. (Describe what you know; don't prescribe what you wish they'd be.) The items you jot down may be short-term specifics such as

1. Bring costs down 10 percent.
2. Install new computer software.
3. Hire new production controller.
4. Debug machine repair system.

or you may include permanent standing items such as:

5. Continue to supervise project groups.
6. Improve and maintain performance evaluations.
7. Maintain customer liaison.

Now, although the items you listed are important, you rank their relative risk/value to your boss this year (1 through 8). Sit down with your boss and validate what you have written so far. Next, in the right-hand column, jot in your own role as a subordinate to your boss. How will you contribute specifically to each of these goals? (You may be involved with only a few—while other managers support the boss on other tasks. Just fill in yours as appropriate.)

HOW ACCURATE WILL YOUR ESTIMATES BE?

Do you imagine that your list of boss's goals will be accurate? Many people assume they are clear about the boss's goals and their relative risk/value numbers. Yet, when we match up presidents and their VPs, or VPs and their division heads, we find wide divergence—as much as 40 percent—even when the pairs get along well and work effectively. Think of the enhanced clarity and targeted energy you'd gain when you *know* where you are both going.

Sometimes, in our seminars, people tell me they'd be afraid to show such a chart to their bosses. They fear the boss would feel pressured, or the subordinate would feel stupid if the entries are way off target. (They fail to see that they've already committed themselves to the goals they *imagine* to be right. Discussing the chart would help them confirm or correct the flight plan.)

I've conducted sessions using these charts at such widely divergent organizations as

- Ciba Geigy (Manchester, England)
- Department of Defense (Ft. Meade, Maryland)
- Boston City Hospital
- State of New York, Department of Education
- Wright Patterson Air Force Base, Dayton
- Southwest Research Institute, San Antonio

No matter how senior or conservative the boss—I found bosses to be fascinated, not frightened, by the process. And for the first time, some of the boss/subordinate teams had quick, concise conversations clarifying issues that had previously taken lengthy debates. What they needed was a simple structure or context for matching goals with each other, and for sizing up risks.

If you've been going through your business year smugly supposing you see eye to eye with your boss, or nervously worrying that you're growing farther apart, this contextual tool, which I call the Risk/Value Chart, will help in either case. Once you've made a success of the Risk/Value Chart to pin down immediate goals, you may need to look at a broader planning tool to help you divide power and responsibility in a new way to accomplish these goals.

If your boss has said that you must "do more with less" this year, you've had a signal that power will be pushed downward to you—and you may have to follow suit, pushing some of your power downward to your subordinates. Because releasing power to the next level down is always difficult for managers (and risky for the subordinate receiving the new powers and responsibilities), you should have a concise context for doing it. Using the Power Sharing Chart that follows, you analyze your boss's present method of handling the classic management functions: Plan, Organize, Delegate, Measure, Control, Communicate, and Perform Routines. Every boss in the world exercises these seven functions, but they do it in different proportions, depending on their level of power and the resources they command. First, jot down all you know about your boss's present modus operandi. Then do a similar chart about your own managerial methods. Then, decide specifically how you would alter those proportions if you are to help your boss in new ways to handle new risks.

Scan the chart and read over the instructions that follow it before attempting to fill it in.

BOSS'S POWER SHARING CHART

FUNCTIONS WHICH ALL MANAGERS PERFORM	PERCENTAGE OF TIME REQUIRED IN THE YEAR BY YOUR BOSS	RISK/VALUE RANK 1-7 AS BOSS WOULD RATE: IT	WHERE I COULD HELP
Plan (changes, new projects, programs)	___%	_____	_____*
Organize (redeploy all resources)	___%	_____	_____*
Delegate (assign, teach, coach, develop)	___%	_____	_____*
Measure (number crunching)	___%	_____	_____
Control (follow-up, corrections)	___%	_____	_____
Communicate (outside and upward in the organization)	___%	_____	_____
Perform routine tasks	___%	_____	_____
	TOTAL 100%		

*By invitation only

↑
BY WHAT
% COULD
I RELIEVE
MY BOSS?

(Fine-tuning instructions follow.)

HOW TO FIGURE THE FUNCTIONS

Before filling in percentages, you might want to think about the functions as your boss uses them.

PLAN If your boss is very senior, planning will be a major responsibility, even if professional planners are available for some of the legwork. Presidents often put in as much as 25 to 30 percent of their year planning. Especially if changes are expected—new acquisitions, new products, new legislation, shifts of manpower, budget cuts. Those changes will involve senior managers in heavy planning sessions.

ORGANIZE If some of the previously-mentioned changes occur, detailed organizing sessions will follow the planning sessions. If you are short staffed, or your budgets are reduced, senior managers must determine who will do what work and what use will be made of total resources? Manpower, machinery, money, property, contractors, may all be redeployed.

Even if your boss is not very senior, you must consider whether experimentation, training, new products, new equipment, or new programs will require your boss to reorganize. If so, there will be many late nights at the desk, mapping things out and many meetings necessary to get agreement on the new organization plan.

DELEGATE If the plan/organize load is heavy this year, the boss will be obliged to assign new tasks, train people, get commitment, debug and adjust assignments, keep up morale, and keep people informed of progress as well as future plans. All this is included in the ongoing process of delegation.

Regardless of your boss's place in the hierarchy, you may need to account for these two factors in delegation:

Worker turnover if your workers turn over frequently, the delegation process has to be repeated over and over again for newcomers. This consumes great quantities of management time.

Boss turnover If the boss is newly appointed, or newly promoted, it takes time for subordinate managers to adjust and for the boss to learn the ropes. The delegation process is fairly intense until both sides come to an understanding on details. (Conversely, if the boss and subordinates are all stable, established, and used to the routine, delegation succeeds with a minimum of explanations or argument.)

MEASURE What percentage of your boss's time goes to measuring and evaluating performance of technical, financial, production, sales, and other tasks? Is your boss a number cruncher? Or are the numbers done by the boss's subordinates? Some senior managers have set strict limits on the kinds of numbers they really want to see daily. Instead of looking at miles of computer printouts, they get one single sheet of data per day that tells them at a glance the state of health of their operation.

CONTROL Must your boss check up, follow through, and adjust requirements until subordinates produce the desired results? If people take direction well, the control function is minimal. If people miss the point at the delegation stage, however, control can become a nightmare—and deadlines are pressing by then. Senior bosses entrust the lion's share of control functions to trusted and powerful midmanagers. In the case of supervisors and junior bosses, however, the boss may perform the control function personally and frequently throughout each day. Delegation may be followed quite closely by control.

COMMUNICATE Remember, all downward communication can be safely covered in the categories *delegate* and *control.* So this *communicate* category is available for upward and outward communication. After all, we cannot control those above us or those outside the corporation, so we communicate with them using persuasion, not power. Senior managers do very little upward communicating: Often they are at the top, themselves. They may do outward communication to press, government, other corporations, and the public. Midmanagers do a lot of upward communication as well as outward. Supervisors may confine much of their communication to peers and people inside their own departments, though supervisors in service and customer liaison departments can rack up big scores in outward communication.

PERFORM REPETITIVE WORK While CEOs do very little of this, and midmanagers do modest amounts, there are many working supervisors who spend half their days doing work very similar to that done by their subordinates. They may break in newer projects or debug problems. Here are three illustrative examples showing different charts at different levels of organization:

FUNCTIONS	TOP MANAGERS	MID MANAGERS	PERFORMING SUPERVISORS
Plan	30%	10%	5%
Organize	20	10	10
Delegate (downward communication)	20	20	20
Measure	8	15	10
Control (follow-up)	5	15	20
Communicate (up & out)	15 (outward)	20	10
Perform Repetitive Tasks	2	10	25
	100%	100%	100%

Of the three levels, the most senior will have heaviest scores on the top three items: Plan, Organize, and Delegate (all tasks that drive the future). Midmanagers will have heavier scores on Measure/Control since they must adjust and monitor until workers meet the plan sent down from on high. Supervisors may have heavier numbers from the middle to bottom of the chart if they perform routines personally. While they may have heavy Delegate scores (this includes coaching of new workers), their opportunity to communicate upward or outward may be limited (unless they deal directly with customers or vendors).

HOW THE TWO CHARTS INTERLOCK

Using the Risk/Value Chart, you can confirm what your boss needs done for the coming period: how much he or she values the various tasks—and you'll know where to volunteer your services. Next, you can work together on the Power-Sharing Chart to see where the boss would like to be less involved—and where you need authorization to get more involved. You must be politically careful as you exchange power.

WORK UP A SET OF THE TWO CHARTS ABOUT YOUR OWN JOB

Create a Risk/Value Chart about your own year to come. Compare it with your boss's chart. See where you need to make yourself available to your boss. See also which items of yours would drop to the bottom (or off the chart altogether) if you attempt to help your boss.

Then create a Power-Sharing Chart regarding your own deployment of time and energies for next year. Ask your boss to go over these charts at your next performance/goal-setting session.

Here are some simple rules:

1. First, be sure your boss is happy with the way you handle the Plan, Organize, and Delegate roles on your chart.

2. Then, be sure you are getting results from Measure, Control, Communicate, and Perform on your chart.

3. When requesting additional work or volunteering to help your boss, stay out of your boss's areas: Plan, Organize, and Delegate . . . these are the source of your boss's power and will not be shared with you easily. Help, by invitation only.

4. When offering to help your boss or save time for the boss, only offer to involve yourself with the boss's Measure, Control, Communicate, and Perform, since these are not the source of the boss's power; they do not drive the future of the department. Also, errors in these four areas can be spotted more quickly and fixed more easily than errors at the upper levels.

Bosses want you to use your initiative, but they don't like you to interfere in theirs. If you can learn this early (and the two charts help you get clear about it), you won't make the political blunders that many hotshot subordinates make without knowing where they went wrong.

Whenever you feel off balance with your boss, spend some quiet time reviewing your boss's upcoming tasks (the Risk/Value Chart) and your boss's current use of time in various functions (The Power-Sharing Chart) so that you go into your discussions with sympathies rather than suspicion, exploring needs rather than motives, and you'll have a forward-looking and fruitful negotiation.

PART

FIVE

THREE RELATED CHECKLISTS: WHAT WE OWE ONE ANOTHER

Since we've been saying that a lot of our pain and anxiety about bosses comes from unrealistic expectations, perhaps these checklists will be helpful to summarize what we discussed in this session.

WHAT BOSSES OWE SUBORDINATES

1. *Direction:* clear, specific, consistent with announced goals.
2. *Information:* on which risks/opportunities require a change of direction, and why.
3. *Support:* adequate facilities, funds, and staff to get goals met. Coaching when the employee falters.
4. *Feedback:* objective and specific performance evaluation with room for employee response.
5. *Strategic planning:* as investment in the department's future growth. Career path advice as consequence.
6. *Inspiration and encouragement:* sincere.
7. *Discipline and correction:* even-handed and positive.
8. *Respect:* for the subordinate's human dignity and achievements.

WHAT SUBORDINATES OWE BOSSES

1. *Performance:* careful and complete to meet or exceed stated requirements.

2. *Information:* on risks/opportunities clear to the subordinate, relevant to boss.
3. *Requests and recommendations:* not complaints and untested "ideas."
4. *Patience:* consideration of the boss's time demands and constraints.
5. *Commitment to the boss's goals:* unstinting investment of time and talent to achieve them (or openminded willingness to be convinced).
6. *Courage and self-discipline:* staying power even in tough times. Willingness to ask what and how rather than assume why.
7. *Respect:* for the boss's human dignity and position in the hierarchy.

WHAT NEITHER OWES THE OTHER

1. Mutual psychoanalysis, mind-reading.
2. Personal affection.
3. Allegiance to the same values.
4. Self-sacrifice for one another's "good."
5. Perfection.

NEGOTIATE: HOW TO GET ALL YOU NEED IF YOU CAN'T GET ALL YOU WANT

SESSION FOUR

NEGOTIATE: HOW TO GET ALL YOU NEED IF YOU CAN'T GET ALL YOU WANT

INTRODUCTION

While many managers think that management virtues like decisiveness, or "getting along" or "communicating well" are keys to career success, I am convinced that getting great assignments and assembling capable work teams to handle them are the real keys. Of course, you might need the former to accomplish the latter.

Early in your career, you work hard in minor roles on the best projects you can sign up for; later you earn middle or specialist spots on larger projects with bigger stakes. Finally, you get to star in or lead your team on some really glorious assignments. These are what help you validate your work and gain access to higher-value tasks.

As you will read in the questions that follow, some people come to seminars because they cannot get their bosses to delegate anything interesting to them, they cannot get into the departments where the interesting work is going on, or they get conflicting instructions about how this interesting work is to be done.

Sometimes, they are right in thinking that they are pawns in some game between sophisticates, but this is rare. More often, they have not made themselves credible candidates for the good assignments that powerful managers give as rewards to those whom they trust.

PART ONE

GETTING GOOD ASSIGNMENTS

When negotiating your niche for any year, you'd be wise to look for assignments with these attractive features:

1. The task will make a difference to your department, organization, or the public.
2. You have particular experience, talent, and interest for the task. (Don't let lack of staff or budget stop you from grabbing the project. You'll have time to negotiate for resources *after* you claim ownership of the task.)
3. There's a 50/50 chance of getting the task accomplished, technically, financially, and politically.

An assignment with these three features will naturally acquire the fourth:

4. Senior executives will notice the manager who successfully completes this assignment; your visibility and promotability will be enhanced.

As a bonus, a really great assignment will have these added attractions:

5. It will inspire respect from a wide circle of onlookers.
6. It will gain you access to important data and stimulating people.
7. The task will be so worthy in itself that savvy subordinates will want to follow you into it. You'll get to lead the cream of the troops.
8. Success in the task will help make you rich and famous (or merely famous if you are in nonprofit work.)

Naturally enough, such a task will be coveted by other canny managers, and competition for it may be stiff. For you, as for others, these peak assignments dotted throughout your career make all the dreary common-place tasks bearable.

TAKING YOUR SHARE OF MIDDLING ASSIGNMENTS

Peak assignments are the "soufflés" that add zest to your managerial banquet, but many months of each year, you'll earn plain bread, doing those routine tasks that underpin every business and public endeavor. What makes a good middling assignment?

- There will always be a need for the function. It serves a basic human requirement.
- The task has enough quirky features to make computerization/automation difficult.
- Heavy communication/liaison are required.
- The function is transferrable to companies of every type and size.

Managers and workers who value job security more than variety and challenge will be attracted to middling assignments.

Beware of that attraction; beware of getting bogged down in these functions. Reduce the proportion of workers in your team dedicated to ordinary maintenance of the status quo. Seek people for administrative functions who question their methods and trim every superfluous step they see. Together, you will open up time slots for handling the better assignments for which you are always on the prowl.

Be specific with your team about your intentions. Be specific with your top management about your availability to handle upcoming projects. Identify unfilled needs and develop ways to meet them, so that your proposals to management will be clear and relatively risk free, as well as compelling and convincing.

Getting good assignments requires vigilant initiative and energy, a fact that seems to have escaped the first few managers whose questions follow.

1. BOSS WON'T DELEGATE

I keep asking my boss for more responsibilities, but the boss keeps putting me off.

AUDIENCE RESPONSES

YOUR RATING

________ **a.** *Pick a specific assignment you want to take over, and volunteer to contribute specific parts of the solution. Be prepared for rebuff. Persist.*

________ **b.** *Gain your boss's confidence. Impress your boss with your sense of responsibility and reliability.*

________ **c.** *Have you been clear with your boss about your desire and ability to take on more?*

________ **d.** *If your boss won't delegate, you will run short of things to do eventually. In case of cutbacks, you could forfeit your job security.*

	★	★★	★★★	★★★★
RATING	*NO!*	*RISKY*	*BETTER*	*BEST!*

a. **Pick specific assignments; volunteer; be ready for rebuff; persist.**

Yes. Be careful about barging into your boss's decision-making/risk-taking domain when you volunteer. Offer to help in the measure/control/communicate functions where you can handle bothersome legwork for the boss. Yes, be prepared for rebuff. The boss may be too harried to hand over and teach an assignment now, but may be willing later. Or the boss may have another candidate in mind. Ask the boss what homework, preparation, or upgrading of skills you might need to be worthy of the assignment later.

b. **Impress your boss with your sense of responsibility and reliability.**

Yes. The second is more vital than the first. You must perform consistently well on current tasks before asking for more. Make it easy, attractive, and low risk for your boss to assign new tasks for you.

c. **Have you been clear about your desire and ability?**

Good question. If you make your request half-heartedly, at the wrong time, or outside the context of your total work load, your boss will find it hard to see your candidacy clearly. Outline your current load on paper. Show how reliably you meet quality/quantity standards now. Plug in the desired new task so your boss can see its feasibility against your standing work load.

Remember, too, you are competing with others in your department who want good assignments. Can you convince your boss, in simple words and numbers, why you are the one for the job? If you can get this on a single side of paper, and make a case in five minutes or less, you may have a chance. Your boss may be inundated with requests from your peers who want more responsibility but who don't bother to clarify what and how.

★★ ***d. If this continues, you'll run out of job security.***

In some bureaucracies this does happen. Bosses take back the work formerly done by their subordinates to hold their own job security through thin times. In such a case, you would start looking lower on the ladder at lower-echelon people *you* can bump. Or you'd start job hunting outside. In many profit-making companies, however, your failure to get new assignments is a more dangerous sign of the boss's low faith in your performance abilities. Get this cleared up; shape up quickly or you'll be let go, not laid off.

Comment—A Technique to Try: Here's a suggested outline for showing your current responsibilities to your boss and proposing that you take on more. For example, let's say you are a personnel manager:

LISTING CURRENT YEAR'S TASKS	TIME FORECAST % INCREASE	% DECREASE	STEADY
1. Recruitment drives	10%		
2. New training (clerks)	10%		
3. Benefits administration			X
4. Payroll coordination			X
5. Performance appraisal coordination			X
6. Liaison: New division		5%	
7. Revision: HR software		Ending	
8. Data search: lawsuit		Ending	
Recommended Additional Assignment: R&D NEW INCENTIVES PROGRAM			

Sample Discussion

1. Items 1 and 2 will add a day per week next quarter.
2. Item 6 (taking a half-day per week) will tail off.
3. Items 7 and 8 (taking a day per week) will end soon.

4. Balance: I will have 1 1/2 days per week to work on new assignment. Incentive program is one of my specialties. I did the original research last season. I know the stats. I have contacts with the legal people. Could begin now and accelerate with the first quarter of the year.

By making such a simple graphic listing for your boss, you can make your request clearer—map out your availability on your calendar, show where and how you would plug in new tasks of greater concern to your boss and department.

Even when you are not short of work, I recommend this simple eight-point chart format to every professional person who wants to keep the boss abreast of what he or she is doing. Such a sheet should certainly be part of your regular performance evaluation sessions.

As you examine your chart, be sure to reserve for yourself those tasks of highest impact and importance to the future of the division. In this way, when layoffs are in the wind, your involvements will be too valuable to cast off.

2. STALLED WITH PLATITUDES

When I try to negotiate with my boss about my frustrations on not moving ahead, he loads me with platitudes as if I were gullible enough to accept them.

A

AUDIENCE RESPONSES

YOUR RATING

________ **a.** *Be more direct. Let him know you doubt the veracity of his statements. Be tactful but firm.*

________ **b.** *When your feelings guide you to doubt what he is telling you, express your contrary views.*

________ **c.** *Take it all with a grain of salt.*

________ **d.** *Listen, then begin telling him specifics which will convince him of your abilities.*

	★	★★	★★★	★★★★
RATING	*NO!*	*RISKY*	*BETTER*	*BEST!*

★ **a. Be direct; show you doubt his veracity; tactfully!**
You cannot attack another's veracity tactfully. Instead, be more direct about what *you* need. Don't describe your frustrations; you'll sound negative, critical, helpless, or accusing. Instead, bring your boss proposals and plans for making yourself more useful to the department. Make them graphic and easy to understand. If you go in with platitudes ("I'm frustrated, I want to move ahead.") you'll be answered with platitudes ("We all feel this way at times."). If you get specific, your boss may get specific too. (Be prepared to hear some criticism of your performance.)

★ **b. Express your contrary views when you doubt him.**
No! Express more attractive options to help your boss say yes to you.

★★ **c. Take it all with a grain of salt.**
If this suggests being relaxed and nonjudgmental when you go to your boss for improvements in your situation, I'm for it. But as written, this answer just adds another platitude to the ones the boss tossed at you.

★★★ **d. Listen, then tell him specifics about your abilities.**
Go further. Tell him specifics about the contributions you are committing yourself to make on his and the department's behalf. Invest, in order to make gains.

Nickerson's Recommendation

For four stars, *Make an offer!* Negotiating means giving something to get something. You want to get better assignments: what quality or quantity or originality in your past and current contributions will motivate your boss to give you what you want? Express these: Make an offer.

Comment: While bosses owe training and development to all their employees, they respond better to a positive stimulus. You don't have an absolute right to interesting assignments; you have to earn them and compete for them when they are scarce. Demonstrate your commitment and ability, not your frustration. Never question your boss's communication style or veracity; this will retard or permanently damage your chances for advancement. Instead, improve your own effectiveness at communicating how your boss and department will benefit by advancing you. If you cannot make a clear and convincing case, your boss has no obligation to select you over your peers.

3. SCRAMBLED INSTRUCTIONS

Upper management makes unclear, contradictory requests/instructions. They act irritated when I question them, making me feel stupid and demeaned.

AUDIENCE RESPONSES

YOUR RATING

________ **a.** *Bite the bullet. Say you don't understand; ask for clarity.*

________ **b.** *Don't be afraid to persist with questions. You may be neurotic about their responses, or they may be neurotic about their instructions. You have no choice but to get things right before proceeding.*

________ **c.** *Remember, there are no silly questions, just silly mistakes.*

________ **d.** *Play back what you think they requested. If the task is important, memo quickly to fix your understandings in their minds before you spend the company's money and time.*

	★	★★	★★★	★★★★
RATING	*NO!*	*RISKY*	*BETTER*	*BEST!*

★★ **a. Say you don't understand. Ask for clarity.**

Normally I'd agree. But irritation has already been expressed against this approach. You must do your part. Diagram or take notes when contradictory sources give you instructions. Sketch out the apparent contradictions. Rather than saying "I don't understand . . ." (which can be interpreted, "I am slow . . .") say, "I see an apparent conflict (risk) when I compare today's orders with yesterday's" (or yours with theirs). "Let's select the approach that will work best." In that way, you are taking initiative rather than complaining.

★★ **b. Don't be afraid to persist. Who's neurotic? You must get things right before proceeding.**

No. I do not advocate persistence in a routine that irritates your boss. Instead of repeating yourself, come up with a new tack that offers options or cites risks meaningful to these bosses.

★ **c. There are no silly questions, just silly mistakes.**

Contrary to this adage, there *are* silly questions, namely, repetitions of questions that have already been answered. Some people fail to take note of instructions given earlier; some people fail to keep notebooks on procedures so that comparisons and extrapolations can be made for later use. Some people fail to look for underlying "rules" governing the answers to previous questions. Some workers feel that doing, not thinking, is the requirement of the job. Learners need to take notes, make diagrams and get management approval for the "procedures manual" that grows from every Q and A session at work.

★★★★ **d. Play back, memo quickly on important tasks, fix your understanding in their minds before proceeding.**

An excellent learning procedure. Your collection of such memos, authorized as correct by your boss, can become the backbone of your "desk manual." In many complex businesses, new variables will change the use and application of rules learned earlier. You must have a starting point in writing before starting to flex the rules.

Comment: Be sparing about these memos of understanding. If you feel you will be seen as featherheaded when you ask questions higher up, ask your questions at a lower less expensive level (of competent peers, for example) and diagram or demonstrate your understanding until you really grasp it. Only take your diagram upward if you're still not clear or convinced you can procced.

PART

TWO

GETTING MANAGEMENT SUPPORT

Bosses and subordinates seem equally puzzled by the subject of support.

Cozy bosses want to keep their subordinates dependent. They get satisfaction, self-esteem and relief from boredom by solving their subordinates' daily problems. Their door is always open. The subordinates who enjoy this safe arrangement stay weak and compliant. The boss abuts, the employee abets. Everyone's happy as long as the work load remains predictable. Strong-willed subordinates extricate themselves from these departments as soon as they get the drift and seek bosses who give plenty of headroom.

Striving bosses want strong, competent subordinates who have read the policy manual, who know how to extrapolate permissions from previous precedents, and who'll read a risk just as the boss would. The subordinates will make up their own minds about appropriate actions and will keep bosses informed as a courtesy, not as a precaution. The boss is always informed, but rarely asked for permission. In these healthy arrangements, the few conferences the two parties arrange are usually to reset the context in which new risks will be evaluated.

At the perilous end of the scale is the abdicator boss who abandons subordinates to their own devices, and who procrastinates so long about new risks that employees are forced to take leaps. The boss then repudiates the subordinate if blame must be later laid at someone's door.

Wily subordinates, finding themselves with an abdicator boss, take the risk of seeking mentors in higher places, knowing they may be punished for their sins against the "chain of command" as well as for their unsupported actions on problem assignments.

How much support is enough? For both boss and subordinate, that subject is always open to renegotiation. Just when you think you have an accommodation, some change of rules, some accident, triumph, or disaster reopens the issue.

Typical problems, like those described in the next few questions, will arise as you test your support agreements in daily practice.

4. MANAGEMENT HAMPERS MY STAFF

How can I convince top management that my people have earned the right to make decisions. Senior managers interfere, delay, and rescind my people's decisions.

A

AUDIENCE RESPONSES

YOUR RATING

_________ **a.** *Talking won't convince them. Outline and put into effect a process by which your people can make decisions without checking, yet without causing risks. Send up a trial balloon. Succeed. Then make new rules.*

_________ **b.** *Demonstrate that your subordinate managers share the same goals as those at the top. That they can be trusted.*

_________ **c.** *Top levels are isolated much of the time. Include them in your positive praise of your people's decision successes. Copy them in on performance reviews.*

_________ **d.** *Suggest a process for gradually undoing this situation. Top management should be negotiating with you, not your subordinates. Reestablish yourself as the linkage between your staff and the top.*

	★	★★	★★★	★★★★
RATING	*NO!*	*RISKY*	*BETTER*	*BEST!*

4. *MANAGEMENT HAMPERS MY STAFF* ANALYSIS

★★★ **a. Talking won't convince. Create a process where your people's decisions don't cause risks. Send up a trial balloon. Make new rules.**

Ah, talking *will* convince them. Use these words:

> I will resume control of my department. No decision made by my people will be enacted without my approval. In the future, you need deal only with *me*, Boss.

You're in real trouble, Questioner. You have allowed senior management and your subordinates to deal directly with one another, and senior management is not happy about the quality of the work being done. You must resume control. You must review management's risks and needs, review the quality of the decisions your subordinates have been taking to cover these risks, get agreement on how your bosses want these risks covered. Then, take charge of your people as they perform to these rules. Tolerate no more "end runs" by your people or management in either direction. This will entail a lot of work for you, but when trust has broken down, the peace treaty will not be made by your subordinates, but by yourself. Get busy!

★ **b. Demonstrate that your subordinates share the goals of the top people and they can be trusted.**

Impossible. If seniors are complaining, questioning, and interfering with your people's decisions, they do not trust your people. You have abdicated responsibility and must now work, internally, to retake that responsibility. Then, you must rebuild management trust in you as leader. Your staffers must duck out of the limelight. You must stand in its glare until your bosses no longer feel at risk.

c. Top levels are isolated. Include them in praise of your people's decision successes.

I would advocate this for a normal situation where you are building your team in a climate of management approval. But your managers are dissatisfied with your people's performance. This is the time to assure them you are cleaning house internally and will directly oversee performance until results meet top management requirements. After a solid period of superior performance, you may want to begin "credentializing" your staff, starting with anointing one strong lieutenant who can stand in for you during an absence. Don't make it your goal to have top management know all your staffers' individual performance gains. As for "copying" top management on your performance reviews: in most companies your own immediate boss would have to be kept informed—but don't feel the need to publicize these widely among top management ranks. Top management is looking for your group's results.

d. Suggest a process for undoing this. Top management should be negotiating with you, not your subordinates.

That's it! The process has just been outlined.

5. ACCOUNTABLE BUT UNSUPPORTED

I'm held accountable for department revenues but denied the tools to get the job done.

A

AUDIENCE RESPONSES

YOUR RATING

________ **a.** *Do the best you can with what you have.*

________ **b.** *Enforce your point of view until it is accepted.*

________ **c.** *Prove you can handle things well with limited resources; then you'll receive more tools.*

________ **d.** *Document what you need. Justify the investment.*

	★	★★	★★★	★★★★
RATING	*NO!*	*RISKY*	*BETTER*	*BEST!*

5. *ACCOUNTABLE BUT UNSUPPORTED* ANALYSIS

★★★ ***a.* Do the best you can with what you have.**
While I'm not for tight-lipped stoicism as a stance, I agree with this response. You cannot withhold performance while waiting for all the necessary tools. Instead, eke out what you can, but inform management specifically what you need to approach their revenue goals more closely. I think you must put forth a vigorous effort or you'll look like a quitter before you've started toward your new goals at all.

★ ***b.* Enforce your point of view until it is accepted.**
Enforcing is not one of the suggested approaches to engaging top management. They, not you, have the powers. Save the energy you'd expend enforcing your view for your race toward the goals. By all means, express your point of view in a positive way while clearly complying with their demands.

★★★★ **c. Prove you can handle things well now; then you'll receive more tools.**
Right. If you perform . . . and if you ask.

★★★ ***d.* Document what you need. Justify the investment.**
Begin. Perform, then request help with their goals clearly in sight.

Comment: Whenever profit makers jack up their revenue goals, lower-level managers scream that they cannot perform without extra support. They want their seniors to invest before they do. When the screaming ends, the performing begins, and management starts supporting those managers likeliest to get big results. Waste no time; chase the new goals; they stir the heart, stimulate the spleen, elevate the spirit. Sketch out the goals as they concern your department specifically. Specify the steps you will take, in detail, to meet these new benchmarks. Set intermediate steps, goals, and timetables. Get your people involved in ways they can contribute directly. Inform your immediate boss of your plan and seek adjustment advice. The more realistic you are, the more influence you can bring to the adjustments top management may make. Put your energy into cooperation, not resistance, and your requests for support will be heard.

6. HQ INTERFERES, THEN WITHHOLDS

Why does HQ interfere where they're not needed, then withhold help when we request it?

A

AUDIENCE RESPONSES

YOUR RATING

_________ **a.** *Make it clear to "corporate" when their help constitutes interference.*

_________ **b.** *Bear with both. They happen everywhere.*

_________ **c.** *Try direct confrontation.*

_________ **d.** *Present a clear outline of the consequences of interference and slow/no response. Ask for their ideas on a better approach. Offer yours.*

	★	★★	★★★	★★★★
RATING	*NO!*	*RISKY*	*BETTER*	*BEST!*

6. HQ INTERFERES, THEN WITHHOLDS ANALYSIS

a. Show where help becomes interference.
Do this only if the interference constitutes a risk to the organization. If it merely represents an inconvenience to you, do you want to bother senior management about it? You may need to bother them about more important things later.

b. Bear with both. They happen everywhere.
As Drs. Beieir and Valens said in *People Reading*: "Behavior that is noticed is repeated." If you notice the interference, it will happen some more. If you notice the withholding, you'll see more of it. Instead, notice real cooperation when it helps; be clear and directive in your gratitude, and you'll be showing management when and where you need and appreciate help. Don't expect to control your seniors however. Only to negotiate with them.

c. Try direct confrontation.
Beware. This case reads like "Goldilocks." The porridge is never quite the right temperature; management help is never quite the right degree or timing. Don't try confronting, rather, try adjusting. It's easier for the requester or underdog to adjust, than for the senior to climb down during a confrontation. Save confrontations for really major acute issues.

d. Outline the consequences of both behaviors; jointly seek a better approach.
Do this, particularly when you can demonstrate a damaging pattern of continuing behavior. In such instances the consequences are more compelling and visible; the offender's awareness is better aroused, and willingness to compromise is enhanced.

Summing up: Combine answers *b* and *d* for a healthy view on handling uncomfortable behavior from above. Complaining may only increase the unwanted behavior. But if the behavior is chronic, outline the costs and jointly seek a remedy.

7. BOSS SIDES WITH MY SUBORDINATE

I had to discipline a valued subordinate. My boss took the subordinate's side. Morale problems are stirred up throughout the department.

A

AUDIENCE RESPONSES

YOUR RATING

______ a. *Be frank. Ask your boss to let you do your job with no second-guessing.*

______ b. *Work to rehabilitate this valued subordinate. Take the long view. The boss and others will respect your constructive, sober approach.*

______ c. *Let this pass. Work on "next time." Come to a mutual agreement on discipline policies that satisfy you and your boss. Then use that approach on subordinates, and get the boss to stay out of it.*

______ d. *Stand and fight. Management and you must find a way to get this subordinate into line; otherwise, your credibility is gone with all your staff.*

	★	★★	★★★	★★★★
RATING	*NO!*	*RISKY*	*BETTER*	*BEST!*

7. *BOSS SIDES WITH MY SUBORDINATE* ANALYSIS

★★

a. Be frank. Ask the boss to avoid second-guessing you next time.

Go further: help the boss to avoid second-guessing you by arming him or her with information when you are taking a disciplinary action that could backfire. Warn your boss what you are planning to do, and why. Armed with information and a viewpoint, your boss will not fold easily when approached by an indignant subordinate of yours. That will take care of next time. For this time, you still have a righteous subordinate who went over your head successfully and an upset department. We need more answers.

b. Work to rehabilitate this valued subordinate.

If this says "Don't cry over spilt milk," I cannot agree (though in the end, I think you *will* work to rehabilitate the person). The present situation must still be ironed out. Sit down with your boss and examine the pros and cons of your decision and the boss's policy in overturning it. If you were wrong and can see it, admit it, and discuss your need to save face and restore discipline to your department, without further overt action by your boss. Express your ideas about this process and ask the boss's views about restoration of order.

c. Let this pass. Work on next time, keeping boss informed.

If you can really let it pass without loss of momentum or loss of face, go ahead. Amen to how to treat it next time.

d. Stand and fight. Get this subordinate into line; otherwise, your credibility is lost.

It is crucial to get this result without a fight. Quell your fears and take the calm reasoned approaches of *b* and *c*.

Nickerson's Recommendation

There are two separate events involved here. In the first, the boss forgave the subordinate's original infringement (the one that brought about your disciplinary action). But the boss has also countenanced a second offense: your employee's going over your head. Suggest (or draft) a memo for your boss's signature that might clean up both issues in one swoop. The memo might caution the employee that the regulations of most companies require disgruntled employees to include their immediate supervisor in any visit "upstairs." Suggest this as standard procedure for any future encounter.

At the same time, the memo might restate the policy now to be followed in the original matter that caused the discipline. In this way, the subordinate is discouraged from further acts of rebellion. With these items laid to rest in a short, clear memo, you can go about your supervisory business, cheerful and satisfied, and your appropriate demeanor in your department will calm your staff. As long as you are successfully defied by a subordinate, with senior management's blessing, you won't be able to lead effectively.

8. *BOSS MADE ME LOOK FOOLISH*

My boss rescinded a decision I hammered out with customers, destroying my credibility with them.

A

AUDIENCE RESPONSES

YOUR RATING

________ **a.** *Let boss know how this handicaps you. Back up your allegations with specific examples. Otherwise, if only your feelings are hurt, forget it.*

________ **b.** *Take notes during your customer meetings and inform boss in writing of promises you make. He may have reneged out of ignorance of the details.*

________ **c.** *When informing boss of promises you make, set follow-up dates on implementation so you can track any slippage.*

________ **d.** *Find out what kinds of promises cause debate. Come up with alternatives that will satisfy customers without having them run to your boss. Convince your boss of costs/benefits of your offerings to clients so your boss will tend to stand firm on your side.*

	★	★★	★★★	★★★★
RATING	*NO!*	*RISKY*	*BETTER*	*BEST!*

8. *BOSS MADE ME LOOK FOOLISH* ANALYSIS

Four stars to all answers.

★★★★ **a.** *a* is saying: "Don't try to get your feelings salved, *only your needs met.*"

★★★★ **b.** *b* gives a wonderful hint for use when clients give you an argument during negotiations. Don't softpedal their demands when memoing your boss. The boss needs to have heard "their worst" if he or she's to stand up to them in their complaints later on.

★★★★ **c.** *c* reminds you to stay on track with the customer in case they start to think ill of the agreement they signed.

★★★★ **d.** *d* suggests you set *principles* for use in the future so the boss's first instinct will be to consult *you*, when remaking a deal with a customer.

Comment: Will all this *guarantee* that the boss will never "improve" your deal when judgment tells him or her it is worth it? No! Your boss is still the boss and has a right to change the deal, whether made by you or even by him or her. It's just that the four suggestions cited will guard against the boss doing it wantonly.

PART

THREE

RENEGOTIATING PAY, BUDGET, STAFF

INTRODUCTION

One of the sorriest sights in the corporate world is a new manager, risen from the ranks of hourly or unionized employees, whose previous appointments, promotions and raises were negotiated *for* him or her in blanket agreements. Having come from a succession of cost-of-living hikes or prescribed steps, grades and increments, the person enters a new environment where no rights are assumed, and where future rewards must be haggled-for and won by competition.

Fear of negotiation is a surprising trauma, too, for many of the experienced managers I meet at my seminars. They equate negotiation with confrontation, quarrelling, opportunism, "chiselling," hard bargaining, or "beating the boss down." They believe that one person's win forces someone else to lose. They see negotiation as begging an inordinate share of the pie, rather than as building a bigger corporate pie so that larger shares are available to many. In many large, highly structured organizations, managers adopt passive, fatalistic stances, assuming that next year's pay raise or budget increase is nonnegotiable, already determined by recent performance factors: a predetermined reward or rebuff. They are shocked to learn, on the contrary, that advanced thinkers see raises as a management gamble, an investment in your potential to perform superbly next year. What you did in the past is merely an indicator of what you might do next.

GOING AFTER BUDGET AND STAFF INCREASES

Passive managers hesitate to ask for added staff. They only dare ask after their exhausted troops yell "Cavalry to the rescue." But astute managers see added staffers as a corporate investment in much greater outputs in the next campaign.

Cynics fear that their managements will withhold help by challenging, "What have you done for me lately?" Astute managers are hardier than that. They take the view that everything "done for management lately" will qualify you to "get in line" with other "winner managers" to *bargain* for more money, staff, and personal incentives that will make next year's accomplishments outstanding.

When both sides understand these principles, negotiation becomes a most stimulating, satisfying collaboration of power and commitment.

But the hesitant managers, whose questions follow, are loath to begin the negotiating process, even though this task must go with us to the final day of every good manager's career.

9. *MY HELPER HINDERS ME*

My boss hired a new staffer to help me out. When the new guy disagrees with me, he goes to the boss who often compromises. I seethe; the boss just coos.

AUDIENCE RESPONSES

YOUR RATING

________ **a.** *Tell the new staffer that his going to the boss violates chain of command rules and that the boss will lose patience soon with all these visits for "reassurance."*

________ **b.** *Ask your boss to send the staffer back to you to sort things out. Then listen. The staffer may have useful ideas.*

________ **c.** *If this person reports to the boss and not to you, he is free to visit the boss at will. You are only a senior colleague. Your hands are tied.*

________ **d.** *Watch your back. This new person may be after your job, and the boss may have hired him for the purpose.*

________ **e.** *Find out what your authority is—and whether you have* any *actual responsibility for this person.*

	★	★★	★★★	★★★★
RATING	*NO!*	*RISKY*	*BETTER*	*BEST!*

★

a. **Caution your new staffer against annoying the boss.**
No. Don't speak for the boss. The boss isn't annoyed, *you* are. (And not with your junior colleague, but with your *boss*, for the boss did not appoint this person to report to *you*, but instead, to report direct to the boss.) As senior colleague, your role can be advisory, but not directive. If you want this person to remain under you in the chain of command, you must arrange that the boss appoint *you* supervisor over this new person and make it official. Otherwise, the situation you describe is quite legal.

★★

b. **Ask the boss to send the staffer back to you: listen.**
This will only work on a permanent basis if the boss appoints you supervisor over this person. Otherwise, you are both subordinates of the boss. You have only *longevity*, not responsibility or authority as it stands.

★★★★

c. **This newcomer is free to visit the boss.**
Absolutely.

★★

d. **Watch your back. The boss and newcomer may be out to get you.**
Possible, but unlikely. You'll undergo a lot of stress if you take this attitude. More likely, you asked for a helper and failed to make clear you'd want the person to report to you. Your boss, accustomed to having everyone report directly may be doing what comes naturally and cheaply.

★★★

e. **Find out what your authority is—and whether you have any actual responsibility here.**
Don't just "find out." *Sell* your boss on the advantages of having you supervise and train the newcomer:

1. *Savings*: Your boss's coaching costs much more per hour than yours. Can you afford to let the boss supervise this underling?

2. *Productivity*: Remember, it did cost your boss money to have this person help you handle a load you once handled solo. You must think of ways to make this investment pay off. What more could the team of two do better than ever before? How can you maximize the two-person performance beyond your boss's current horizon and make this investment really pay?

Take care that your boss feels rewarded for getting you that help rather than criticized for the positioning of the employee along side you. Now, improve things further.

Nickerson's Recommendation

The next time you need help, write a request stating that the helper should be interviewed, selected, and supervised by yourself. Your boss will be involved only in the authorization of this process. Such a "helper" will be lower-paid and less knowledgeable than yourself. Otherwise, the boss will be free to hire a colleague, whom you may not supervise. One other point: Hiring "help" is never trouble free. These individuals are not robots; they have ideas of their own which may not coincide with yours. Some ideas may be better than yours: orientation, training, and continual negotiations will ensue.

10. RESPONSIBILITY WITHOUT AUTHORITY

When my boss is away, I'm left in charge—but I get slow or no cooperation from adjoining departments.

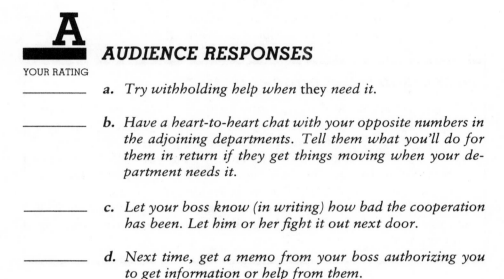

AUDIENCE RESPONSES

YOUR RATING

_________ **a.** *Try withholding help when* they *need it.*

_________ **b.** *Have a heart-to-heart chat with your opposite numbers in the adjoining departments. Tell them what you'll do for them in return if they get things moving when your department needs it.*

_________ **c.** *Let your boss know (in writing) how bad the cooperation has been. Let him or her fight it out next door.*

_________ **d.** *Next time, get a memo from your boss authorizing you to get information or help from them.*

	★	★★	★★★	★★★★
RATING	*NO!*	*RISKY*	*BETTER*	*BEST!*

10. RESPONSIBILITY WITHOUT AUTHORITY ANALYSIS

★ ***a.* Withhold help when they need it.**
Sure. Their boss and yours will rate you incompetent, uncooperative, insubordinate.

★★ ***b.* Make a deal with your opposite numbers there.**
In any long-standing relationships between groups, these obligations and favors grow up naturally, building goodwill—and therefore the right to call on that goodwill when you need it. But the "underdog"—that's you—cannot promise to start building that goodwill now, while you're in trouble. You will probably have to go to them hat-in-hand, explain the consequences to your boss, and ask for their help. Then you will "owe them one."

★ ***c.* Memo your boss about the bad cooperation. Let the boss fight it out.**
This will make you "so nice to come home to!" While a pattern of noncooperation from next door would have to be discussed with your boss, your complaining now will show the boss you do not know how to negotiate, and that you neglected to set up your authority limits *before* the boss's departure. (See next suggestion.)

★★★ ***d.* Next time, get a memo from your boss urging their cooperation.**
Even easier, prepare such a memo for your boss's signature. Have a few, like blank checks, to use when you need them. Your boss must be able to trust your discretion in the use of these. A sample might read

TO XYZ Dept.
FROM: A.L. Bigwig
RE: Cost Estimates for Raja Project: Due 5/5

I will appreciate your having these estimates on the due date when Ken Smith will pick them up from you. He'll be in regular touch with me on these urgent items while I'm out of town.

Thanks.

Nickerson's Recommendation

Answer *d*, slightly upgraded, is the four-star reply. While it is, legally, the boss's duty to make your temporary authority clear—it is *you* who will feel the pain and strain if cooperation is half-hearted. Therefore, it behooves *you* to do the work of writing a memo your boss can feel comfortable to sign.

By the same token, it may be important for customers/clients to be introduced to you (on the phone if personal introductions are impossible) so that they will feel safe in your authorized hands during the boss's absence. Set up these calls or arrange a note for your boss to sign for use outside the corporation. It is always your boss's authority that's needed to sell you as a temporary stand-in.

11. "ACTING" DIRECTOR TOO LONG

My boss resigned suddenly. They made me "acting director" while seeking a replacement. A year later, I wish I'd negotiated better. All work. Low pay.

AUDIENCE RESPONSES

YOUR RATING

_________ **a.** *Threaten to quit. They'll be left standing.*

_________ **b.** *Ask if there's anything you can do to hurry the search for your boss's replacement.*

_________ **c.** *Tell them how much money you want and how much official authority you'll need if you are to remain in the slot. Give them a tight deadline, in writing.*

_________ **d.** *It's not too late. Write up your accomplishments in the job and ask for the "acting" designation to be dropped, with a commensurate raise in pay.*

	★	★★	★★★	★★★★
RATING	*NO!*	*RISKY*	*BETTER*	*BEST!*

11. "ACTING" DIRECTOR TOO LONG ANALYSIS

★ **a. Threaten to quit. They'll be left standing.**
Never threaten. Not even if you mean it. Always negotiate. Say what you need.

★★ **b. Ask what you can do to hurry things up.**
Good for opening the conversation. But saying what you need is much better. To do that, you must decide what you need. Most people who accept an "acting" title do so because they absolutely do not want the job and are willing to fill in on parts of the job, within their knowledge area, while the organization finds someone who can do it *all*. Was that your situation? *Never* accept an "acting" title because your company isn't sure of your ability, or because *you* aren't sure. Everyone else will *presume* that you and the company aren't sure of your abilities. Everyone's lack of confidence in you will cause your very quick mummification. Go-getters will get what they need by going around you, and your whole department will end up "acting."

★★ **c. Tell them what money and authority you want to remain in the slot. Give a deadline.**
By the time a year has passed, what still remains negotiable? What tasks, formerly done by the old director, have been neglected? Where have they gone? Is someone doing them? What have *you* been doing all this time? The full job? Parts of it?

If you hold the company at ransom for remaining "in the slot," they may use this opportunity to tell you that your year as acting director has been lackluster. Or *you* may use this opportunity to prove that your performance has been so good you should now be appointed permanent director. Your performance review is the key now. (Only if you've been acting director as a lead up to retirement—and you're doing the company a favor by staying—can you expect to be rewarded for sticking around.)

Otherwise, your only way to get enhancements now is to do more to earn more. Offer to take over all of the director's roles for full pay—or more of the roles for more pay, with a recommendation that some specialist/consultant fill in the missing pieces where necessary. (Be sure the cost will not be greater in total than the director's salary, upgraded for the current year.) The company may like the new downgraded director's slot and want to continue getting this bargain. Unless you can give them a reason to change, they won't.

d. **It's not too late. Write up your accomplishments and ask for the full job, full pay.**
Again, I like this reply because it says: Prepare your year-end performance review. *But* it suggests that you'll be given a raise for your good performance in the past year. No you won't. You were already paid for that good performance. The only way to get more money now is to contribute more. You must propose ways that the company's increase in pay to you will be an investment.

Nickerson's Recommendation

Build on reply *d* for four stars.

It's not too late to look at your own strengths as a director. What *new* enhancements are you bringing to the job? Do these counterbalance any benefits that were sacrificed when your old boss left? Your achievements of the past year are significant if they show a trend that you will improve on in the year to come. You will get a raise for what you're going to do next, not for what you already did. Work on that. Then write a new job description for what you want to do, and suggest a new rate for it.

When your agreement is struck, be sure your full-power job is well publicized inside the organization and outside to your clientele.

12. *I MADE MY BED . . .*

I accepted a job that looked tough. It is! Gossip has it that my predecessor coped by working every night and weekend . . . before his heart attack! My boss just says "You're smarter. You can do it."

AUDIENCE RESPONSES

YOUR RATING

_________ **a.** *Your boss probably needs to deny what happened to the other employee. That employee was responsible for his own health. You are responsible for yours.*

_________ **b.** *Do a desk audit. Record the items you have to do each day, the time they take. If the time required cannot be reduced, they must be cut out of the process altogether. Negotiate this.*

_________ **c.** *Tell your boss what kind of help you need. Insist on it.*

_________ **d.** *Unless your job is unique, there's another job like it in a similar company. Ask around. Find out how others do it, with how many staffers. Then, negotiate with your boss.*

	★	★★	★★★	★★★★
RATING	*NO!*	*RISKY*	*BETTER*	*BEST!*

★★★ *a.* **Your predecessor was responsible for his health; you are responsible for yours. Your boss needs to deny.**
Right. You must take care of yourself, assess the work, prove whether the job is structured incorrectly, and sell your boss on a remedy. Whether the boss "needs to deny" a role in the heart attack of your predecessor cannot be proved, so why get into it?

★★★★ *b.* **Do a desk audit. Reduce time requirements or cut out some tasks. Negotiate this.**
Right! If you've never done a desk audit, you may find it hard to validate your findings. Try your public library (reference section) for two government publications: *The Dictionary of Occupational Titles* and the *Occupational Outlook Handbook*. These will provide relevant *job descriptions* with details on the *duties* of jobs like yours, in various settings and sizes of organization. You may find that you are combining two full jobs under one heading. Ask your library for addresses of professional groups or societies you can contact. They can add precise information on how many staffers are usually needed to do how much work. For example, your local personnel society may tell you their rule of thumb: "one personnel professional per one hundred employees." Beyond that, overwork may cause errors and inefficiencies. That's the kind of data you would need to help educate yourself and your boss. Then, you can start trimming work, upgrading your methods, or negotiating for personnel/equipment/software to get your job done to the boss's satisfaction, while keeping your health and life intact.

★★★ *c.* **Tell your boss what kind of help you need. Insist on it.**
Not so much insist on it, as prove it. Also, when bringing in help over the resistance of your boss, go easy at first. Bring in part-time or half-day helpers. Work study experts tell us that half-day people produce about 65 percent of a day's work in half a day. Two half-timers may give you

more productivity than one full-timer, and they can be brought on, one at a time, until your boss sees the benefits of having the help. Make sure these benefits are visible.

d. **Find your opposite number in another company. Find out how they do it. Negotiate with your boss.** Another excellent suggestion. There's nothing lonelier than the feeling you're going against your boss with no information. "Real-life" testimony, added to the library research you should do in any case, will add dimension to your findings. Don't go up against your boss with *only* the testimony of a single other worker from another company, but add it to your package.

Very rare are business contracts that bind you for a lifetime. There is never a need to say "I've made my bed, now I must lie in it." If you negotiate an item, make sure it is for a term of months you can tolerate. Even if the term is not up, you can always *ask* your boss to reopen the negotiation. Trials are reopened if there is new evidence. Negotiations are reopened when there are new advantages visible to both sides. All you need do to reopen a negotiation that appears closed is to find an advantage to your opponent as compelling as the advantage you see for yourself. The other party will reopen.

PART FOUR

FINE TUNING: FINDING A NEED, NEGOTIATING A NICHE

Whether you're going after your next major "push" in midcareer, or trying to get unstalled at some later point, bear this easy lesson in mind:

> *When seeking to improve your position, always sketch out a simple organization chart, showing your proposed new niche, its effect on adjacent "boxes" on the chart, and its beneficial effects on the whole locale around you.*

Dozens of times a year, I listen to litanies of complaints from managers of all kinds—from go-getter supervisors to disgruntled directors. They're unhappy about their niche in the corporate edifice. They feel passed over or outmaneuvered. I always ask, "Show me the chart. Draw the boxes for me. Show me where you are, and where you're headed."

Once they start drawing the changed chart (showing the effects of their proposal on several positions), they see, without further help from me, what other positions and tasks will be affected by the proposed move. Their perspective widens. The hardest part is remembering that you are negotiating *positions*, not personalities. You must draw a chart where every *new* niche fulfills a need your boss cares about. Be ready to show what advantages your boss will reap by reorganizing in the way you propose.

This process ought to be obvious to anyone with ambition, but it clearly eludes many frustrated managers.

Yes. You may rightly say that other people's boxes are none of your business. But if you change one piece of the puzzle (yours), you may jostle adjacent niches, and your boss must be reassured about these to be attracted to your proposal.

To do a good job of this, you must know a good deal about other job descriptions in the organization chart, to avoid overlap, duplication of effort, or the risk of leaving requirements uncovered.

In the questions you've just read, you saw some of the agonies people endured when their niches were neutralized: "Responsibility Without Authority," "Acting Directorships," "Doing Double Duty" all were cases where the victim's position on the organization chart was unclear to people whose support was needed. The victims' job descriptions had become overgrown and confused.

The saddest and angriest people I meet on this subject are those who feel they've been passed over, left in a backwater. Their sense of personal worth collapses, and they cannot see their own situations clearly enough to negotiate new niches for themselves as company needs grow. They feel cheated when really they've neglected themselves, rendered themselves invisible.

THE PASSIVE ARE PASSED OVER

I see any number of these cases each year. For example, one personnel manager did a creditable job for years, using experience, common sense, and judgment in her job. She handled recruitment, hiring, payroll, benefits, personnel records, compliance, counseling—all without benefit of a college degree—and she depended on her long-time boss, the personnel director, whenever a matter got too hot to handle. When he became ill and retired suddenly, she carried a double load for months and assumed that help would be hired, below and around her, to handle the specialties she knew little about. She never got around to sketching things out for the president, assuming that he would approve her choices as soon as she got "dug out" enough to recruit and hire help.

Instead, the company hired a Ph.D. consultant as the new personnel director. When he arrived, and asked her congenially to "Tell me your ambitions for yourself," she fumed: "My ambition *was* to do *your* job, but I wasn't given the chance to grow into it!"

This wise new director got down to graphics immediately. He pulled out his job description and a new organization chart. The unhappy woman was flummoxed to see at a glance that her company would be taking an entirely new direction shortly.

1. The president would sell out to a large manufacturer proposing a takeover.

2. The company would move from nonunion to union in the takeover.

3. Some manufacturing operations would be scrapped which duplicated the parent company's work.

The personnel director's job description revolved around these coming events; he was an expert on transitions of family firms to public ownership. He was also expert in union-management relations.

This woman now saw that her company, and her old job would change radically as this transition became effective. She realized at once how passively she'd behaved for months. How could all these changes be in the works without her knowledge? She recalled, with embarrassment, her narrow replies to conversations with the president over recent weeks. When he'd tried to open a subject, she'd closed it, pleading that she was too busy to talk just now.

The same fate has befallen many. I've met more than one law firm administrator who starts out in the "back-room" operation for a single attorney and hopes to hang on twenty years later when there are dozens of partners, huge billings, and several *categories* of professionals working there. The administrator is shocked and resentful when the company hires a personnel manager and a financial controller.

Early probes by the boss to test the administrator's flexibility are met by "I'd rather do it myself" responses. Even when the personnel manager and financial controller arrive on the scene, the administrator still fails to draw up a new organization chart, carving out a coordinating/administrative niche that will keep interest, dignity, and income percolating. Passivity turns to frantic activity in a job hunt outside the walls. "After all I've done for them, *look* what they're doing to me!" wail the victims of such events.

BRAINSTORM YOUR NEW ROLES

Whenever you spot a new corporate *need*, born of competition, growth, legislation, or new technology, brainstorm about your role in meeting this need.

- What talent have you for handling it? What experience?
- What powers would you need?
- What staff/budget/equipment would you need?
- Why would you be the *best* person to handle it?
- What title and positioning would you need to make a go of it? Would this be accepted by others?
- How could you save time and money while getting it covered?
- Who would you need as allies?

- What risks would your boss want covered? What would be the most attractive timing and context for introducing it to your boss?
- Will your proposal enhance other long-term goals of your boss and company? How? Demonstrate this.

Once you've answered some of these questions in prose form on paper, start sketching it out in list format with pros and cons, costs and benefits.

When sketching out your new proposed title, and your relative placement among peers, seniors, and subordinates, draw the boxes on a proposed new section of the organization chart. Play devil's advocate as your boss and your colleagues would do. Look at your organization chart as a chessboard and imagine your varying routes to reaching your hoped-for destination. Use corporate needs to propose new tasks/assignments that will benefit your organization and your boss.

Finally, be willing always to go back to the drawing board if your first proposal meets resistance from allies, collaborators, or executives. Let respected friends "blue pencil" your charts if they have a better idea, and keep involving them until you all can endorse your proposal.

Don't tell me that this would be a waste of time, that your corporation is rigid and unwilling to entertain such ideas. *You* must develop flexible thinking for yourself, so you can do this "what if" exercise at the drop of a hat—*yours*—into a new and better box on the organization chart.

CHECKLIST: ESSENTIALS OF NEGOTIATING WITHOUT GETTING NASTY

The most important element of negotiation is *knowing what you want at all times*. This may shift as the other side makes counterproposals and fresh offers. While most inexperienced negotiators concentrate on what the *other* guy is saying, the really savvy ones keep auditing their own reactions to new proposals against their original very clear goals. So, the most important part of negotiation is

PREPARATION

1. Know what you want. Write a simple sentence that states the result you want in the end. (It can be useful also to list what you *don't want*, but many unfortunate negotiators enter the meeting room knowing *only* this element.)
2. List the consequences and benefits to you of getting all you want.
3. List the consequences and benefits to the other party of your getting all you want.
4. List your best guess about all the other fellow's wants. Where can you help the other guy win?
5. Forecast how your negotiating partner (opponent) will react when you start winning. Know which items you'd be willing to relinquish when bargaining heats up.

6. If money is involved, *know your numbers*. Take the time to calculate the dollar outcomes of all the positions likely to be proposed. Keep a crib sheet on this if you can.

(As you see, the preparation phase may be the most arduous.)

THE MEETING

1. Assume the essential goodwill of your bargaining partner (opponent). He or she will only be trying to get needs met—as you are doing. Assuming this to be true is much easier on your emotions than is entering negotiations in a spirit of mistrust.
2. In your greeting, contribute to the climate of respect, cordiality, and trust.
3. Say what you want as simply as you can. Cite only two or three main goals in outline form.
4. Ask the other party to do likewise. If the person verbalizes at length, *you* make a list of what you think is being proposed. Show this "graphic" openly. You are seeking to validate your understanding.
5. Show any points on which you clearly agree with one another. Highlight or initial these to make progress.
6. On any points where you disagree, state the disadvantage you see for yourself, and ask for concessions. Invite the other party to do likewise.
7. Give way on small issues to show goodwill and pave the way to winning on bigger ones. If you give a concession, don't hesitate to ask for a reciprocal one from the other side.
8. If you come to serious loggerheads, call for a "time-out." Agree to search for creative ways to find a *third option*, beyond "yours" or "theirs" to break the deadlock.
9. Sketch out your conclusions; list simple points of your emerging "contract" so both sides can see what you are agreeing to.
10. Thank your negotiating partner for the joint effort to reach agreement.

FOLLOW-THROUGH

1. Memo your negotiating partner to confirm your agreement. Detail any benchmarks, inspection, or trial period items agreed to, as these steps may commence almost immediately.

2. If, on reflection or review with others, you feel you were hasty, or "could have done better," remind yourself that the negotiation was a success the way you envisioned it. If you got what you wanted, *try not to want more now*. Make yourself happy.

3. Decide what would be a decent interval before you reopen negotiations, if your new evidence shows further benefits available to you—or better still—to both parties.

This is a much gentler checklist than you find in the literature by hardened professional negotiators. For them, negotiating is their only game, and they've developed an elaborate dance beginning with extreme opening gambits, intimidation, and outrageous demands; then after several hours or days, both sides retreat from their extreme demands, reaching a more reasonable central set of agreements.

I take the view, however, that you have a more varied job to do every day—production, public service, health care, research, whatever—and that you want your negotiations to be simple, straightforward, and quick. Open with an honest outline of what you want, get the other guy to do the same, and shorten the span you must cross from your original proposal to your final positions.

CHANGING TECHNOLOGY: HOW TO SURVIVE THE PACE

SESSION

FIVE

CHANGING TECHNOLOGY: HOW TO SURVIVE THE PACE

INTRODUCTION

The people you'll meet next happen to work in technology-based industries: computers, aerospace, defense, medicine, research. They are challenged daily by the turbulent change that advancing technologies bring. Most of them enjoy the pace. For others, it's disturbing.

Managers brought up with paper must move to computers. Managers reared in hierarchies must move over to matrix organization styles. Supervisors whose staffs once came from a single discipline must now coordinate efforts of people from many disciplines, some only vaguely understood by the supervisor. All these are difficult transitions.

If the pace of transition is so fast as to reduce choice, managers feel threatened. As a colleague once put it, "It's not *change* we fear; its *being changed.*" That notion will echo for you as you read the fear, frustration, and conflict in the questions that follow.

In his classic book *Effective Management Leadership*, James Cribbin distinguished *frustration* from *conflict:*

> When the obstruction is environmental it is called frustration. The person finds that his ongoing

> behavior or efforts to satisfy his needs are foiled by things or people outside himself.... One can generally learn to live with externally provoked frustrations, however bothersome they may be.[1]

But conflict is another matter, much more painful. Here, according to Cribbin, the sufferer "seeks to satisfy two antagonistic drives or need patterns simultaneously, despite the fact that this is impossible in a given set of circumstances."[2]

The first few managers in this session are dealing with frustration caused by outer forces—by a failure of policy above them—or by misinformation about policy around them.

The final speakers are suffering internal conflicts, wanting two opposed values at the same time. Some are "generalist" managers marooned on a planet inhabited and soon to be ruled by specialists. They want to earn their bread in a technology company, but they resent technological "star players." Some want to perpetuate their tenures in dying functions. Some fear the challenge of the proffered promotion.

You'll read audience answers that offer superficial solutions. You'll read daring answers that chide: "Change your own thinking. You cannot hide from advancing technological change." These cause apprehension at first, but the message starts to sink in, bringing acceptance, quieting of internal conflict, and the beginning of a new plan.

If you suspect that you cannot hide from advancing technology, you'll be encouraged by the progress these managers are making, down a road you must travel soon.

[1]Copyright © 1972, James J. Cribbin, EFFECTIVE MANAGERIAL LEADERSHIP (New York: AMACOM, a division of American Management Association), 1972, pp. 200–201.

[2]Ibid., p. 202.

PART

ONE

NEW "STARS," NEW STANDARDS

As you've seen throughout your career, management behavior perceived as blatantly unfair will produce worker resistance in many forms, overt and covert, explosive and corrosive. But perception is the problem. Far too many people define "fairness" as "sameness"—and give grudging service to their organizations, hoping for the day when all rewards will be homogenized.

For the troubled managers in Part One, "different" treatment is "unfair" treatment. This is particularly blind thinking in a high-tech company where career ladders have been "dual," "parallel," or "alternative" for years. Xerox, 3M, ITT, GE, IBM, Honeywell, and scores of other organizations give their managers at least two routes to the pinnacle: Some managers aspire to vice-presidencies on the sales/finance/administration side; others rise to VP level with the title senior scientist, senior research fellow, or corporate scientist on a parallel track.

Only a modest proportion of entry-level managers can expect to reach the VP/fellow level in any company, but the scarcity of brilliant technical people causes some companies to woo these wizards early with jazzy attractions. This irritates the generalist plodders whose talents are seen as somewhat more common.

Developing a flexible mind-set that lets you accomplish your mission, negotiate for what you need, and stop scrutinizing what the other fellow is getting—that calls for a maturity of outlook rare in ordinary mortals. But it neatly avoids that splintering of attention and rending of energies that signals internal conflict. Frustration comes from noticing outer events that threaten us. Inner conflict comes from obsession with what we can't have. Watch the first three questioners wrestle with these problems.

1. VP FAVORS "BOY GENIUS"

Our VP overlooks tantrums, erratic behavior, unauthorized expenses from our new "star" while project administrators must cover up or take flak from established team members.

AUDIENCE RESPONSES

YOUR RATING

______ **a.** *How likely is this genius to produce the "inventions" your VP wants? If this kid fails to perform, his welcome will wear out. Just wink and wait.*

______ **b.** *Talk it over with your boss. If favoritism is denting the enthusiasm of other valuable people, he may be willing to pull in his horns a little.*

______ **c.** *Help the boy genius do the administrative stuff right. Make it easier, so he can concentrate on the work he was hired for. You'll all come out on top if he fulfills his technical promise.*

______ **d.** *Some people deserve more freedom than others. Freedom is a reward to shoot for, just like promotions and raises.*

	★	★★	★★★	★★★★
RATING	*NO!*	*RISKY*	*BETTER*	*BEST!*

1. VP FAVORS "BOY GENIUS" ANALYSIS

★

a. If the genius fails to produce, his welcome will wear out.

Winking and waiting will wear you out. Administrators must negotiate a peace with VPs about latitude for star performers. Then the covering-up can ease, and policy can be applied consistently and without apologies. You must set standards for what behavior is considered a tantrum, what latitude can be allowed on expenditures, what freedom on hours, what dress code constitutes an outrage—whatever is bothering you.

★★★

b. Discuss limits with the boss to avoid denting the enthusiasm of other valuable people.

Okay. Do this on the grounds that "X behavior" is disruptive to you and those around you, rather than on the grounds that "stars should have to live like the rest of us." Many companies now operate on the principle that attracting and holding great researchers means they can work on anything they want—within product line strategy—and that they can do so with more budget latitude and more administrative support than others get. If that is your company's policy, accept it. Otherwise, you may be tempted to throw some tantrums of your own, without star status to protect you.

★★★

c. Help the genius do the administrative stuff right.

Or not at all. It may be easier for another team member to handle administration by being teamed with the genius for experimentation, writing, editing, or other vital support work.

★★★★

d. Freedom is a reward to shoot for.

Absolutely. As true in sales, administration, editing, accounting—and a host of other fields, as it is in science.

Nickerson's Recommendations

For a four-star answer, project managers must contribute to and abide by company policy regarding the treatment of promising scientists and technicians. If you have dual career ladders, don't think of them as "double standards"; they are based on policy, not on unfair practices. As long as creative genius is a scarce and highly marketable commodity, companies will continue to create attractions and perks to hold the creative genius. Project managers will learn the care and feeding of these rare birds—and will make concerted efforts to satisfy in other ways those ordinary mortals who take the ideas of the genius and administer them into existence.

So long as there are high levels for all to aspire to, and several different tracks for getting there. there will be not only double, but triple and multiple standards for people to keep meeting.

Comment: While magazines, newspapers, and management books are extremely lucid on the subject of parallel career ladders, the technologists and middle managers who are climbing these ladders seem unaware of where they are or where they are going. One wonders what discussions take place at the annual performance review when they get to the last paragraph about career paths! Certainly, senior managers, R&D directors, and human resource managers have thought the problem through and made policy decisions—but the participants at seminars seem to think it's all a matter of management style or personal preference by bosses.

2. *MY DOUBLE STANDARDS HAUNT ME*

I tolerate administrative infractions from my star technologists; now I am paying the price as other good employees point out my unfairness.

A

AUDIENCE RESPONSES

YOUR RATING

_________ **a.** *Clean up your act. Sit down with your "good" employees and cite the penalties that will apply in the future.*

_________ **b.** *Simply make flexibility available more widely if employees deserve or need it. (Transportation and child care problems and other emergencies befall all your employees.)*

_________ **c.** *Suggest a "peer review" in which co-workers discuss this issue and agree some set of standards for "star performance" that merits stellar privileges.*

_________ **d.** *Compliment workers on their good work, but don't bend rules for them. Enforce rules evenly; offer* rewards *specially, without breaking rules.*

	★	★★	★★★	★★★★
RATING	*NO!*	*RISKY*	*BETTER*	*BEST!*

2. *MY DOUBLE STANDARDS HAUNT ME* ANALYSIS

★★

a. Clean up your act. Cite future penalties even for star performers.
You may be overreacting. These "infractions" may involve nothing more serious than tedious paperwork or rigid attendance rules or routine reporting requirements from which your star technologists might better be freed. Only serious matters would require "penalties."

★★★

b. Make flexibility more widely available for all—many people have emergencies that need coverage.
If attendance or lateness were the "infractions" involved here, this answer would apply. But if serious reporting requirements, purchasing rules, equipment use, or other vital items were at issue, giving wider easements might result in confusion or neglect.

Regarding hours, I believe that *flexing* the workweek for all your employees can result in much greater productivity for the company. "Gliding time"—a system where all employees work their full, agreed hours per week, but some elect to start the day early and finish early, others pick a later start-finish sequence, and so on—lets employees tend to personal business, early or late each day, making absenteeism and lateness unnecessary. Once chosen, the pattern is consistent and easy to monitor. It has improved output by 18 percent for many companies, without increasing stress.

★★★★

c. Engage in peer review to set "star status" privileges.
Unorthodox, creative, laudable. So long as the boss is part of the review team. This should be negotiated, not imposed, either side. Then, star status would be a target worth shooting for, and the target behaviors and standards would be clear.

★★ *d.* **Enforce rules evenly; offer rewards specially.**
Sounds okay in principle, except that for knowledge workers, freedom from rules *is* the supreme reward, more prized than raises, bonuses, and other attractions that appeal to mere mortals. Freedom to break trail without going back to signpost it—that's what explorers want. They need co-workers and assistants to do the follow-up.

Comment: It is not the double standard that is really coming back to haunt this questioner. It may be his or her failure to get the drudgery *covered* by someone other than a star, so that no failure occurs and no benefit is lost to the company. Failure to announce a policy of parallel standards—that's the real failure here. Employees will think you have a single standard unless you announce the contrary.

3. *SIGNALS CHANGE TOO FAST*

Top management keeps making radical changes of direction. Before we've made headway with one system, they've changed to another. I and my people feel paralyzed. They want quality too!

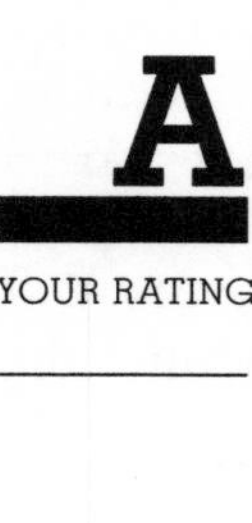

AUDIENCE RESPONSES

YOUR RATING

________ **a.** *Tell management you need time to make the first idea work before disruption is imposed.*

________ **b.** *Always respond to directives with written pros and cons. When a change occurs, show how the change contradicts previous requests, or retards progress, or increases costs. You cannot afford to leave this to verbal means.*

________ **c.** *Inform management immediately of any damaging consequences you see in a directive.*

________ **d.** *Management may be forced to respond to government, legal, and competitive moves. Find out* why *these changes are occurring so rapidly. When your own commitment improves, you may be able to get better compliance from your people.*

	★	★★	★★★	★★★★
RATING	*NO!*	*RISKY*	*BETTER*	*BEST!*

★

a. Tell management you need time to make the first idea work.
While you could argue for consistency/stability in accounting or personnel work, you may go down in flames in a high-tech setting, where the *speed of change* is often geared up to respond to or beat out competition. You may have to work on your people's paralysis, not on management's rapid response.

★★★★

b. Don't leave your response to verbal means. Write up the contradictions and costs you foresee.
By all means, so long as you find a neat, quick way of doing it. Management will insist you spend more energy on compliance than on resistance.

★★★★

c. Inform management immediately of any damaging consequences you see in the directive.
By all means. And ask for a response that may settle your fears and help you motivate your people. Your compliance will be much more enthusiastic if it is informed. When you write up the *risks* you see, *write up possible remedies* for these, and you may be able to spare management and yourself a lot of argument.

★★★★

d. Find our why these changes are occurring rapidly, whether government, legal, or competitive reasons compel these changes.
Yes. If you can find out without challenging your boss (asking peers, vendors, consultants, other contacts), you may save yourself some embarrassment. Having done some research, you will go to management (if you must) with speculative questions satisfied. Showing a simple graphic flow chart of increasingly rapid change would convince management that your inquiry is not frivolous.

Comment: Just as competition between high-tech companies forces rapid and vigorous experimentation, so competition among rival departments in high-tech companies forces progress along divergent paths, and more brutal decisions to dump unpromising projects, despite early enthusiasm.

Such companies as IBM and Data General are famous for assigning more than one design group to work on a single concept. The competition can be stimulating for some people, threatening for others. In larger companies with plenty of creative people to go around, this tough-minded approach pays off. If you come from a smaller company with limited creative resources, you'll be disquieted, at first, with the internal competition of the "gladiator school" style.

PART
TWO

CONFLICTS WITH CUSTOMERS AND COLLEAGUES

When Peters and Waterman drew up the *Eight Basic Principles* that keep America's best run companies on top, they opened with "a bias for action" and listed as number 2; "Staying close to the customer—learning his preferences and catering to them."[3]

Why is this so obvious to the owners and builders of businesses—yet so dimly perceived by many midmanagers and technologists? I believe the problem is one of *isolation*.

To one of the complainers in this next section who castigates clients, a helpful responder suggests, "To know our clients is to love them. (Ha!)" But the irony is—the joke is right. Many of your technical staffers work on your most vital contracts without ever meeting, talking with, or coming to know your clients. Some of your people ignore your client's company, its marketing problems, its successes. They focus on details without enquiring which *risks* your company is helping the client to manage. Therefore, when the client flies into a panic, makes an eleventh-hour demand, or overreacts to your late delivery, your people may put it down to bumbling or malice, when your client—if understood—would be seen as innocent of both.

INTERNAL "CUSTOMERS"—YOUR BREAD AND BUTTER

Familiarity breeds irritation with some of the departments you service internally. Often they are seen as nuisances rather than as "customers." Suc-

[3]Copyright © 1982, Thomas J. Peters and Robert H. Waterman, Jr., IN SEARCH OF EXCELLENCE (New York: Harper & Row, Publishers, Inc. 1982), frontispiece.

cessful internal service groups take pride in their role as "internal consultants" with expertise to share. They see their fellow departments' needs as "our reason for being here," and they rise to the occasion.

Think of the most successful salespeople, entrepreneurs, consultants, field engineers you know. How do they look when they're in a room with a real, live customer/client, talking over the client's problem? They look most alive, most stimulated at these times. Their phenomenal energies are released when they're in the presence of *their* reason for being. That's where the action is, and they relish it.

That heady experience is self-denied to some of the people who speak next.

4. CUSTOMERS AS ADVERSARIES

How can I help my technical people accept that customers' needs will often create inconveniences. Our researchers balk at every last-minute change.

AUDIENCE RESPONSES

YOUR RATING

_________ **a.** *Remind them that clients pay our salaries and produce our profits.*

_________ **b.** *Explain the overall advantage of creating and maintaining good client rapport: You cannot get promoted without it, in any service business.*

_________ **c.** *Invite them to client meetings; let them in on conference calls. To know our clients is the love them. (Ha!)*

_________ **d.** *Keep educating people that we are a service company, not a production line business. And we have competitors! Our clients have choices.*

	★	★★	★★★	★★★★
RATING	*NO!*	*RISKY*	*BETTER*	*BEST!*

★★ **a. Remind them that clients pay our salaries.**

That will increase your people's feelings of powerlessness. Take time to explain what risks the client is trying to cover with the last-minute changes. This stimulates the creativity of your worker instead of resentment. Grumbling about customer/client requests is natural enough, but as a boss, you want to curtail it or ease it every chance you get. All work is easy when you're willing—hard when you're not. Faults are easier to accept in a client whom you generally admire than in clients for whom you have little esteem. Assign your people to client companies in which they really have great interest—and focus on the worker's strength to improve that client's business rather than on the worker's powerlessness over the client.

b. Explain the advantage (career-wise) of maintaining good client rapport.

Yes. And tell them *how*, too—using the specific context of the last-minute request. In a lasting relationship between your organization and the client, these last-minute favors can be used to trade off at some future time when your company comes up short. Get your people to take the longer view and to *bargain* with the favors they do cheerfully.

c. Invite them to client meetings. To know clients is to love them.

Absolutely! Invite clients to meet your staff, too. Set up the most favorable possible conditions. In some good contract situations, staffs at client and service companies all know each other well, meet fairly regularly to work out problems, and develop a collaborative relationship. This comes in very handy when the going gets tough.

d. Keep educating people that service companies have competitors and clients have choices.

Yes. If you also add that "because of our technical and artistic merit—as well as our ability to respond to emergencies, we *are* their *best* choice." Appeal to your people's superiority, never their inferiority, when mentioning that clients have choices. It makes a huge difference.

5. CUSTOMERS CANNOT COMMUNICATE

How can I reform customers who do not give clear directions and do not understand processing language?

AUDIENCE RESPONSES

YOUR RATING

_______ **a.** *Ask if client company has technical people with whom you can communicate. Often they do, and will put that person on the project team. You should suggest this at the outset of a project.*

_______ **b.** *They need not speak our language, we must speak theirs; as the service company, we must do the translating. We must show them that they benefit by "filling in the blanks" for us.*

_______ **c.** *Sit down face to face with customers. Explain what we* both *need to* do *to ensure the success of a project. Explain* why *they save money and get benefits by doing things a certain way (ours).*

_______ **d.** *I find it easiest to* draw pictures *of what I think they've just said—to be sure we understand each other. Avoid technical jargon.*

	★	★★	★★★	★★★★
RATING	*NO!*	*RISKY*	*BETTER*	*BEST!*

5. CUSTOMERS CANNOT COMMUNICATE ANALYSIS

★★★ **a. Ask customers' technical people to "interpret" from the start.**

Sure, if they have them and can assign them to you, your technical people and theirs can collaborate. But, failing this, you must speak *their* language and help them begin to learn yours.

★★★★ **b. As a service company, we must do the stretching; we must do the "marketing" and give them benefits for reaching toward us.**

This is a great attitude for Earthlings to take when attempting to market their services to Martians and Venusians.

★★★★ **c. Face to face, explain why they save money and get benefits by doing things our way.**

Another excellent approach. If you can provide them with *tools* for getting their needs met quickly and with reduced chance of misinterpretation, go ahead. Don't expect the customer to create the tools for translation. If *you* do it, you add *customer education* to your array of attractions. It may give you the edge over companies more technically able but less good at building communication bridges.

★★★★ **d. Draw them a picture.**

Yes. Give them a chart, a checklist, a graphic tool for continuing, consistent, shortcut communicating with you. The original effort is paid back very quickly.

6. GOOD CUSTOMER: IMPOSSIBLE DEMAND

My best client requests deadline changes that DP cannot meet. Neither side will budge. I'm in the middle, as account manager.

AUDIENCE RESPONSES

YOUR RATING

______ **a.** *Explore what your customers might sacrifice or pay to get their needs met. Can they take less detail? Will they pay for DP to work overtime? Unless there is a cost to them, they will become even more unreasonable next time. If they balk, go to your boss.*

______ **b.** *Perhaps we can provide some other service or data at low/no cost (summary tables, management summaries, usable interpretations) instead of the total answer they want so fast.*

______ **c.** *Offer them their "most needed" information only, with detail to follow. Next time, allow for unanticipated bottlenecks when committing to a deadline. Watch for patterns of changeable demand in some clients. Point it out; charge for it.*

______ **d.** *Seek trade-offs. Clients don't always need all they ask for. If client "gives a little," you may get DP to match them.*

	★	★★	★★★	★★★★
RATING	*NO!*	*RISKY*	*BETTER*	*BEST!*

6. *GOOD CUSTOMER: IMPOSSIBLE DEMAND* ANALYSIS

★★★ *a.* **Explore trade-offs: detail, overtime. Unless they pay, they'll demand more. If they balk, go to your boss.**

Yes. If this is a precedent-setting demand with big consequences, I concur, *provided* your manner is calm and judicious throughout. If you panic, you may cause client and in-house services to dig their heels in. If you keep the climate cool, you may be able to bring in your boss as adviser, not arbitrator. The boss will appreciate that.

★★★ *b.* **Try for a temporary pacifier, if you can't provide the whole answer.**

Yes. Good thinking. But be careful. They may want the pacifier service as a matter of course for all future orders; or they may take *it* and demand the full treatment too, *this* time. You must be clear that the temporary service is in lieu of instant provision of the full demand, and that it, too, is a benefit.

★★★★ c. **Offer them "most needed" information only. Watch for patterns of unreasonable demand; build it into future scheduling and pricing.**

Excellent, given that you find the demand "impossible."

★★★★ *d.* **Seek trade-offs. Get both sides to "give a little."**

If you can do this regularly, you make an excellent negotiator. Let both sides know that the other side is "giving"; increase goodwill, and you'll reduce tension and improve energy for everyone.

7. DP VERSUS MARKETING: STALEMATE!

How can we call a truce between the DP programmer/ analysts and the marketing folks. Continual complaints reach me from both sides.

A

AUDIENCE RESPONSES

YOUR RATING

______ **a.** *Have joint workshops with small groups from each area. Involve more than one level of manager/worker.*

______ **b.** *Have representatives of each department sit down and live inside the other department for a few days. Really* seeing *what goes on would improve understanding.*

______ **c.** *Explain* why *you need what you need . . . both sides. Give feedback and specific thanks when needs are met.*

______ **d.** *Marketing must explain its* objectives *better. Half-baked requests to DP are met by half-baked results from DP.*

	★	★★	★★★	★★★★
RATING	*NO!*	*RISKY*	*BETTER*	*BEST!*

7. *DP VERSUS MARKETING: STALEMATE!* ANALYSIS

a. Set up joint workshops with several levels from each area.

Right! When a couple of managers from each area communicate successfully, don't lose the momentum; pass it on. Getting the groups together under the leadership of convinced parties from both departments—and doing it regularly (after hours if necessary) focusing on a current work problem—will give your informal workshop some oomph. You need to build a chain of communication successes to offset the communication blockages of the past.

b. Live in the other person's department a few days.

Well worth the investment. Sharing to some degree in the actual work (having to achieve a *result* in the other department) gives you appreciation of the other person's value. Cross-training often achieves this benefit—Japanese companies wouldn't live without it. In one U.S. company (NFO Research, Toledo), the people who "built the communication bridges" between marketing and production (computers) were people who had served terms in the other fellow's department.

c. Explain the why of your requests. Give feedback and specific thanks when needs are met.

Indeed. But go further. DP departments usually create a request form for use by "client departments." It should start out with the why or the goals of the project and then urge requesters to be clear about all the information needs their system should serve.

Internal DP projects should be handled as if the two parties were contracting: one a customer company, the other a DP consulting firm. If the requester were paying directly for DP consulting services, and the DP people couldn't get paid until they delivered satisfaction, the original contract discussions would be a lot more thorough than they are, typically, when two departments of the same company make a contract.

★★★ *d.* **Half-baked requests get half-baked results.**

Yes. If you do not have to pay for the services of the DP people, you often enter negotiations with only hazy ideas about your needs. Or, encouraged by the gung-ho attitude of the DP people, you agree to have advanced technical feats performed on your project—when all you need is something simple. Behave as if you have to pay for every moment of contact with them, and you'll be much clearer at the outset and keep your project from mushrooming.

Comment: I applaud the companies who do insist on internal budget charges for internal services. This causes the requester to read, study, get hands-on experience with computers to make intelligent, rational requests. If you are not ready to do this yet, assign a lieutenant who is computer friendly to oversee your request-for-proposal and to keep the lid on costs and complexity of the service provided to you.

PART THREE

CAREER PATH PROBLEMS: RENEGADES TO RETREADS

Now come the painful problems—those in which inner conflicts confuse the managers in question. You'll recognize the issues—they are present in every fast-moving company where demand is relentless—and managers grow tired, frightened, distracted, outrun by events. The first three managers are afraid of their own subordinates; they do not trust the team to voice ideas effectively, implement company policy, or handle disappointment.

Fortunately, when some bosses approach burnout, their hotshot subordinates may rise to the occasion, setting up "skunk works" to chase the goals the boss is too tired or timid to try. The boss is "saved."

Fortunately, when some groups approach burnout, senior management remembers its mission—to keep lighting up the "big billboard" with the company goals emblazoned on it. They put heart into the managers, who put heart into the team. The group is "saved," to fight another day.

But the managers must overcome their dangerous deficiencies in clarity about corporate policy. The first three managers you'll meet *are resisting reality* and are waiting for events to overtake them. Subordinates and senior managers may not forgive repeated failures by the leader.

The final two managers have broken faith with themselves. For them, and possibly for the groups they manage, the good days may be over. Events *will* overtake them. As Hans Selye said in his book, *Stress Without Distress*, regarding middle managers, administrators, or public servants with limited responsibilities,

> one of the major sources of distress arises from dissatisfaction with life, namely, from disrespect for their own accomplishments. As they grow older and progress toward the completion of their career, they

> tend to doubt the importance of their achievements. They are frustrated by the conviction that they really could have done, and would have liked to do much more. These people often spend the rest of their lives in search of scapegoats, grumbling about the lack of opportunity, excessive responsibility towards their relatives—anything will do to avoid the most painful confession: that the fault was really their own."[4]

The forgiving respondents to the next five questioners view the insanity as temporary, and offer—among others—replies designed to help the askers snap themselves awake.

[4]Copyright © 1974, Hans Selye, STRESS WITHOUT DISTRESS (New York: Harper & Row Publishers, Inc., 1974), pp. 74–75.

8. *CAN'T MUZZLE MY MAVERICKS*

In our knowledge business, there are too many independent types who want to debate every decision. How can I discipline them?

AUDIENCE RESPONSES

YOUR RATING

________ **a.** *Make your limits clear on what latitude you allow for debate before moving ahead. Then insist on unreserved support.*

________ **b.** *Show them who's boss.*

________ **c.** *The right to debate must be earned. Keep a track record on how many arguments fizzled when put to the test. Silence these people until their performance matches their mouthiness.*

________ **d.** *You hire mavericks for a knowledge business because you need people who can think. Just insist they do their homework. Don't let them repeat themselves once they've voiced their point.*

	★	★★	★★★	★★★★
RATING	*NO!*	*RISKY*	*BETTER*	*BEST!*

a. Make limits clear on debate; then insist on support.
Good. You gain enormous value from letting your team contribute to decisions *before* they are final. Specify what parts of the decision are still up for grabs: the *how*, not the whether, or the *method*, not the budget, for example. This helps to limit the debate. Rather than insist on support from uncommitted people, you may be able—in a large department—to assign those who can feel total commitment to a project—while letting others work on other things. You cannot *force* unreserved support—not at the speed American companies work. (In Japan, they start planning a lot earlier, so that concurrence can be gradually gained from all. A process we might well emulate.)

b. Show them who's boss.
And they'll show *you* how painful it can be to be boss.

c. The right to debate must be earned. Silence those who performance fails to back up their arguments.
This may sound like justice, but it's a high-stress route, open to endless seesawing and bickering. Naturally, you may give much more credence to the arguments of your strongest performers, but your newer people may have brilliant insights you all can use—and neophytes deserve a chance to be heard even while they are developing their track record. Like it or not, your team will tell people to "pipe down" without any help from you. You may have to act as peacemaker more often than "pipedowner."

d. You hire mavericks to think. Insist that they back up their debates and don't let them repeat themselves once heard.
Correct. In a knowledge business, expect much more discussion and debate of ideas; expect to say "maybe" or "maybe later" a lot more than you would in cut-and-dried affairs. You need to keep encouraging your best and

brightest to keep pumping in ideas even if their current ones are not meeting with instant acceptance. If you don't want people to "repeat themselves," just ask for new wrinkles or new approaches. As you know from your own life in technology, persistence pays off, sometimes after exploring hundreds of avenues leading to a tantalizing possibility.

9. *CAN'T ENFORCE POLICY*

How can I demand that my dedicated staff take time from clients to handle "accountability" paperwork that is really redundant but "counts" upstairs.

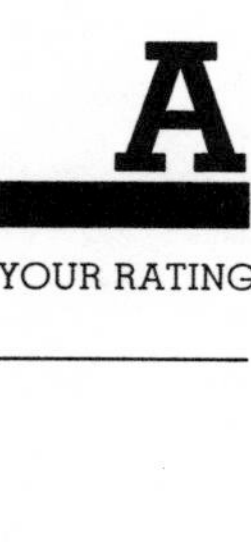

AUDIENCE RESPONSES

YOUR RATING

______ **a.** *How can you? How can you* not*??? Meet your staff. Explain the "long-run" necessity of this paperwork, even though it hurts, short run.*

______ **b.** *Face your role in the process. Will you rebel or conform with regulations? Remember that you represent senior management; they pay your salary. Your group will follow if you lead.*

______ **c.** *Make peace between technical and administrative requirements; only then can your people do it. Remember what the mission is.*

______ **d.** *Can you find a way to divide the labor so that some people with heavy client work don't have to do the paperwork? Can some staffers be dedicated only to paper?*

	★	★★	★★★	★★★★
RATING	*NO!*	*RISKY*	*BETTER*	*BEST!*

a. Explain the long-run necessity, even if it hurts, short run.

Yes. But to do this, the manager must be convinced the paperwork is necessary and *not* "redundant." The manager needs to understand why it "counts" upstairs. Is it required by government regulation that justifies funding? That's necessary, not redundant. Are there legal liabilities that this paperwork covers? Then it's not redundant. As long as the manager devalues this work, the "dedicated" staff will too.

b. Will you rebel or conform? Senior management pays your salary; your group will follow your lead.

I agree. But, again, the manager must *understand* in order to decide upon reforming or conforming. It's best if the group follows an *informed* leader. When a manager feels unable to conform with regulations, he or she must pursue information and make a decision, not just withhold enthusiasm.

c. Make peace between your technical and administrative requirements, based on your understanding of the total mission.

This is it! Just as corporations calibrate the relative value of both administration and science to the corporate mission—just as corporations create parallel ladders for people in both careers—so department heads must carry out this policy in daily practice, making the requirements very clear to all staffers, and then dividing the pieces of the workload in a rational way.

d. Divide the labor so people with client-heavy work need not do paperwork; other staffers handle that.

Involve your staffers in designing a system that divides work equitably (not equally) along talent lines. Design recognition and rewards so that *both* necessary functions are attractive enough to ensure completion by appropriate staffers. Staffers are already dedicated to "information" (not "paper")—they are called secretaries, research assistants, writers, editors, administrators, and project coordinators. In some companies, people more senior than the scientists handle the paperwork—they consider it so vital.

10. CAN'T BREAK THE BAD NEWS

How can I tell my people that top management has canceled a project we've all committed to. My own disgust is bound to show.

AUDIENCE RESPONSES

YOUR RATING

________ **a.** *Be honest. Have a choice replacement project to offer.*

________ **b.** *Tell subordinates that the work done up to now has been great but that circumstances beyond your (or the company's) control have put the project off—and that they will get other good projects to replace it.*

________ **c.** *Ask your team if they would consider pursuing the project on their own, if it is so good.*

________ **d.** *Call the group together. Explain the situation. Ask for a thorough report on progress made up to now—so that all plans and progress are preserved in case the project arises again.*

	★	★★	★★★	★★★★
RATING	*NO!*	*RISKY*	*BETTER*	*BEST!*

★★

a. Be honest. Have a choice replacement project.
Here's an optimist talking. I'm all for this approach, except that the questioner is worried about his "disgust" showing. That's the feeling he has to deal with before communicating with the troops. I've watched managers announce a policy they find hateful—and the troops take their signals accordingly, causing havoc in the aftermath.

★★

b. Compliment their excellent work up to now, cite circumstances beyond the company's control, promise replacements.
Yes, to part one. No, to part two. Yes, to part three. Your staff may deserve compliments on work done so far. Give them and be specific, but don't cite circumstances beyond your or the company's control—this worsens their feelings of powerlessness and makes the company seem rudderless too. Cite the real reasons for the cancellation; the *cause* may be something you can all work to eradicate. Unless you do this, they may have as little faith in the replacement project as they now have in the canceled project.

★★★★

c. Ask your team if they would consider pursuing the project on their own.
Wow! That's good. If you remember Tracy Kidder's book, *The Soul of a New Machine*, this was the challenge thrown out by Tom West at Data General; it resulted in a triumph. Anything that brings your people back to full power is a good move. Anything that gives people *choices* rather than "faits accomplis" I'll applaud.

 *d.* **Explain the situation. Ask for collection and preservation of all progress to date in case project arises again.**

If you lack the daring of responder *c*, this is a second best possibility. Follow up by keeping these "good but not yet" projects listed in plain view. Resurrect them in meetings from time to time, asking for new wrinkles, new approaches, new applications. Build on the good engineer's natural aversion to throwing ideas away. They keep turning up in the next project, in disguised form, just the way authors keep writing the same books, over and over.

11. OVERAGE, OVERQUALIFIED, ALIENATED

We've been invaded by young technologists who see an older administrator like me as redundant. My seniority is becoming a liability to me.

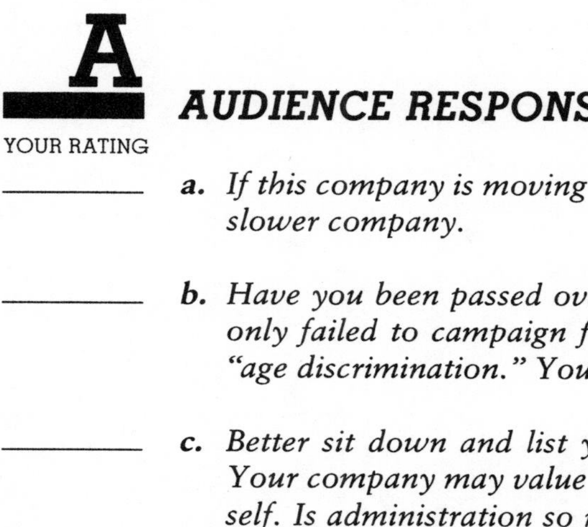

AUDIENCE RESPONSES

YOUR RATING

_________ **a.** *If this company is moving too fast for you, find yourself a slower company.*

_________ **b.** *Have you been passed over for promotion—or have you only failed to campaign for it? Your comments indicate "age discrimination." Yours or theirs?*

_________ **c.** *Better sit down and list your virtues and contributions. Your company may value you more than you value yourself. Is administration so nonimportant at your company that the firm can use someone "adequate" instead of someone terrific?*

_________ **d.** *If you are older, how recent are those "qualifications" of yours. Administration is a new ballgame now that computers are here. Keep making yourself current. Become more technical yourself.*

	★	★★	★★★	★★★★
RATING	*NO!*	*RISKY*	*BETTER*	*BEST!*

11. *OVERAGE, OVERQUALIFIED, ALIENATED* ANALYSIS

★ **a. If you're too old a fish for this pond, find a more congenial spot.**

Not so fast. You need to understand the company's strategy first. At what stage in its life cycle is your company? If your company has come through a period of growth through mergers and acquisitions, it may have carved out its market share without needing heavy R&D innovation. It *bought* innovation for a time. During such a stage, the company needed extra managerial layers in the financial, legal, and administrative wings where all the action was. Today, with new competition and the drive for greater innovation, your company may be looking for more technical people and, perhaps, fewer administrators. You must explore this with the Personnel and Human Resources departments. This is not a personal issue involving "young technologists versus older administrators." It is a much larger issue about company strategy for the next five to ten years. If the company is offloading administrators, you need to know this, but don't assume you'll be the first to go. Find out. You'll then know whether to retool for a stay, or start peddling your resumé to a different type of company in a different stage of growth.

b. Have you been passed over, or did you campaign? Who is discriminating? The company or you?

Worth thinking about. When a manager uses words like "older," "redundant," "seniority," and "liability" about himself or herself, the age discrimination may be internal. On the other hand, seniority and the high pay/benefits packages that go with it are a real liability for seniors in many companies, unless these seniors show ability to produce *added value* for the added cost. This is the real challenge for this administrator. Can he or she *add on* rather than simply linger on?

★★★★ *c.* **List your contributions; your company may value you if administration is important and you are terrific.**

Yes. And once you've got your act together, take it to your boss and Human Resources before you "take it on the road."

★★★★ *d.* **How recent are your qualifications? Are they up to date with the new technologies your company is hiring?**

There's a pertinent question! Rather than fighting the progress that's obviously here, fit your administrative skills to it. So many questions in this session show a crying need for *appropriate* administrative partnering of technological "stars."

12. PROMOTION MEANS OBLIVION

After years as senior technical field man I'm faced with promotion to district manager. Flying a desk will kill me, but policy requires it.

AUDIENCE RESPONSES

YOUR RATING

________ **a.** *Change the policy, or at least question it strongly with your boss.*

________ **b.** *How long does the district manager posting extend? What comes after that? Don't you have a career ladder of which this is only a necessary rung? Focus on what you could learn in this post.*

________ **c.** *You can't stay a sales rep forever. If your boss has faith in you, believe it.*

________ **d.** *Talk it over informally with some friendly district managers. How did they make the transition?*

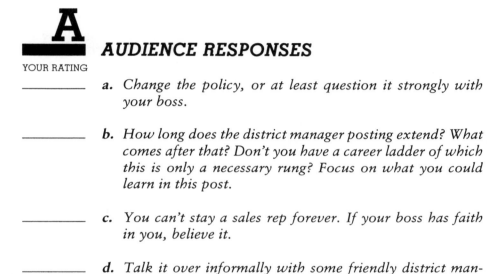

	★	★★	★★★	★★★★
RATING	*NO!*	*RISKY*	*BETTER*	*BEST!*

12. PROMOTION MEANS OBLIVION ANALYSIS

★★★★ **a. Change the policy or at least question it strongly with your boss.**

If you were less than senior technical field person, I would think this reply too optimistic. But a person about to be promoted has a voice. Many sales organizations have dual career ladders with very high field slots—running parallel to HQ management ladders: 3M is one such organization. You might want to research this with your professional sales organizations locally and get some ammunition to use in your discussions. Many companies are seeing the folly of turning a great field sales rep into a mediocre district manager. 3M leaves its great field people on a field ladder, but promotes them into larger territories, or requires that they train, help field test products, or assume other *field-based* responsibilities to keep earning promotions and share their expertise more widely.

★★★★ **b. What rung on your ladder will this post represent, and for how long?**

Yes. Some companies require every manager to assume certain posts for a time. Without demotion, they can then return to the field in another capacity. See what you can negotiate. You may *change* the role of district manager while you are in that slot. Prenegotiate that!

★★★ **c. You can't stay in field sales forever. Have faith in your boss's judgment.**

If you can't stay in field sales forever, why not? Because your volume declines when you can't keep up with technology? Because your salary and benefits are too high compared to those of newer salespeople with better track records? Is this district manager slot a challenge, a promotion, a reward? Or is it a dumping ground for played-out seniors in the field? When the questioner says, "Promotion means oblivion," it makes me wonder. Either take the promotion as genuine and make a go of it, or assess your real value in field sales, and make a case for staying there, and adding value.

d. Talk it over informally with friendly district managers.

Here, as in any midcareer crisis, some informal discussions with people who've been there can be manna in the desert. This is a good time for chats with former bosses who appreciate you and with friends from your professional group, friendly vendors, and others whom you can trust. Don't pour your heart out; just get a sense of wider options than the ones that frighten you. You may find a whole new approach that benefits you and your company.

PART FOUR

FINE TUNING: TECHNOLOGY MEANS TRANSITION

Adventurers. That's what you need if you run a technology business: people willing to test, discard, argue, experiment, push, risk, respond, invest, without many guarantees and despite "laws of nature" that portend failure. You need people with high energy who don't expect to rest long on their laurels and who can react to disappointment with resiliency.

You need people who relish rigor, who devour new data voraciously, who digest disparate ideas and create new ones, without flagging. You want energetic, enterprising optimists. Then you start wanting more.

You want people who can fly, yet you want their feet on the ground. You demand total commitment and concentration, yet you want them to let go, without a fight, when business logic says "cut our losses."

You want them to *think* like explorers, yet *apply* knowledge like marketers.

You want scientists with business sensitivity, technologists with tactical and financial insight. You want it all. Of course.

What are you willing to do to get it?

FOUR ENTICEMENTS

As you've seen, companies use many options for reward and encouragement of their best people. Most of them spring from four simple elements: *recognition*, *protection*, *respect*, and *leadership* that is caring as well as daring. These enticements would attract talent to your team.

1. Recognition Intel's president Andrew S. Grove puts it this way:

> The Ph.D. in computer science who knows an answer in the abstract, yet does not apply it to create some tangible output, gets little recognition,

> but a junior engineer who produces results is highly valued and esteemed. And that is how it should be.[5]

In many companies, I find, there is value in teaming both kinds of engineer to get advanced thinking and applications.

2. ***Protection*** You've seen how vital and desirable this is for technologists. Describing 3M's "executive champion" system, authors Peters and Waterman say,

> The executive champion is an ex-product champion himself, who behaved "irrationally," got shot at, was committed to something, and probably hung in there for ten or more years on some pet project of his own. But now, as the executive champion, he is there to protect the youngsters from premature intrusions from the corporation staff and to push them out of the nest when the time is right.[6]

Often, something as simple and effective as the help of a good coordinating secretary can provide tremendous protection—ensuring progress—for a group of engineers bent on meeting a deadline or making a discovery reveal itself.

3. ***Respect*** Your outstanding scientist/technologist *will* take no for an answer, but not always peaceably. Can you set limits without getting macho about it? Here's how D. Quinn Mills suggests dealing with impassioned resistance from your people. It's the best of them, the most committed who may be the most questioning, he opines:

> For employees who have a long term investment in the firm, or hope to, this questioning should not be interpreted as resistance to change. Rather than being discouraged by this reaction, some managers welcome it and hear that the employee may really be saying: "How can I continue to contribute? Can I make a place for myself in the new environment? Will the organization help me make the change if I need to?"[7]

[5]Copyright © 1983 Andrew S. Grove, HIGH OUTPUT MANAGEMENT (New York: Random House, Inc., 1983), p. 166.

[6]Peters and Waterman, IN SEARCH OF EXCELLENCE, pp. 225–226.

[7]Copyright © 1985, D. Quinn Mills, THE NEW COMPETITORS (New York: John Wiley & Sons, 1985), pp. 345–346.

The more the dedicated worker has invested, the more respect his or her fears deserve, and the more honest reassurance or rationale he or she needs to hear.

4. ***Leadership*** Is leadership tougher in a high-tech environment? Definitely. This is true whether you perform feats with computers, polymers, chemicals, petroleum, aerospace, medicine, weapons, microwaves—or banking, legislation, automobiles, toys, construction, sports, the stock market. Nothing is simple any more.

   If the technical team must concentrate harder than ever, and move faster than ever on the next breakthrough, those who lead them must keep the team on course, all through the voyage, from the lookout position.

   Do you provide your technical teams with glimpses of broader victories to counteract their "bench myopia"? Do you encourage their memberships in professional societies? Do you foster field contacts with customers, vendors, learned journals—to counteract the sclerosis that comes from concentrating too long? Do you make yourself available, informally, for those after-hours chats that help people see ways to solve problems, that assure them you are alongside. Do you act as "silent guardian," clearing away barriers so that their next steps will be easier? Do you do it in unassuming fashion?

   In *The Soul of a New Machine*,[8] Tracy Kidder related how the engineers relished their "ownership" over the new machine and did not realize until after the launch, how many "saves" their boss had made, silently, along the way. Magic!

   For both workers and leaders, building a career in technology means giving up that vision of "someday when everything will settle down and be orderly"—and getting comfortable with controlled chaos.

   Once having agreed to accept turbulence as a way of life, you will then need protective armor against burnout.

BURNOUT PREVENTION

If you've been living in this high-risk environment, you are familiar with the early signs of burnout: irritability, trying too hard, unaccustomed rudeness, complaints over loss of home life pleasure.

Rest-and-relaxation is the approved prescription. Rather than let a job run on and on to endless overtime, the leader's job is to set limits: name a date by which certain team members can expect a rest. Then stick to it.

[8]Copyright © 1981 Tracy Kidder, THE SOUL OF A NEW MACHINE (Boston: Little Brown and Company, 1981).

The work plan must allow for rotation of team members through various phases of a project. This practice pays off over the life of the project, reducing errors, illness, absenteeism—and avoiding the fatal step, namely, having the employee walk off the job for good. Weekends off at intervals mean better projects and work force stability, no matter how important the project. Build it into the plan.

Has the situation gone beyond that point in your company? Do your technologists exhibit bitten nails, skin eruptions, sleeplessness, headaches, facial pain, crippling back pain? These are signs of deepening fatigue. Now, they must be encouraged to formulate a plan for cutting back. They need your support to do this. Without it, they will tend to hide their fatigue as if it were a shameful weakness. They risk going into "stage 4 burnout" or "crisis stage" burnout, according to Robert Veninga and James Spradley, with self-doubt, visible depression, escapist thoughts, even suicidal leanings as typical signs. Rescue from stage 4 will not be by self-help and is difficult without professional support.

Failure to get relief at stage 4 takes most sufferers to the stage referred to as "hitting the wall." Here, Veninga and Spradley warn, the worker suffers "loss of life control, crippling pain, substance abuse, mental breakdown."[9] This is the stage that turns brilliant scientists into street people.

Here, too, the values of the leader and the common sense displayed on a daily basis makes the difference between technologists who take their transitions with verve and teams who get dragged through the hedge backward into change. As Bennis and Nanus put it, in *Leaders*,

> A number of firms we know of have installed the most expensive state of the art gymnasiums/health centers imaginable. At the same time, these firms induce an unbearable amount of stress through prodigious work loads, unhealthy plant conditions, heavy travel schedules, and anxiety-laden situations, all of which nullify the presumed benefits of their formal "health programs".[10]

No. Industrial leaders needn't become physicians or psychiatrists either. But they can provide the balance and values that allow dedicated people to take care of themselves.

Long hours and hard work are not harmful. They can stimulate "eu-

[9]Copyright © 1981, Robert L. Veninga and James P. Spradley, THE WORK STRESS CONNECTION (Boston: Little Brown and Company, 1981), pp. 63–70.

[10]Copyright © 1985, Warren Bennis and Burt Nanus, LEADERS: THE STRATEGIES FOR TAKING CHARGE (New York: Harper & Row, Publishers, Inc., 1985), p. 116.

stress" rather than distress. *Frustration* is the dangerous ingredient in the long workday, and leaders can provide the perspective and support to reduce it.

In a Swedish retirement home near Boston, I recently met a gentleman, still vibrant, independent, healthy. During our first conversation, when he learned that I do management consulting, he volunteered that he used to work the clock around with Ned Land, founder of Polaroid. Glowing with pride, he described the many times when he, as the older technologist, worked alongside Land hour after fascinating hour, until both of them nodded off exhausted, at the workbench. Did he develop ulcers? No. In fact, those arduous workdays made the high point of his work life—with stories he can "dine out on" to this day.

If you manage a high-tech business, get informed about simple stress-reduction techniques. Practice them personally; make them available to those vital people on whom technical transitions and corporate triumphs will depend.

TEN STEPS TO STRESS REDUCTION

Kathy Nielsen, consultant and clinician, recommends a simple ten-step program[11] to keep medical and technical managers challenged and healthy: How many of these do you use to control your stress?

1. ***Budget Your Energy*** Sketch out on a large sheet of paper the commitments you've made for the next few weeks or months (the term of your big new project) at work, home, community—all your commitments. Seeing them on one sheet of paper makes you realistic and helps you seek help from family, colleagues, and subordinates if you tend to carry too much alone. It helps you "dis-volunteer" where necessary.

2. ***Rest/Sleep*** Compare the hours of sleep you normally need with the hours you get now. Make up for lost sleep by returning to saner patterns.

3. ***Relaxation techniques*** Read up and practice simple meditation and mild self-hypnosis techniques. Audio tapes and books are widely available to help you do this. Slow, rhythmic breathing can be done almost imperceptibly, to calm your racing pulse during a hectic or trying day.

[11]Copyright © 1985, Patricia Nickerson and Kathy Nielsen, MANAGING MULTIPLE PRIORITIES (New York: Dun & Bradstreet, 1985), p. 11.

4. ***Nutrition*** Cut down on sugar, salt, caffeine, nicotine, alcohol, all substances that lift and slam the body, wearing out your adaptive response mechanisms.

5. ***Positive Addictions*** Indulge in your fascinations; engage in hobbies, sports, and artistic endeavors that give balance (and *exercise*) to a day filled with thinking, negotiating, and evaluating.

6. ***Assertion*** Say what you think and what you need: stop "stuffing" things until they explode. Focus on the present and future. Assert with courtesy, inviting the other person to assert feelings and needs too. Then, barter.

7. ***Active Listening*** Offer more "uh-huh's" and fewer prescriptions to troubled colleagues. They benefit more from concerned listening than from coercive advice.

8. ***Changing Old Tapes*** Any injunction you give yourself, starting with "Unless I do this, they'll think that . . ." is coming from an "old tape" that may be forcing you to neglect your own needs.

9. ***Humor as healer:*** Think of the two funniest or most light-hearted people you know, and seek them out on the occasion of your next frustration. They may not make light of your problem, but they may make your heart lighter while you unravel it. Most of us seek out grim associates when we want to be confirmed in our grimness. This just makes things worse.

10. ***Friends and Allies*** While these people are just plain comforting in times of trouble, the recommendation here is to remember friends who "owe you one" and to "collect" when you're close to burnout and really need help. Being asked for help makes them feel valued and strong—a feeling they may relish now, just as you have done in the past.

These steps are utterly simple. They are also *not* natural to stress addicts. You and your team can cultivate them to ease your burdens and increase your sense of control over your environment. Protect your mental health during periods of intense labor and sacrifice.

PART FIVE

CHECKLISTS FOR ATTRACTING AND HOLDING TECH TALENT

The same attractions that draw the brightest graduates to your company tend to hold the best performers at higher levels. If you want your innovators to stay with you, giving dedication, energy, stamina, and devotion . . ,

HERE'S WHAT THEY WANT

- *Excitement.* Hot projects with major impact on the company's profitability but even bigger impact on the world outside. They want to be "famous" among their peers for having worked on a particular product or project. Only this chance at fame will keep them at the lab bench, making miracles for weeks at a time.
- *Control.* Autonomy over their own portion of the work without frivolous interference from the boss, mates, or worse—nontechnical outsiders.
- *Compatibility.* A good match between the tasks of the project and the team's specific talents. This improves the odds for advanced discoveries.
- *Information.* Especially in environments where several teams compete on projects. Your genius wants a boss who keeps his ear to the ground and saves the technical group from tunneling in the dark toward a dead end.
- *Insulation.* From bureaucratic interference and imposition of nontechnical criteria on innovation.
- *Powerful bosses.* Bosses who keep flashing the "big picture" on the

screen, especially when the picture changes. Bosses who nudge, empower, and protect without hovering.

- *Worthy colleagues*, with commensurate and complementary knowledge who will share the midnight watches and supply the missing links that strengthen a project.
- *Recognition.* Not just at the final victory celebration, but minicelebrations to mark important intervals.
- *Ownership.* Credit for their specific contributions to the finished product—given loud and clear at the "launch," the trade shows, the press parties, and writ large in the corporate history.

Compared to these, the honorific titles that await at the pinnacle, the pay raises and bonuses along the way are aspired to, appreciated or assumed as "a right."

HERE'S WHAT THEY DREAD

- *Dud projects.* Being assigned to something inelegant and klutzy, hastily conceived or panic driven.
- *Tiresome competition.* Infighting among technical staffers inspired by political, not technical nudging from above.
- *Technical humiliation.* Making a gross error or miscalculation that drags down the team effort and loses team respect. Especially an error "we should have seen coming."
- *Being outclassed.* Competitive moves which bring out a product much better than the one you've been struggling with. A string of these will tarnish your company's holding power. The misled, misused genius will depart.
- *The end of the project:* What Tracy Kidder called "those post-partum blues."[12] You must have another winner in the wings: "Follow that act" to keep your talented people inspired but not exhausted. Determine in advance what "rest period" is required; make them comfortable about taking it, but keep the new goal at the ready.

The suggestions made in this chapter are simple, appealing, but difficult to apply in companies with only short-term targets and shifting values. Other organizations, new or old, with strong cultures and consistent codes of ethics, use these *ideas* to endure and override crisis or challenge. You may know these values; you may live them.

As one manager exclaimed at the end of a stimulating seminar day, "I *knew* I knew it! Lord help me *do* it!"

[12]Kidder, THE SOUL OF A NEW MACHINE, p. 286.

NO-GUILT DELEGATION

SESSION SIX

NO-GUILT DELEGATION

INTRODUCTION

Delegating is so natural and necessary, it's amazing we have such trouble with it. When did delegating start? When some primitive hunter divided the work load among the club wielders, rock tossers, and snare throwers in his clan to bring down a saber-toothed tiger? What early master mustered the courage to let younger runners do the chasing while he strategized for future forays? Perhaps anthropologists could tell us.

Most managers seem able and willing to delegate routines when the risks are low and the chances for glory have declined. But when the work is vital, exciting, rewarding, you and I may stumble over the real meaning of the word "delegate," *to authorize*. We want the burden lifted, but we hesitate to empower others. And we ignore the great truth that power sharing multiplies success for the many when leaders forge ahead on the efforts of the led.

Perhaps you are one of the rare ones who felt comfortable with delegation from the start. But before you count yourself among the good delegators, ask yourself how often you have said, "Aw, heck, it's quicker to do it myself!"

Perhaps you were right that once. It *was* quicker to do it yourself. But if the task must be repeated weekly or monthly, how can it be quicker next time, and the next?

TO DELEGATE, TO AUTHORIZE, TO TRUST

Time is not the main deterrent to delegation. Many of the blocks are ego driven. Perhaps you hesitate because

- The task is your favorite.
- You seek perfection—no one will do it as well as you.
- The task requires finesse—no one else is as talented as you.
- You fear losing touch with the clients, customers, or seniors your delegate will now contact.
- Your delegate may botch things, involving you in clean-up, apologies, embarrassment.
- Your delegate is lean and hungry, out to prove it's time for you to step down. Why test that assumption?

You may care to add some deterrents of particular poignancy to you. But if you can identify with any of the reasons just cited, you will have some sympathy for the managers whose questions follow and some appreciation for the views of those who reply. You are not alone.

PART ONE

TRUSTING COMPETENCE BELOW YOU

In an ideal world, you'd select your own subordinates and let them learn, try, adjust, test in safety, until they can handle the job under all conditions. They'd have your views on the risks and opportunities involved at each plateau, and they'd resolve priority conflicts according to *your* policies and sensitivities. You'd have built yourself some clones.

But in real life, things work very differently. You may be hired from outside to head up a group whose alliances—holy and unholy—are already in place. You must deal diplomatically with those who were passed over to make way for you. Sometimes you inherit a mess that must be cleaned up, with troops who are tired of trudging.

In real life, you must often delegate under pressure. Competitive moves or economic events may force you and your team into risky campaigns before you're ready. The saber-toothed tiger may invade your camp when the fire's gone out and the sentries are asleep. You have to spread your best troops thin and defend your territory with peach fuzz kids who still need seasoning.

Indeed, you may need seasoning yourself. Trust, you will learn, must flow from the led to the leader, even more vitally than from the leader to the led. That fact has not penetrated yet for the first managers who speak in this session.

1. CAN'T LET GO

My subordinates insist they are ready for more: I know they won't do my work as well as I do it. I fear the hand-over process.

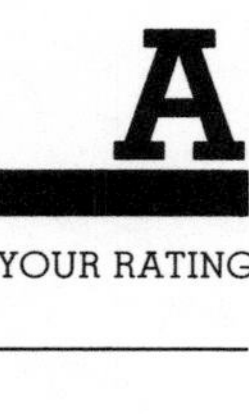

AUDIENCE RESPONSES

YOUR RATING

________ **a.** *Release work on a gradient. Start easy with lower-risk items.*

________ **b.** *Accept volunteers from among your best to teach tasks to juniors. Let them monitor performance.*

________ **c.** *It's humbling to admit others can do work acceptably, even if they do things differently from you. Different need not mean better or worse.*

________ **d.** *You'll be forced to delegate when overload conditions reach the "sink or swim" stage. Do it now before panic sets in. Delegate to qualified staffers.*

	★	★★	★★★	★★★★
RATING	*NO!*	*RISKY*	*BETTER*	*BEST!*

Four stars to all four answers. They acknowledge the emotional turmoil you feel when handing over work that "made you famous" or that marked some passage in your corporate life. Even if you are an experienced manager, convinced intellectually that you will gain relief and multiply your effectiveness by delegating, you must still control the emotional loss you feel when giving up "your baby"—that problem you once solved or that task that signaled a new competence for you. The responders' advice should make it easier.

a. Release work on a gradient, starting with low risks.
This is safer for you, and safer for your delegate. It will build a series of successes for you both and strengthen your relationship through mutually good experiences. Delegation by this gradual process builds confidence in both the delegator and the learner.

b. Accept volunteers from among your best to teach tasks to juniors. Let them monitor.
Wonderful. If you know you'll suffer a jolt with each detail you have to release, then release the whole task to a trusted mature subordinate and let the delegation proceed further from there. After a second translation, of course, the methods used may depart considerably from yours. But will they work? Adequately? If so, be at peace.

Sure, you broke trail across the original icefield. Once there are many sets of tracks out of the wilderness, you can release, without regret, your memory of the pristine days when your footprints were the only signs of glorious progress. Find new wildernesses to conquer.

c. Humbly admit acceptable work. Different need not be better/worse.
"How good is good enough?" That's the question you must ask yourself when you feel reluctant to let go. If you have structured your solutions to an old problem so that others can follow your trail, if you've reduced the old risks

to a minimum, it will not take a person as swift or strong to follow where you led. The clients or customers you helped may no longer have risks or needs as great as they once had either. Decide how good is "good enough," now.

d. **Don't wait until you "sink or swim." Delegate now.** Certainly it pays to delegate early so that correction, practice, and progress are reached before the schedule gets tight. Often, managers hang onto work, thinking they will be underoccupied if they give up too much to subordinates. Then, an unexpected heavy work load arrives, giving a double burden of teaching the old while struggling with the new. An enterprising senior will *always* find plenty of new worlds to explore.

2. *AIDES WANT GLAMOR JOBS*

My aides press for "more interesting" work while neglecting the scutwork pegged at their level. This irritates me, as well as their peers.

AUDIENCE RESPONSES

YOUR RATING

______ **a.** *Involve them in projects where all peers must share the "cleanup" tasks. Let the team "give 'em hell" if they shirk.*

______ **b.** *Explain your terms of employment: that each person must complete all work in the job description. Keep an eye on things so you can insist that the employee "volunteers" for such work when his or her turn comes around.*

______ **c.** *You might have a staff meeting where the group gets to list "dumb and tedious" jobs. Involve humor as you ask how these jobs might be done with least pain. Perhaps one person doesn't mind a certain job but wouldn't touch another.* Ask*!*

______ **d.** *Find out what these aides do enjoy. Praise them for good work on that; then insist on their cooperation on the tedious stuff. Explain that even you have your share of this to do.*

	★	★★	★★★	★★★★
RATING	*NO!*	*RISKY*	*BETTER*	*BEST!*

★

a. **Let the team do your disciplining.**
No. Discipline is one task a supervisor cannot delegate. If these aides have the wrong approach to their work, *you* must teach them the right way, not immerse them and their peers in an experiment designed to embarrass or trap the out-of-line worker. This can damage group relationships, confuse the issues, extend the bad behavior to a larger arena. You must warn your subordinates when their behavior increases your risks, as this particular behavior does.

★★★★

b. **Explain terms of employment. Monitor closely so they must volunteer for their share of boring tasks.**
Yes. Review the job description and desk manual of any worker who seems to neglect an aspect of the job. Be quantitative when you show that they carry a disproportionately small amount of the "clean-up" work. Show them that you give points for *finishing*, not just starting or half-completing a task. Always show the consequence of failure to complete a task (consequences on customers, your department, fellow workers). Clarity is the first step in discipline.

★★★

c. **Try a staff meeting; openly list "dumb" jobs; seek creative ways of getting them done; seek volunteers to trade one scut for another.**
Very interesting and worthwhile, but watch your timing. If you were to do this *first*, before disciplining your glory-hungry aides, you might be winning them an advantage at the price of hurting other conscientious members of the group. First, get your aides to follow department discipline, and once they are pulling their share, you might try this creative approach to getting dreary details handled painlessly for all. Your suggestion system will benefit, but get those aides in line first.

d. Find out what the aides enjoy; praise that. Insist they do their scut as you and others must.

Good suggestion for opening the conversation. While you are insisting they do their scut as you all have to, consider what you would reply when they ask why you don't delegate *your* scut to them!

Comment: When your aides ask you for more glamorous work, they are asking for pieces of *your* job, since one assumes that is the next level where the work gets more glamorous. A little soul-searching may be required of you here. Are *you* hanging onto work that's really appropriate for them. Can *you* get them to do their routines, with the proviso that more exciting work will come from you when you are satisfied they are fully covering the risks already entrusted to them?

3. *TALENT SCOUTING TRAP*

How do I find and develop my people's strengths to complement mine rather than compete with mine.

AUDIENCE RESPONSES

YOUR RATING

________ **a.** *Look for people who think as you do, who do not resist your basic values. Look for ways you match or complement your own boss; duplicate that method of matching by encouraging it in your subordinates.*

________ **b.** *Observe their work habits for a period. Listen. Coach and compliment. They'll trust you gradually; they'll listen when you tell them where to develop, and they'll volunteer to help in the places you ask.*

________ **c.** *Give the "comers" a variety of tasks; see where they excel. Interview: Ask what tasks they find easy, hard, challenging, up their alley. Develop along their natural talent lines to cover department needs.*

________ **d.** *Tell them, up front, where you need particular strengths, particular coverage. Ask them to demonstrate/discuss their capabilities for providing that coverage.*

	★	★★	★★★	★★★★
RATING	*NO!*	*RISKY*	*BETTER*	*BEST!*

3. TALENT SCOUTING TRAP ANALYSIS

★★ *a.* **Look for people who think as you do. Copy the good match you had with your own boss.**

While this method might work for owners of small companies seeking to build their inner circle—or for presidents of larger companies, choosing among qualified VPs for a successor—it would run counter to Equal Opportunities Act rulings for most organizations as a promotion/employee development policy.

For midmanagers and supervisors building talent below them, you may not anoint princelings on the basis of shared values and personal preferences (at least you must not be seen to do so.) Instead, you appoint people whose ability to do the *tasks* in hand can be demonstrated. You focus on *tasks* to be done, and you appoint/promote/train/develop people according to their demonstrated aptitude or ability to do the work—whether you happen to warm to their values and personalities or not.

Some bosses who once preferred the "crown prince" method can now appreciate the value of *rotating* all possible candidates through the major tasks in a department. They *cross-train* to build coverage in a department while developing skills in a wide number of candidates.

b. **Observe their work habits. Listen, compliment, coach. They'll cooperate with your development plans.**

Much better. Whatever size your corporation, this method relies on *observed behavior*, not supposed value sharing.

When you offer personal warmth, acceptance, encouragement, and coaching in an atmosphere of equal opportunity, you've got a winning combination of factors that makes you feel good about yourself, and your team feel good about themselves and you.

c. Give the "comers" a variety of tasks. Interview; develop people along their natural talent lines to cover department needs.

Yup! A continuing dialogue develops as your group grows stronger.

d. Tell them where you need particular coverage. Ask them to demonstrate/discuss their ability to provide it.

This could be your continuing "process" for asking your people for more and more excellence as you and they grow in competence. As your department shows its strength, top management will throw tougher challenges your way, making this method practical for a strong, competent team to pursue. A really self-confident boss knows that he or she need not have all the answers; you can ask your people to provide answers when you have reason to trust their judgment. If you keep growing yourself, competing comers cannot catch up with you. Look ahead, not behind.

PART

TWO

SETTLING TERRITORIAL ISSUES

Two dangerous ideas block effective delegation; they revolve around territoriality and fairness:

1. Some managers and subordinates believe that *fair* means *equal* in task distribution as well as rewards. They insist that work be *evenly* distributed as if it were all burden, instead of competed for as if it were part privilege. But work flows from one end of that continuum to the other.

2. Some managers feel guilty about asking others to take on "their" work, especially if the subordinate claims overload. Both bosses and workers see tasks as "mine" versus "theirs" rather than "the company's" or "department's."

Two fresh ideas may help you to delegate without guilt:

1. *Fair means unequal.* No one really wants equal treatment; everybody wants special treatment, with other people's approval or ignorance. We maintain a myth about fairness for our morale's sake, and we keep upping the ante as our appetites grow stronger. What was fair last week is not quite good enough now.

2. *Fairness is only noticeable when glaringly absent.* Otherwise, it's a bore.

So many people are essentially bored with the contents of confining jobs, they raise equity/territoriality issues to the status of a mythical dragon which must be slain by management, with a lot of attendant tumult. When the job is quite fascinating, however, and choices are attractive, people stop seeing every fine crack in the corporate plaster and start looking for ways to exercise, walk, run and plant bigger gardens out of doors. The corporate garden will offer many exotic and tasty fruits to workers in the next decade: flexible working hours, job sharing, multiple reporting relationships, technology that will keep people excited by the new. Many-faceted reward systems—high salaries, bonuses, merit pay, contests, cafeteria-style benefits, profit sharing, stock ownership, sabbaticals, paid travel—appeal to people's specialness. People invest themselves to gain rewards of their own choosing, and do far less comparing with co-workers. Fairness, when rewards and assignments vary so much, declines to the level it always deserved: a minimum requisite, not a meaningful quest.

But for the managers who speak next, this utopia seems millenia away.

4. I FEEL GUILTY DELEGATING

My people look martyred when I approach with new work. But I** must **delegate to meet the demands of higher management. The guilt gets to me.

AUDIENCE RESPONSES

YOUR RATING

________ **a.** *Encourage your people to give you an estimate on* when, *not whether, they can do the work. Ask them to clarify their scheduling problems.*

________ **b.** *Don't let your people communicate with martyred looks. Ask them to state what effect the new assignment will have on other current obligations. Ask them to reprioritize and let you know the new order of things.*

________ **c.** *What's their track record? Do they start off with martyred looks; then do the work smartly? They're manipulating you. Tell them your opinion of manipulators!*

________ **d.** *Yes, you must delegate. But do you need more staffers to complete the work load? Gather the group; ask for a run-down on their work loads; make a judgment and follow through.*

	★	★★	★★★	★★★★
RATING	*NO!*	*RISKY*	*BETTER*	*BEST!*

★★★ *a.* **Get an estimate; ask them to state their scheduling problems.**

Yes. By stating that this is a when, not whether, issue, you are showing that the work is appropriate to the department and to the workers' level. Then it does become simply a problem of available time. By asking *when*, you drive the workers' minds forward to positive possibilities.

★★★★ *b.* **Don't allow martyred looks. Ask them to state what effect the assignment will have. Have them reprioritize.**

Yes. Teach your subordinates always to state consequences or risks that new assignments will incur. Then have them reprioritize their work and let you make a judgment if they cannot. Once they regain a sense of logical control over the structure of their work, the fear that drives their "martyrdom" will be relieved, and you won't have to forbid or preach about it.

★★ *c.* **Do they enjoy complaining, manipulating? Cite the record.**

No need to speculate on their motives or intentions regarding you. Only look at your own motives and intentions regarding them. It's a pity that people's *resistance* often takes more energy than the work itself requires, but that's human nature.

★★★★ *d.* **Delegate! Ask for a report on their work load and bring in help if it's needed.**

Yes. The group may express martyrdom because its members *are* overloaded. But they must find a quick way to illustrate this unequivocally for you. Then you can confidently negotiate for more help or postpone some less vital portion of the standing work load. If, like most managements, your bosses are reluctant to hire part-time or full-time extras without evidence, you must provide that data, and you must get it from your staff.

5. LIGHTING A FIRE UNDER LOAFERS

My least productive people think they have a license to loaf. They set low goals, resist every prod, take up supervisory time.

AUDIENCE RESPONES

YOUR RATING

________ **a.** *Log their work in. Estimate time required. Distribute to each "in turn." Consciously avoid giving every load to your good people simply as insurance. Depend on your secretary to track distribution, logging, follow-up.*

________ **b.** *Assign your "lesser lights" to help your productive workers—taking some of the pressure off your best people and giving your good folks supervisory experience.*

________ **c.** *Establish work groups. Empower each group to schedule and upgrade its output. Rotate co-chairmanship of each group, teaming strong people with weaker ones, so that each group experiences success.*

________ **d.** *Illustrate the schedule and work flow of the new projects at the start, so loafers can see how their track interlocks with others. When they fear group retaliation, they'll start pulling.*

	★	★★	★★★	★★★★
RATING	*NO!*	*RISKY*	*BETTER*	*BEST!*

5. *LIGHTING A FIRE UNDER LOAFERS* ANALYSIS

★★ **a. Log, estimate time, distribute work in turn, track, follow-up.**

This is a pretty elaborate program for gaining control over unmotivated workers. When you make them the centerpiece of a rotation scheme, they promptly take a few "rest days" off, forcing you to rotate without them. By all means, assign your loafers quantifiable work for which fair standards have been set. Prove that their performance falls below acceptable standards on a consistent basis. Warn; move to dismiss them.

★★ **b. Assign them to help your productive people. Give your good folks supervisory experience.**

Can you imagine the thanks you'll get for dumping your problem people as "helpers" on the necks of your best workers? This discipline problem is yours; don't pass it down. I'm all for buddy systems, but not as dumping grounds for your worst performers.

★★ **c. Establish work groups in charge of their own output. Team strong with weak people as co-chairs.**

Again, I would like this scheme if you were talking about teaming innocent but inexperienced people with your best. This buddy system works very well on good-intentioned workers. But for resistant goldbrickers, like these, *you* are responsible for applying discipline. Don't saddle your best racers with lead balloons.

★★ **d. Illustrate the work flow so workers can see they must pull their share or incur group anger.**

Once again, I'd be very reluctant to *create* a plan where the loafers had any key or pivotal role in getting a project completed. The sensible people in your group can foresee the dangers from the start. Working together in the production process, they will carry the risks when loafers fail to perform. Group pressure may have some effect on the loafers, but this burdens the group with both the work load and the discipline load. Once again, *you* must carry this responsibility; you cannot abdicate it.

Nickerson's Recommendation

For a four-star answer, *you* must counsel and discipline your loafers, directly. Specify what *you want*. Quantify. Measure and discipline for failure to meet your requirements. Do not shift this responsibility to your group, however strong the temptation to do so. Your best workers certainly can stimulate your beginners and encourage your tryers; they can certainly gain supervisory experience with promising newcomers, but they cannot perform your disciplinary duties by default. If your loafers have "a license to loaf," you must rescind it.

6. OVERLOADING MY BEST PEOPLE

Is it wrong to concentrate the most gratifying work in the hands of my best people? I feel safer, but worry about overburdening them.

A

AUDIENCE RESPONSES

YOUR RATING

_________ **a.** *Learn to trust other employees. Let your trusted lieutenants work with new people to develop a team.*

_________ **b.** *Give new people at least a taste of the jobs where they can contribute successfully. Small doses of good experience build confidence and gradual reliability.*

_________ **c.** *Assess skills and assign work accordingly. Give the less skilled people the routine work; save decision-heavy tasks for your best people. Praise the work of both kinds of workers; ask the better people to help develop the poorer ones.*

_________ **d.** *Avoid concentrating work. Log assignments in and spread out the work. Record the results. Critique and train so your new people learn. Don't let variances in assignments be seen as rewards/punishments, but as natural matching of tasks with talents.*

	★	★★	★★★	★★★★
RATING	*NO!*	*RISKY*	*BETTER*	*BEST!*

6. *OVERLOADING MY BEST PEOPLE* ANALYSIS

★★★ ***a.* Trust others. Get lieutenants to help develop new people.**

Now, you're talking. Once you are speaking of new, not resistant, workers, you can bring your trusted people in as coaches and team leaders. Remember to reward them, both emotionally and tangibly, for their coaching efforts.

★★★★ ***b.* Give the new people a taste where they contribute well.**

Yes. Notice their particular skills. Whether mathematical, technical, verbal, manual—let them make a contribution. Do this carefully so as not to offend your best workers who are handling the lion's share of the task. Ask your best workers *where* they see the newcomer's talents as useful, and help them welcome the newcomer's contribution as a relief.

★★★★ ***c.* Assign work according to skills: routines to the new, decisions to the experienced. Praise both.**

Excellent. I'd just change the word "praise" to "thank." Praise is for dogs, thanks is for people.

★★★ ***d.* Avoid concentrating work. Log assignments. Spread the work. Vary assignments as you match tasks with talents.**

In a large, busy department, keeping a log for yourself to ensure smooth work flow makes sense. Publishing such a log and emphasizing "fairness" to your folks would be a trap, however, requiring you to keep this up forever and exposing you to hairsplitting discussions over each and every assignment. What you must generate is a general sense of fairness that arises from sensible, self-disciplined delegation. Responder *d* says something piquant like "Don't let variances in assignments be seen as rewards/punishments but as natural matching of tasks with talents." I'd say, "Let them be seen as *all three*."

7. FIELD PEOPLE DISADVANTAGED

Some of my field people complain that they are overlooked for good assignments, hence retarded in chances for promotion. "HQ people get it all."

A

AUDIENCE RESPONSES

YOUR RATING

_________ **a.** *Is it true? If so, find special projects to give exposure and experience to your field people. Show a proportional chance to field people.*

_________ **b.** *Reassure these folks that they count. Be specific.*

_________ **c.** *Help these people perform and* report *their contributions in ways that HQ cannot overlook.*

_________ **d.** *If they are mistaken, give them information and reassurance about their prospects.*

	★	★★	★★★	★★★★
RATING	*NO!*	*RISKY*	*BETTER*	*BEST!*

7. *FIELD PEOPLE DISADVANTAGED* ANALYSIS

a. Is it true? Give proportional chances to your field people.

While deciding if it's true, decide why. How is your corporation structured? In some retailing companies, you cannot expect to rise beyond middle management *unless* you have been through the fire in the field; otherwise, you cannot have any credibility with the field managers under you. Then, you may need special training to handle technical inside jobs. Career ladders are often spelled out on a full-scale map of the corporation, so you can see all the routes to the top (from starting points inside headquarters *and* out in the field). In that way, employees and their supervisors can decide what steps are next in the climb to the middle and beyond. Without such a logical overall plan, you will keep incurring anxious complaints from befuddled employees.

b. Reassure these folks that they count, specifically.

Can you reassure them? In certain companies, the only field positions are customer service or maintenance slots. Will these—can these—lead to good assignments at headquarters? Don't promise unless you intend to fulfill the promise. Can the field be a dead end? Call this person in, ask what he or she has in mind for a career path. Do some counseling based on the person's actual chances. If the person shows aptitude, you must provide the training required for advancement over a reasonable period of time—to meet the company's needs and the employee's ambitions.

c. Help these people perform and report their contributions.

Yes indeed. Once you have established a career path leading from the field to senior positions, once you have specified benchmarks along that path, do help your field people to meet the requirements and report them so they get full credit for their overall excellence. It is easy to lose sight of people who are not performing under your nose. You may be grateful that this employee rang a warning bell for everyone's benefit.

d. **If they are mistaken, give them information and reassurance.**
Right. And if they're correct, be truthful and take steps to right the situation.

PART
THREE

TEAM BUILDING ON TEAM STRENGTHS

Once you overcome your own resistance and the fears of your subordinates, your facility with delegating gains momentum. You understand and accept the *process* and can now focus on *people*, helping them pick up their pace as a team. You begin to acknowledge and enjoy the individual strengths each person adds to the group's overall impetus.

Try this exercise in team building: list your subordinates on a sheet of paper, then ask yourself which roles you've seen them take in this year's major projects and meetings.

- Who *leads*, technically, administratively?
- Who *facilitates*, greasing the skids with other departments or groups when cooperation is needed?
- Who *sustains*, offering new options when the group sticks over some point?
- Who *steadies* or questions the group when emotions or snap judgments threaten the peace?
- Who *follows through*, signing up for the legwork so that planned work gets accomplished?
- Who *excites* or *reignites* the group when fatigue or frustration slows them down?

It need not always be you, the boss, who keeps the chemistry healthy. The group can gain its own momentum and sustain it.

You need not psychoanalyze your people in order to observe their interactions. You are noticing observable behavior, not probing for inner motivations. You will detect clear patterns after a while. You will discover that your people gravitate naturally toward certain roles when the group works as a unit. To acknowledge and thank them for performing these roles is to notice positive behavior you'd like to see repeated.

People are complex. Members of the team may adopt multiple technical and administrative roles as well as interpersonal patterns, in various combinations. What matters is that they see each contribution as necessary, different, complementary, and valuable if they are to achieve synergy, that level of excitement, energy, and output as a group that far surpasses the power of any single member.

That's what team building aims for—and achieves often—if your leadership and your luck hold out.

This synergy is built, however, on a thousand days of ordinary, down-to-earth trying and debugging when a team is first learning how to come together. That's the stage our next four managers are facing.

8. *IMPROVING EMPLOYEES' JUDGMENT*

My people can do prescribed tasks well, but they shock me sometimes by their lack of judgment. When anything arises out of the ordinary, they flounder.

AUDIENCE RESPONSES

YOUR RATING

______ **a.** *Be sure they understand the end product of what they are doing: what we make, for whom, why it is needed, what can go wrong, what constitutes excellence. Teach!*

______ **b.** *Some people mistake good intentions for good production. Others mistake good production for good judgment. Each level takes increasing maturity at the job. Spell this out. Coach them.*

______ **c.** *Give people time to mature. People develop good judgment only from experience; it cannot be taught.*

______ **d.** *Include them in low-pressure planning.* Before *a decision is due, outline the factors. Ask a few chosen subordinates to outline an approach. You outline the way you'll go. Compare and discuss until they understand how you make these judgments.*

	★	★★	★★★	★★★★
RATING	*NO!*	*RISKY*	*BETTER*	*BEST!*

8. *IMPROVING EMPLOYEES' JUDGMENT* ANALYSIS

★★★ **a. Be sure they know what we do, for whom, why, what can go wrong, what constitutes excellence. Teach.**

And when you've finished teaching, educate! Draw from them what they *do* know. Ask your subordinate to list the key results required of them this year. Ask them to cite the risks they will face in getting these results. Ask them to list their tactics for avoiding these risks. The simple listing process will help them to stay on target as they open their minds to you. If you like, make the *tactics list* a mutual exercise. You list how you would handle the risks; they list how they would do it. The matching and contrasting exercise you share when comparing the two lists will help you to transfer your thinking about risks/opportunities. This kind of thinking *can* be taught. Keep it up 'til you've learned to appreciate your subordinate's mind, and vice versa.

★★★ **b. Spell out the difference between production and decision making. Coach.**

Go ahead, but ask your learner to do it first; so you can see how much thinking ability is already there. Let the teaching be mutual. (Try such a list on your own: what activities of your department have become *prescribed* production actions? Which are still open to question/test/experimentation/change? In short, which still require decisions? What are these decisions *about*? If you can clarify it on paper, you can then ask your people to do so.

★ **c. Give them time to mature. They develop good judgment only from experience; it cannot be taught.**

I disagree. Good judgment can certainly be taught. No sense having your people learn judgment by trial and error. This can be unpleasant both for customers and for your company. Take several decisions you made recently. Jot them down. Put three multiple-choice possibilities under each. Make a quickie quiz out of this and administer it to your people. The discussion that would follow would make a practical teaching session. You can also teach judgment through *role playing a "live problem"* with your nominees. You play the angry customer making an unreasonable demand. Your subordinate plays the manager, "making it right" while adhering to corporate policy. In your discussions of this experience, you will cetainly teach judgment.

Once your people can reliably handle technical and routine tasks, teaching them judgment is your next logical step. Be sure to do it in safe "laboratory" sessions before exposing your people to real-life experiences that raise your risks as a company.

***d.* Give them a planning exercise; ask them to outline an approach. Compare with your method and discuss.**

Excellent. Some naturally good supervisors do this several times a week. When a good "object lesson" opportunity arises, they get everyone to gather round, outline the situation, and ask for suggested approaches. They then describe the likely outcomes of each approach, to *teach risks/consequences* of decisions in a real-life situation with a real-life current time frame. Great!

9. PUT "THINKING" IN THE JOB DESCRIPTION

How can I teach and develop creative thinking among my competent doers. They seem to imagine that thinking is my job and doing is theirs.

AUDIENCE RESPONSES

YOUR RATING

________ **a.** *Promote informal after-hours sessions with your elite workers. Make them social and fun so people will seek to be included.*

________ **b.** *Give your staffers some guidelines for handling the decision responsibilities around each set of tasks they've mastered. Help them build confidence through discussion/trial/error on the lower-risk items. Show them how promotion depends on developing these thinking skills.*

________ **c.** *Regular staff meetings where everyone can chip in ideas and analyze problems can make thinking about things as natural as breathing. Beware isolating people with drudgery. It kills thinking.*

________ **d.** *Tell people when their ideas are good. Get excited.*

	★	★★	★★★	★★★★
RATING	*NO!*	*RISKY*	*BETTER*	*BEST!*

9. PUT "THINKING" IN THE JOB DESCRIPTION ANALYSIS

★★★★ *a.* **Promote after-hours rap sessions where thinking is demonstrated.**

Yes. As a young manager, I saw these going on in all the best departments. These sessions drew people from many disciplines to cook up exciting solutions to problems. Much sophistication was learned here, and lasting friendships were made. Once invited to these "bull sessions," you knew your legitimacy was accepted. You were *in*.

★★★★ *b.* **Give guidelines for moving up to the decision level on tasks they've mastered. Build confidence through discussion/trial/error.**

Most people respond well to being told they've demonstrated excellence on all phases of a task so far . . . now they are ready for the next phase, and this can lead to promotion. By all means do this.

★★★★ *c.* **Regular staff meetings where thinking is encouraged. Avoid isolating workers.**

Yes. "Regular" is the operative word. If you hold these meetings only when you are dissatisfied with the thinking level, people will sense the implied criticism. If you hold them every week, people build tolerance for both good news and bad, and they build confidence that their contributions will be welcomed and respected, whether immediately usable or not.

★★★★ *d.* **Celebrate good ideas.**

Great. Management fabulists and theorists all agree: *Notice good behavior when you see it.* It will then be repeated.

10. TURNING LONE WOLVES INTO TEAM-MATES

As a business owner, I have trouble melding the different types who report to me into a team. Production, finance, marketing heads—each must "star."

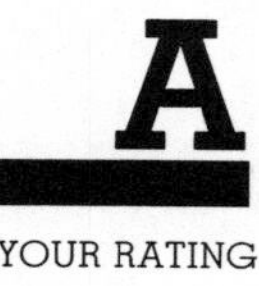

AUDIENCE RESPONSES

YOUR RATING

______ **a.** *Use team involvement at each stage of planning and execution, on a task campaign or product launch. Point out that you expect them to consult one another.*

______ **b.** *Create assignments that force them to reach beyond their demonstrated capabilities to accommodate total company needs.*

______ **c.** *Share problems early so each can share in creating potential solutions. Reward, accept ideas that mold objectivity and build mutual cooperation.*

______ **d.** *Respond to individuals appropriately: assert with the assertive ones, joke with the comics, but maintain your own program and insist that they support it.*

	★	★★	★★★	★★★★
RATING	*NO!*	*RISKY*	*BETTER*	*BEST!*

10. TURNING LONE WOLVES INTO TEAMMATES ANALYSIS

★★★★ ***a.* Involve them as a team at each stage of project life. Point out they must consult one another before proposing.**

Although it may seem obvious, the way people learn they are a team is to be together in their boss's presence a good deal of the time. You'll often find neophyte managers dealing one-on-one with their subordinates and then wondering why they don't operate as a team. People must *experience* themselves as a work group functioning together under a boss. If you make it a requirement of proposals that objections from fellow members be anticipated and covered, you'll save a lot of consultation time and further enforce team cohesiveness. Don't overdo it, but do it.

★★★ ***b.* Create assignments that force them to reach beyond narrow interests.**

You won't need to create such assignments. The needs of any company trying to serve the public or compete in the marketplace will create such assignments naturally. You may need to do a little demonstrating, and applaud when they stretch, together, to accommodate wider interests.

★★★★ **c. Share problems early for wide involvement. Reward cooperation.**

Another good but not so obvious suggestion. Some managers consult first with "close buddies" only, get things locked down, and then present *faits accomplis* to the rest of the managers. This retards group cohesiveness, builds competitiveness, and leads to distrust.

Whatever time you save in favoring the few, you then lose in beating down resistance from the last managers in line. At least until group trust and cooperation are built, invest the extra time in early involvement and joint communication as this response suggests.

d. **Respond to individuals on a personal basis, but insist that they support your programs as a team.**
Also correct. You need not lockstep your relationships with the individuals involved. You'll warm to some more than others, share backgrounds and interests with some more than others. But when something important is brewing, bring them together and let them know you need *all* their strengths and talents to interlock for maximum coverage and minimum risk as you fly the project together.

Comment: Aw, go on; let 'em each "star" whenever you can. There'll be times when they really *have* starred and should get their share of the afterglow.

PART
FOUR

FINE TUNING: TEN MUSTS OF DELEGATION (AND FIVE MOST MANAGERS AVOID)

THE BASIC IRONIES

If you've done your management reading, you've been exposed to the two most obvious facts about delegation:

1. *That despite the risks in delegating, there are limits to what you can do, unaided.* In addition, you are told, the more work you delegate, the more time you save for new business and exciting pursuits. But what new business and exciting pursuits are you chasing with the time you save? Ask yourself that. If you can't list something pretty convincing, you *ought* to feel guilty about delegating (or dumping) work on others.
2. *That all work should be done at the lowest possible level where it can be done right and cheaply.* Some writers insist, convincingly, that once you remove or reduce the risks, any minion can do your routine work. But, again, your competitors may get *their* routines handled by slightly smarter people and machines than you, enhancing their products and services in the eyes of the consumer.

So these "simple" rules of delegation aren't so simple after all. You *must* delegate, but you must think carefully about why, how much and to whom, at what cost? The ten steps that follow may make delegation easier and more comfortable, but they won't make it a cinch. It simply isn't.

THE TEN "MUSTS"

From my continuing survey of how managers handle delegation, I've found these ten steps to be minimum for safe, effective delegation. You may want to add your own special "English" at the end. Some of these steps are a pain in the neck to apply, but the penalties for failure to observe them are even worse. (As you read, you might detect the most neglected five among the ten.)

Steps 1, 2, 3: Preparation

1. ***Analyze the task or job. What skills and steps does it demand?***
   - ***a.*** List the required *skills*, specifically ("ability to do full-charge bookkeeping to balance sheet stage" or "ability to type accurately 80 words per minute in general correspondence," etc.). In this way, you make clear the *abilities*, not character traits, required of candidates.
   - ***b.*** List the *steps* required. Summarize briefly the key items in the procedures manual for this task. *Use nouns and verbs* (not adjectives) so that a candidate can see *what one must do, not what one must be like*, to do the job. In that way, you will comply with Equal Employment Opportunities rules, and you'll get candidates who really *know* what they're signing up for.

2. ***Advertise and interview candidates.*** Ask for the technical skills you need: statistics, typing, vocabulary, lab skills, mechanical skills, physical strength, judgment, human skills, languages—whatever the job requires. Check out references and qualifications, even among insider candidates. Then judge which person will care enough about the work to do it best. What do you gather from their track record and interview comments?

3. ***Get the job written up in detail.*** If you or another person will have to teach the task to the winning candidate, you'd better have an excellent teaching outline. Does a write-up already exist in the department's procedures manual? If not, sketch out the job in outline form, or get a current performer to do so, who knows the details involved.

Be sure to do your write-up in *list* or *graphic* form, step by step. Graphics appeal to the eye, which *receives* data far better than the ear in a "live" encounter. The eye *remembers* better than the ear too: nearly twice the retention for a visual versus verbal message.

Steps 4, 5, 6: Handing It Over

4. ***Assign and teach the task.*** *Assigning* means presenting the task to the candidate, making it attractive, describing its virtues and vitality to the department—getting the candidate to reach for the task. *Teaching* means presenting the steps one by one, demonstrating, inviting questions, and letting the candidate try out the steps, one by one. Before releasing the task, you need to let the delegate "play back" the job for you from start to finish, using his or her own words and pace.

   Don't interrupt. Go back and correct any missed points at the end of the recital. (If you interrupt in the middle, you throw the learner into a tight-lipped panic, and you will not hear how he or she really plans to do things when out from under your gaze.)

5. ***Transfer goals from yours to theirs.*** If time allows a pause after step 4, give the learner space for "thinking things over." Ask him or her to "interfile" this task into the rest of the work load or, if it's a total job, into the rest of the career plan. Ask the person to bring you a list of ideas about how *committed* or *reserved* the various parts of the task make him feel. Ask him to put some simple jottings on paper about
   - **a.** *Quantity*: How much can be done how quickly?
   - **b.** *Quality*: What does the candidate think about the level of quality required and the margin for error or scrap?
   - **c.** *Costs*: What space, supplies, time or money does he or she envision needing?
   - **d.** *Authority*: What approvals will the candidate need . . . how much room to question, get guidance and support as he or she learns and finally takes over the task?

   If you give your candidate the preceding list, the thinking may take a couple of minutes or a couple of days, but the writing should take only half a sheet of paper.

   This paper is an outline contract or employee commitment to do the job with some sense of ownership of it.

6. ***Invite and allow time for feedback.*** Before sealing the agreement, invite further comment: Use open questions such as: "What did we leave out?" "What questions still linger in your mind?"

   Relax the person enough to elicit questions where they make sense: "Most people have questions about the transportation section. What puzzles you?" Sit back and listen.

Steps 7–10: Empowering Your Delegate

7. ***Agree on Benchmarks.*** Together, set specific intervals for monitoring progress and allowing adjustments. You might say, "Want to check progress after the first four hours?" Watch for a reaction. You might say, "Get my initials on this before sending out the first layout. Then you should be all right on your own." Or you might feel secure enough to say, "I'll leave this with you, then. With your background in production, I'll expect to hear from you only if you get the problem you anticipate on the color mix."

   The monitoring schedule must be negotiated until it is comfortable for both of you. The degree of control must be understood and accepted by both sides. Otherwise, your supervision may be seen as uncaring or oppressive. Some boss/subordinate teams set up the monitoring plan, not on the clock or calendar, but around the critical go/no go steps in a process. But set up your plan and follow it.

8. ***Authorize Your Delegate Publicly.*** If you want this person to act in your place, make it comfortable for all by informing peers, supervisors, subordinates, suppliers, clients—whoever must cooperate with your delegate—that this person is fully authorized by you. Failure to so inform people will result in their end running your delegate and coming back to you. This will undermine your delegate's confidence, waste your time, and cause embarrassment when you must chide or correct uncooperative people.

   You can kill two birds with one stone with the following memo or message:

   > Effective August 1, DELEGATE will be taking over project X. I will expect you to give him the same fine cooperation you have always given to me. His decision will be binding.

   In this way, you compliment everyone—your delegate and those whose cooperation you are requesting. You can frame this message with your own personal courtesies, but make sure your authorization is clear. Should anyone "in house" come trotting back up to see *you*, instead of your delegate, rummage around on your desk mumbling, "Where's that memo I sent everyone . . . didn't you get one?" Send them down to your delegate, forthwith.

9. ***Reward Effort as Well as Achievement.*** As with all thanks, be specific and timely. Not "Great job, Harry," but "Great job on

that fabric refinish, Harry," so the person knows what to keep on doing. Note *progress* high points as well as *finished* achievements, particularly if the task is lengthy and the person needs encouragement.

Offer praise in public, so that "old guard" employees know the new candidate is working out. Take these opportunities to show your respect and thanks to the regulars, too. Note your delight about your delegate's progress in your little black book so you will not forget at performance review time. (Do this with all your employees, and you'll be a better boss to everyone.) While I tell your employees that it is their responsibility to keep track of how they are doing, I admonish you bosses to keep an eye on it, too. You'll be glad, at review time, to have a balanced view.

10. ***Critique, Correct Errors, or Withdraw the Assignment*** Some of this work gets done at step 7, when you conduct your benchmark discussions. But despite these, not every delegation effort succeeds. Even the best boss and the best willed subordinate can submit to a gross mismatch of worker and assignment, especially when time pressure interferes with good judgment.

Be a big guy. Take the responsibility for the mismatch; let the delegate comment, in an open-ended way, about his or her frustrations with the job. Ask them to write up (again briefly and simply on a half-sheet of paper) the cautions they would bequeath to their successor if there were one.

When things do go wrong, your adherence to the *task requirements* rather than the candidate's personal shortcomings saves embarrassment for the candidate and may encourage willingness to correct errors and pursue task requirements more closely. At other times, you will both agree that the person cannot accommodate the requirements in the time available, so another person will be asked to take the job over. A feeling of failure may well demoralize the "failing" candidate despite your avoidance of personal criticism. (See Chapter 8 for more on performance review technique).

Caution: If a worker *can* do the work, but does a half-baked or sloppy job, never be seen to redo the work you have delegated; get the learner to do it right. Some people fail because an impatient boss grabs the work back and completes it, to make a deadline, without explanation or discussion. This humiliates the learner and impedes his or her willingness to relearn the task. (If you *have to* redo the work yourself, do so "in the dark" and keep your delegate on it until the learner can do it effectively.

WHY MOST MANAGERS EVADE FIVE OF THEM

While reading through the steps, did you detect the five steps most managers neglect?

You were right if you guessed steps 1, 2, and 3.

In their haste to teach and transfer a job, many people start with step 4, only realizing in the process that they must backtrack and get some details in writing. Arduous homework.

Step 5 is another neglected step. Many managers rush through the goal commitment stage. They assume the worker is willing and get a straight "yes," instead of asking for the how of the job. Listen acutely.

Finally, step 8 is often neglected through ego problems and lack of trust. Managers feel they can "sort of" delegate some work and then "sort of" take it back again if the candidate flubs the job. That almost guarantees the failure of any but the strongest candidates.

CHECKLIST: INSTANT AUDIT ON DELEGATION

TO BREAK DOWN YOUR OWN RESISTANCE

1. List tasks that you do daily, weekly, or monthly.
2. List the five or six *key* steps involved in doing each task. Now select the task with the clearest procedure.
3. Write up a careful, step-by-step list of exactly how you do this "clearest task"—a page or two.
4. If you still feel resistant to delegating the task, jot down the following:

   How many years have I been doing this task?

   If more than two years, compare your earnings per hour two or more years ago with your earnings per hour today. Is this task worth the differential any more? Or has it merely become more expensive per hour without any added value?
5. What specific *risks* are there in performing the task? (How could an inexperienced person err?)
6. What corrective steps would forestall such errors?
7. Go back and write these corrective steps into your procedure at step 3.
8. Go over your revised list and highlight which steps are *critical checkpoints* where both delegator and delegate could check and make corrections before proceeding further into the task. These are *benchmarks*.
9. Estimate the time you'll need for training and handing over the task.

TO AUDIT YOUR PERFORMANCE AS A DELEGATOR

1. Did your candidate understand and use your written procedure to learn and adopt the job?
2. Does your candidate check with you on the agreed-to critical benchmark dates? Is this process now complete? Has the learner adopted the job?
3. Did any unforeseen errors arise? Were corrective measures written into the procedures list?
4. Did you meet your training/handover timetable?
5. Using the learner's pay rate and your own, what was the cost of the delegating this task? At what point will these costs be amortized, as the task is done repetitively by a lower-paid person than yourself? Calculate so you know the date on which this job becomes self-supporting.

Why would you go to so much trouble—doing an audit of the delegation process? Because you will convince yourself *exactly* how much it pays to delegate . . . and you'll pass on this conviction to your whole team. Throughout your company, if delegation can be accomplished sooner and more cheaply, your company will move ahead faster, and people's energies will go into results, not resistance or repetition.

How Enlightened Bosses Appraise Performance

SESSION

SEVEN

HOW ENLIGHTENED BOSSES APPRAISE PERFORMANCE

INTRODUCTION

It's a scandal! The way some American workers wait for a decent experience with performance reviews. In some small companies, employees complain that they've *never* had a formal assessment of their work. They subsist on their sense of self-worth alone, because the boss refuses to put their year's work into perspective. The boss justifies this neglect by quipping, "Don't worry. If I'm *not* pleased, you'll be the first to know!"

Some bosses say they are too soft-hearted to play judge, jury, and executioner with employees; they insist that casual reassurances will do the trick. Managers complain that frequent reviews are too time consuming. Some do the paperwork but avoid "the chat." In companies that pretend to comply with EEO regulations, employees suspect they are reviewed regularly, but they are not allowed to see the paperwork or discuss their "sentence." While the law protects them in principle, lack of funding for inspection leaves the goodwill up to the individual company and manager.

Nonetheless, the law of equal opportunities grants every worker in medium-sized and large companies the right to an annual performance review in writing, with space for the employee to comment. Still, there are many unsolved problems and inequities.

SETTING STANDARDS THAT BUILD EXCELLENCE

In the enlightened company, performance evaluation is part of a continuum that starts when a job is created and continues for the lifetime of the position, not the person filling it. First, the required tasks and their relevant observable behaviors are set down in a *position description*.

Then the candidate is sought, interviewed, and evaluated against these behaviors. (Interviewers check your references, experience, education, and work samples to assure that you can perform the required duties and behaviors.) The standards focus on what you must do, not what you must be. Candidates are judged against the job *standards*, not against each other. Equity is the result, in the hiring process.

Later, these same standards, spelled out in greater detail, drive the employee's performance, training, measurement, and development on the job. If job conditions change, or the candidate gains expertise in the same slot, the position's standards may be upgraded. Or the employee may move up to a higher job with tougher standards (promotion).

In performance appraisal, the reviewer in an enlightened company avoids the cliché adjectives "enthusiastic," "cooperative," "vivacious," "creative" that once littered our illegal evaluation forms. Now, they comply with the law that says *Describe required behavior using a noun and verb*. For example, instead of "helpful," use "Helps overloaded colleagues without endangering own deadlines." For key behaviors, a "critical incident" or working example would be used to clarify the behavior desired.

This careful setting of standards applies not just at the formal review but is the heart of all actions regarding employee progress: hiring, training, assignments, transfers, promotion . . . even discipline and dismissal.

Do you handle performance evaluation this way? When you need to delegate a task to someone, do you sit down and *specify standards of behavior* for performing the tasks? Do you select a candidate who can perform those behaviors rather than seek a clone of yourself with the "right attitude"? Do you look for the "right personality" to handle the job, or do you comply with fairness regulations by focusing on observable behaviors instead?

P A R T

ONE

HASTY HARSH JUDGMENTS

HASTE ENDANGERS EQUITY

When I mention the spirit of the law at seminars, people immediately come back with

> Who has time for such detail? When I have a rush job or urgent need, I look around for whoever's not busy. I can't bother to set standards. I hardly have time to describe what I need. I have to "dump" on the handiest person, and though I don't like it, I have to hope and pray they understand the job; I have to assume willingness.

This is a recipe for failure. In your haste, you force the employee to submerge his or her doubts; the employee with questions may hesitate to "bother" you; your delegate may struggle in silence when the job goes sour, increasing the risks for both of you; the employee may beg assistance from equally ignorant peers. Complaints and errors pile up; the employee hastens to cover them. Before you know it, your subordinate is muttering to friends about your unsupportive management style. And you are muttering to your buddies about worker incompetence.

Both boss and subordinate sense one another's discomfort, but they rush to meet deadlines, and shrink from each other's silent scrutiny. The problem worsens.

That all-too-common process may have broken the trust of the teams you'll read about next. And a return to correct and legal performance appraisal may begin to mend the damage.

1. STALLED BY UNDERACHIEVERS

My staff has done great things, but not lately. They've plateau'd, and I fear that our whole unit will be passed over from now on.

A

Audience Responses

YOUR RATING

_________ **a.** *Call a meeting. Review their strengths and successes. Set new goals to enhance or build upon them. What project would you like them to compete for?*

_________ **b.** *Offer an incentive to increase performance levels.*

_________ **c.** *Examine company policy. Are your salaries fair? Is there participation in company growth, profits? Are benefits below average?*

_________ **d.** *Provide financial rewards and incentives; try something fresh, like travel incentives involving the whole family.*

	★	★★	★★★	★★★★
RATING	*NO!*	*RISKY*	*BETTER*	*BEST!*

a. Meet. Review strengths, set goals, offer projects to stimulate competitiveness.

If you make this a periodic "group performance audit" where the group does the review and, more important, the planning for its next climb, you'll experience a revitalization of the group. You can set up a flip chart and let the group fill it in together:

A. *Peak Achievements, Recent*
   1.
   2.

B. *Talents, Strengths Used*
   1.
   2.
   3.
   4.

C. *New Corporate Needs Where Strengths Apply*
   1.
   2.

D. *Training/Updating/Empowerment Still Needed*
   1.
   2.
   3.

E. *Action Steps to Take Now*
   1. What?
   2. Who?

F. Results/Rewards Aimed for
   1.
   2.

This would help the group to analyze its own progress and needs without any preaching or pep talks from above. All you need to do is have data at hand on projects still "up for grabs" in the company and some ideas on how to facilitate "ways and means" once the group starts wanting to run again.

★★

***b.* Offer incentives**

No. Don't offer. *Ask*. Ask the group what kinds of incentives (monetary and nonmonetary) would turn them on. Ask the group to assess the likelihood of management's heeding their desires. Open it up. Then offer only those incentives that respond to their needs—and that company policy might allow.

***c.* Examine the company's conscience on policy, benefits.**

I'm not against it. But the person who asked this question would certainly *know* about any glaring deficiencies in company policy. He or she is *puzzled* about the staff's low morale. More likely the problem is more subtle.

Where are they in the hierarchy? In large organizations with lockstepped grades, people often hit plateaus. When they were reaching for the bottom rung of a whole new grade, they were motivated. But once on the new ladder, they see a daunting set of rungs reaching high above them. Having climbed Annapurna, they now face Everest. Worse—some have reached the step just below the top—with no hope that those above them will vacate their positions, short of death. Smart organizations, sensing these hazards, offer special project work, contests, achievement awards and bonuses to ease the paralysis of having one's shoes nailed to a rung on the ladder.

***d.* Provide financial incentives, family travel, fresh ideas.**

Yes. If the financial incentives are open to competition. If the employee's behavior can really trigger the amount and frequency of awards, good! Straight pay raises don't work, however, for they become a "right" as soon as they are given.

Poll your employees. Seek their ideas about novel or even "chance" awards. For example, some companies reward above-average performance by putting "winners" in a drawing for a single fabulous award. Being nominated for the "academy award" is almost as good as winning it.

2. *AFRAID TO INVADE PRIVACY*

How can I probe a sudden, unexplained drop in a subordinate's performance without invading privacy. This person is aloof by nature.

AUDIENCE RESPONSES

YOUR RATING

________ **a.** *Take the person aside. Let him or her know that you are available to talk about more things than strictly work. Perhaps they have a personal problem you should know about?*

________ **b.** *Ask "why" performance is off. Insist that they improve or you will place a memo in their personnel file.*

________ **c.** *Have a head-to-head confrontation.*

________ **d.** *If you keep up a practice of quarterly or monthly information reviews, it will be easy to let this person know that you notice a slippage. Keep the talk going and the core problem ought to surface.*

	★	★★	★★★	★★★★
RATING	*NO!*	*RISKY*	*BETTER*	*BEST!*

2. AFRAID TO INVADE PRIVACY ANALYSIS

★ **a. Privately make yourself available; perhaps they have a personal problem you should know about?**

No! No! No! Perhaps the employee has a personal problem you should *not* know about. You are not a licensed physician, psychiatrist, or clergyperson. This tactic, while practiced by authoritarian or paternalistic bosses in days of yore, is more a cause then a cure of distress. As this person's boss, you are merely a fellow human of slightly higher rank. You have no credentials for listening to or advising on personal problems, no matter how well meaning you may be.

Instead, always ask a troubled worker if there is a business/work problem you should know about—or if there is anything you should do as a boss to help out. If the answer is "No, it's personal," you must take it no further yourself. Be clear that you care but you dare not speak out as an amateur. Then, strongly urge your subordinate to seek help from the proper source: EAP (Employee Assistance Program) or from professional health, financial social, family, marital, or other counselors who can often simplify a seemingly impossible problem.

b. Ask "why" performance is off. Insist that they improve or you'll place a memo in their personnel file.

No. Don't ask "why." Instead, ask "what" the person can do to restore his or her usual level of excellence. That helps the person focus on what's still possible. What's your rush about writing up this employee? Ask what options the employee seeks for help: reeducation, assistance, equipment, whatever. Ask him or her to sketch out a plan for upgrading performance. Ask for deadlines or benchmarks that would constitute a fair test. By asking the performer to suggest these, you are seeking commitment instead of seeking causes that may be none of your business.

★ **c. Have a head-to-head confrontation.**

Only good for those with very hard heads. No. The boss here is puzzled, not angry. Confronting would be overreacting at this point.

d. With regular reviews, it is easier to signal about slippage. Keep talking: the core problem will surface.

That's it. Regular informal checkups, adjustments, and support minimize the danger of sudden downturns. If the flagship stays in sight of the fleet at all times, no one turns up lost.

Comment: Performance deficiencies are *not* a private matter of the employees. They are your business, but stick to business.

3. *CAN'T STAND SUBORDINATE*

How do I survive daily encounters with a subordinate I cannot stand–who sees me as a mentor?

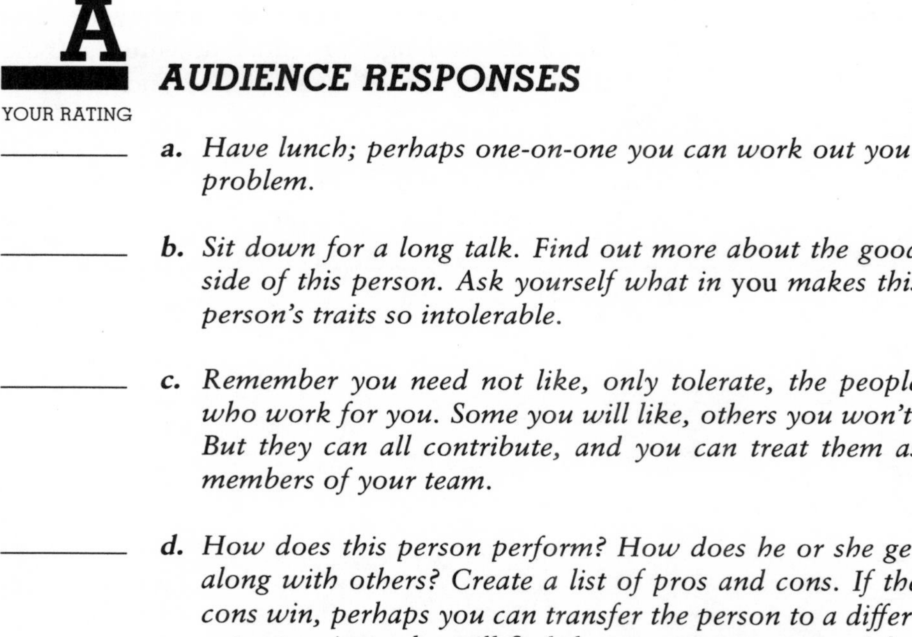

AUDIENCE RESPONSES

YOUR RATING

________ **a.** *Have lunch; perhaps one-on-one you can work out your problem.*

________ **b.** *Sit down for a long talk. Find out more about the good side of this person. Ask yourself what in* you *makes this person's traits so intolerable.*

________ **c.** *Remember you need not like, only tolerate, the people who work for you. Some you will like, others you won't. But they can all contribute, and you can treat them as members of your team.*

________ **d.** *How does this person perform? How does he or she get along with others? Create a list of pros and cons. If the cons win, perhaps you can transfer the person to a different supervisor who will find the person more congenial.*

	★	★★	★★★	★★★★
RATING	*NO!*	*RISKY*	*BETTER*	*BEST!*

a. Have lunch one-on-one; work it out.

Wrong signal. If you can't stand this person, don't send confusing signals with chummy lunches. When you are approached for mentoring, suggest the abilities and experiences (not yours) of a more suitable mentor and assign this person to the right coach. I doubt that you personally "mentor" all your subordinates, so you won't be unfairly discriminating in this instance.

b. Sit down for a long talk; discover the good side of the person. Ask what in you makes the person intolerable.

Perhaps if you do the second thing, you don't have to do the first. You can temper your reactions to people and reduce your psychic pain in their presence if you ask yourself what behavior bothers you. If you can't put your finger on it, you're guilty of personal prejudice that may hark back to the kid at the next desk in grade school or some sibling rivalry. Clean up your act. If you can think of specific behavior, you can ask the offender to exchange that behavior for something else.

c. You need only tolerate, not like, everyone on the team.

Try simple respect for whatever virtues all of them have, and then put them to use—don't just tolerate. If your aversion seems irrational, assign the person to a good lieutenant so the subordinate will get the developmental attention he or she needs, and the assignments and rewards required for growth.

d. List pros and cons of performance and compatibility with others. If the cons win, transfer the person to a more congenial supervisor.

Not if your action would constitute "dumping" of a dud employee on a fellow supervisor. If the cons signal real deficiencies in performance or ability to get along with others, you must teach discipline, or get rid of the employee, not shuffle him or her off next door. If the pros win, and the employee would constitute an asset next door, then arrange for a transfer with your blessing.

Nickerson's Recommendation

For a four-star solution, if the employee has promise, get the person positioned, trained, developed, and deployed in your department by appointing a coach if you can't be one. Personal mentoring is a choice for the mentor, an extra, not an obligation.

4. *TIGHT WITH CREDIT*

My subordinate wants more credit than I'm willing to give for doing ordinary work.

AUDIENCE RESPONSES

YOUR RATING

_________ **a.** *Gently and privately, explain that although he or she has good points, the work is ordinary, and the bragging/begging for credit discounts it even more.*

_________ **b.** *If you are generous in giving credit, people won't have to grab for it.*

_________ **c.** *Does it hurt to "praise" even if you think the work performance is ordinary? This person may lack confidence and need bolstering. What harm does it do?*

_________ **d.** *The person may not have any standard by which to measure ordinary/outstanding. Provide such a standard at an informal performance "chat."*

	★	★★	★★★	★★★★
RATING	*NO!*	*RISKY*	*BETTER*	*BEST!*

4. *TIGHT WITH CREDIT* ANALYSIS

a. Explain that the work is ordinary and bragging discounts it.

Don't just explain it, illustrate it. You owe your employees a clear set of standards for the job, against which they can assess and upgrade their effectiveness. Give comparative figures on speed, accuracy, innovativeness, productivity—at learner, intermediate, and advanced stages of a job. Do not compare this worker against his fellows but against the job standards you have listed on paper from the beginning. Help the employee to see that he is only at the midpoint on performance you require, and spell out the "next steps" for reaching excellence. Be generous with credit when the employee reaches the next stage and encourage him or her to go further, to the "expert" level.

b. If you are generous with credit, people don't have to grab for it.

Yes. But the problem here is—the boss thinks the subordinate should be doing better than he or she is. Again, return to a clear discussion of the *standards* the employee should reach—and give credit when he or she does.

c. Praise even if you think the work performance is ordinary. What harm does it do?

It builds the blah performer's appetite for unearned rewards. It demeans the efforts of the heavy hitters who are *really* scoring for your departments. Ordinary or blah performers do need encouragement, good examples, and coaching to reach the level of performance you need. You can be "nice" while being directive, but be direct!

d. The person may lack standards. Provide formal standards at an informal chat.

Yes. And provide these at *formal* chats too. Keep standards uppermost in your performance talks with this and any employee. Work together to develop steps that will guarantee reaching your goals.

Comment: When I first read this question, I worried that this might be a mean-spirited boss who hated to thank or encourage employees. But since only one worker was cited as greedy for credit, it's more likely that worker is overly-eager. Should you ever find yourself the victim of a boss who can't thank or encourage, don't break your own heart trying to change the boss. Arrange to get your minimum daily requirement of appreciation from an array of others in your business and personal life. Then, the boss's lack of warmth affects only the boss.

PART TWO

FORMAL APPRAISAL CONFLICTS

Common sense tells you that preparing a *negative* annual performance appraisal will produce anxiety in you and defensiveness in your subordinate. The amazing news, carefully and conclusively proven by Gary Latham and Kenneth Wexley during ten years' research, is that all your efforts to "level" without hurting the reviewee's ego are futile; infrequent annual reviews make the damage worse.

Here's how they put it in their scholarly book, *Improving Productivity Through Performance Appraisal*:

> Performance appraisals that are given to employees once a year have little or no positive impact on their behavior.[1]
>
> When criticism is included, performance frequently fails to improve and often drops to a level below where it was prior to the appraisal.[2]
>
> Those areas of job performance that are most criticized are least likely to show improvement.[3]

What they recommend—along with many wise respondents in this section— is continuous *charting* of progress, timely resetting of goals, and continuous two-way communication for joint problem solving as the employee develops capabilities.

[1]Copyright © 1981, Gary P. Latham and Kenneth N. Wexley, INCREASING PRODUCTIVITY THROUGH PERFORMANCE APPRAISAL (Reading, Mass.: Addison-Wesley Publishing Co., Inc., 1981), p. 172.

[2]Ibid., p. 171.

[3]Ibid., p. 151.

MISMATCHED PERCEPTIONS

In the cases that follow, the problem of mismatched perceptions between boss and subordinate is patent. The boss wants more performance than the subordinate is willing to give. Each sees the other as unreasonable.

It may help both parties to learn that many employees imagine they are doing better than they are. When asked to rate their performance against others in their company, all respondents tend to rank themselves in the top 20 percent of performers, according to a national study. Yet, according to Quinn Mills, outstanding and excellent performers combined are about one-half of the total distribution in the United States today.[4]

Let the employee tell you how he or she is doing; you tell him or her what you still need. Say not so much that prior actions were "wrong" but that revised actions will get the desired result.

Sadly, the managers whose questions follow have their eyes locked on the past. They are documenting, record keeping, self-defending, while doing nothing to move the employee forward to improved performance. They are still focused on "who was right" rather than on "what will work."

[4]Copyright © 1985, D. Quinn Mills, THE NEW COMPETITORS (New York: John Wiley & Sons, Inc., 1985), p. 142.

5. *REVIEW REJECTED*

My subordinate insists her quality is excellent while I say it is poor. She argues endlessly.

AUDIENCE RESPONSES

YOUR RATING

________ **a.** *Give direct and prompt feedback on quality problems, in writing. Ask for corrective action with written commitment from this person. Build a dossier to convince her and others.*

________ **b.** *Break the quality elements down in detail. Acknowledge those elements she does fulfill; specify those she has yet to fulfill.*

________ **c.** *When making assignments, specify quality standards in detail . . . areas covered, accuracy levels demanded. Benchmark during performance to provide added direction. Review quality of completed work in writing.*

________ **d.** *Document thoroughly and bring in a third party to arbitrate once and for all. Or document and get your boss's agreement to discipline this person.*

	★	★★	★★★	★★★★
RATING	*NO!*	*RISKY*	*BETTER*	*BEST!*

5. *REVIEW REJECTED* ANALYSIS

★★★★ ***a.*** **Give prompt feedback in writing. Ask corrective action with written commitment.**
Yes. This can be done clearly and kindly, for all subordinates.

★★★★ ***b.*** **Break the quality elements down in detail. Acknowledge correct performance; specify requirements still to be met.**
Yes. This avoids glossing over or misunderstandings. It's good coaching for a troubled performer.

★★★★ ***c.*** **Specify standards at the start, and benchmark during performance. Review quality at completion of job.**
Yes. Good follow-up.

★★★ ***d.*** **Document thoroughly, bring in third party, or get boss's agreement to discipline the person.**
Do this only if the behavior is extremely disruptive. A third-party arbitrator would not normally be called in unless your position were 50/50 or 51/49—and you expect legal action from the employee. Bringing in a third party just because of your own annoyance would overblow the importance of this employee's rebellion. You might inform your boss of intended discipline if this is standard procedure in your company, or if later repercussions would embarrass your boss. Otherwise, proceed courageously on your own authority.

Comment: To avoid the "my word against his" condition, some companies give multilayered reviews. These are very helpful in management and military positions where there are many subtleties in performance requirements:

- *Peer reviews* by those who witness daily performance

- *Field reviews* by those to whom the worker is assigned for special projects
- *Subordinate reviews* to rate leadership skills as seen by those led

Some companies use *simulation exercises* and close observance by a team of senior managers to find promotable talent. Once your argumentative person has to compete with peers in a fair trial judged by strangers, she will learn how her overblown self-esteem stands up in the light of multilayered reviews. Companies save this expensive set of procedures for workers in whom they will have to invest heavily.

The military finds it worthwhile because lives are entrusted to the promotable officer.

6. *SAVVY SALESPERSON, POOR PRODUCTION*

One of my veteran salespeople has superb job and product knowledge but low production. He blames it on "circumstances."

AUDIENCE RESPONSES

YOUR RATING

________ a. *Stress the requirement for combining knowledge with production. Insist he develop his bottom line and ask him* how *he will go about it.*

________ b. *Make sure he is satisfied with the job and surroundings. He may be disgruntled about something.*

________ c. *Maybe a change will jolt him. Change his job for a couple of months and do a review then.*

________ d. *Ask him if he is thinking about early retirement.*

	★	★★	★★★	★★★★
RATING	*NO!*	*RISKY*	*BETTER*	*BEST!*

6. *SAVVY SALESPERSON, POOR PRODUCTION*

ANALYSIS

a. **Stress the requirement for combined knowledge/production.**

What percentage of his total performance requirement rests on product knowledge? What percentage on production? If you could show him on a simple graph, he might start chasing it. Then focus on your other idea: the *how* of beating those "circumstances" he complains of. What are they? How does he diagnose them? Does he face competitive moves, product obsolescence, pricing competition, changing customer needs? Why don't his peers face the same problems? Is his territory or clientele different? Ask him to draw up a chart on special circumstances together with his recommendations for coping. Ask him to cite his own professional concerns: Does he have a career requirement that is not being met? As a valued senior, he has a right to a hearing, but be directive about what he should show and tell you. Instruct him to make you proposals, not complaints.

b. **Find out if he is disgruntled about something.**

Even better, ask him what you can do—in your professional capacity—to help him reach his customary level of performance. If he is disgruntled, it will emerge anyway. Get him to comment on the future, not carp about the past. He may ask for technical help, more personnel, budget and advertising support, any number of things. Ask him to forecast precisely what each "boost" would net the company. Be sure to graph out these elements as you talk. Don't allow free-ranging chat with nothing to pin it down. Work together to sketch out an action plan.

c. **Jolt him with a change of assignment; review after a couple of months.**

This is a higher-risk option. Unless you have plenty of spare capacity among salespeople, who will cover his territory while he enjoys this "change"? Whose territory will he invade? If you change this senior person's job, it should be to accomplish specific goals. He is expensive per hour.

If he is bored or tired, or unequal to front-line pressure, you might discuss a slot where his *knowledge* would be an asset: analytical work, setting up new applications or training for incoming salespeople, consulting, or follow-up servicing—rather than direct selling. Think it through, discuss it. But don't pay for a "tread-water" job designed only to "jolt" him.

***d.* Ask if he's thinking of early retirement.**
Is this a sincere question or a threat? It will be seen as a threat. Be careful about giving the appearance of "trashing" people, especially seniors who have served long and well and may only be experiencing a slump.

Nickerson's Recommendation

For a four-star answer, sit down with this valued veteran and map out the situation graphically, with him doing most of the mapping and most of the planning. If he is disgruntled—or is thinking about retiring—it may come out, but you are not threatening or insinuating. You are working to rebuild.

As D. Quinn Mills puts it,

> Getting rid of people believed to be burned-out does not necessarily get rid of the problems. In some cases the employee may have a better idea than the manager about how to begin to make a contribution again—perhaps a very different kind than the current job assignment allows.[5]

Allow yourself the excitement of finding out from the guy who'll have to do the growing or the going.

[5]Ibid., p. 185.

7. *STIFF STAFF DEFENSES*

My whole group reacts to constructive criticism with stiff defenses, hurt reactions, lots of "yes-butting." Review time is sheer hell.

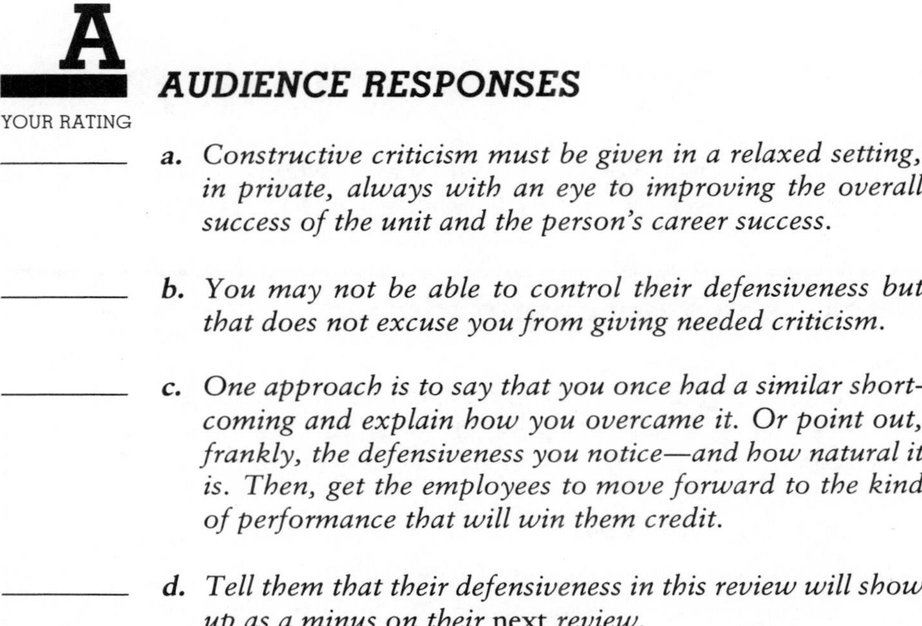

AUDIENCE RESPONSES

YOUR RATING

________ **a.** *Constructive criticism must be given in a relaxed setting, in private, always with an eye to improving the overall success of the unit and the person's career success.*

________ **b.** *You may not be able to control their defensiveness but that does not excuse you from giving needed criticism.*

________ **c.** *One approach is to say that you once had a similar shortcoming and explain how you overcame it. Or point out, frankly, the defensiveness you notice—and how natural it is. Then, get the employees to move forward to the kind of performance that will win them credit.*

________ **d.** *Tell them that their defensiveness in this review will show up as a minus on their* next *review.*

	★	★★	★★★	★★★★
RATING	*NO!*	*RISKY*	*BETTER*	*BEST!*

a. Offer constructive criticism in a relaxed setting, privately. Then look for individual and group success.
Remember: Experts quoted earlier maintain that all criticism is destructive. Instead, make constructive requests regarding "what next." Don't say what they should have done; ask what they can do next. *Coach*, don't criticize. Privacy from outsiders may be necessary, but you can coach a whole group, thanking them while asking for more, within your walls.

b. Despite their defensiveness, you must give needed criticism.
Change that word to coaching, and I'll buy it. Give them a goal, not a reprimand.

c. Say you once had a similar shortcoming and show how you overcame it.
Forget the parables in which you are the hero. Any fiction is quickly seen as manipulative. Let the group come up with today's solution, since yours of long ago may no longer apply.

d. Tell them that their defensiveness now will show up in their next review.
A bit totalitarian, don't you think? It's natural to defend against criticism. If you criticize, the group feels shame. If you challenge, they feel there are still some events they can influence. Take them forward.

Nickerson's Recommendations

★★★★ Now that you know criticism is destructive, *ask* for what is possible now.

Comment: About fairness and privacy, if the group is being held back by poor performance or rule breaking by a few, you must do your supervisory duty and counsel in private with the laggard individual. Don't call the group to account for the failings of a few.

Because this questioner cites defensiveness from the whole department, I suspect that some communal brow-beating has been going on. Apologize, start fresh, focus forward.

P A R T

THREE

FACING THE CONSEQUENCES

Despite all the jokes about "Dad" in the woodshed saying, "This'll hurt me more than it hurts you . . . ," the last-ditch interview—for a demotion or discharge of an employee—gives the boss days of suffering before the fact—and the employee days of suffering afterward. No matter how many times in your management career you've said the big and final "no," it's never easier next time.

You ask yourself, should you have foreseen that the faltering "star" was unready for promotion? Should you have insisted sooner that the outmoded manager go back to school? Should you have scrutinized a job candidate's references more closely? Could you have prevented that fatal stumble? Regret and wistfulness tinge the questions that follow—sympathy wells up in the replies. Managers hate to admit powerlessness to rescue.

The managers in this session express shock, anger, fear at having to prune "deadwood." They fear that embittered employees may make trouble before they go. They hope that some miracle will bring a reprieve or that lawyers and personnel specialists will shield them from the final interview with the failing employee. They turn over every option, looking for escape from the disciplinary burdens placed on all who take command.

Denial—clinging to unrealistic hopes—wondering if "one more chance" will bring a change increases the pain and tension of demotions and discharges. Once you reject unrealistic rescues, once you embrace a decision that your conscience can accept, your tension eases. *Doing* the deed is not nearly so hard as *deciding* to do it.

Yet the *doing* must be handled with care. And you must allow the employee—blind as he or she has been to previous warnings—to experience the same process: facing the fear, hoping against hope, admitting the guilt, mourning the loss, subduing the shock, accepting the hard facts of the situation.

There are no shortcuts before, during, or after the facing of the consequences.

8. *AFRAID TO DEMOTE*

How can I demote a once-excellent employee who is now outclassed by up-and-coming types. His health is poor, he says, from overwork.

A

AUDIENCE RESPONSES

YOUR RATING

______ **a.** *Just do it. Privately and gently.*

______ **b.** *Don't demote. Separate the employee and give him a face-saving way out. (Help with job hunt, recommendations, etc.)*

______ **c.** *Create a more ambiguous "lateral" slot where the employee can be useful but not used up.*

______ **d.** *Get some help from Human Resources or Personnel. This problem may be more complex than you think.*

	★	★★	★★★	★★★★
RATING	*NO!*	*RISKY*	*BETTER*	*BEST!*

★★★ **a. Just do it. Privately and gently.**

And unequivocally. Here, if ever, is your proof that you need to conduct regular, orderly, written performance evaluations (not just once a year, but quarterly if possible) so that such a demotion will not come as a shock. To build your own certitude so you can do this cleanly and kindly, review the record for yourself. List on paper your earlier efforts to train, develop, retrain, coach, work out deficiencies, and cover the employee when health concerns kept him from doing his best. Did the employee refuse any of these offers? Was the employee warned of obsolescence? Did the employee receive new goals and benchmarks with previous performance evaluation? Did he or she fail to meet these goals, benchmarks? Was the consequence spelled out? If so, the final demotion interview is only a formality.

★★ **b. Don't demote. Separate the person to save face; help with job hunt.**

Demotion may not be as repellent to the employee as you think. He may see that he needs a reduced pace or fewer risks in his daily work. If you have not filled his old slot successfully, you could benefit by having him back there, trained and competent. You may be able to "save face" by the kind of announcement you make.

If you discharge this employee, you could end up with an inexperienced trainee in his old slot and another inexperienced trainee in the new. Ask the employee how he or she feels about it. The employee may feel able to step back into the old slot without losing self-worth. An announcement might indicate he was too valuable in the old slot to be moved. And his health may improve once more.

★★★ **c. Create a more ambiguous "lateral" slot where the employee can be useful but not used up.**

Let the ambiguity exist briefly as a transition. Perhaps the person can resume the old slot, with one or two added responsibilities—allowing you to "title" the job in a face-saving way. Sometimes, the more senior slot, made smaller, can be held by a part-time expert, keeping the company's salary outlay in control.

d. **Get advice from Human Resources or Personnel. This problem may be more complex than you think.**
Yes. The health element that the employee blames on overwork may need examination. If you suspect the company may be held culpable for the demoted employee's failing health, seek advice. If your company shows a trend of burning out "once-excellent" people and trashing them, you may lose in court. Formulate a policy and program for avoiding employee burnout and obsolescence. Take Personnel's advice; then face your duty as first-line supervision to deal with this employee.

9. SINKING AT THE DOCK

My new-hire hotshot is failing at the first task I assigned. I'm shocked and angry.

AUDIENCE RESPONSES

YOUR RATING

______ **a.** *Compliment the learner for whatever is working; be polite but frank about specific shortfalls. Offer training or other help.*

______ **b.** *Find out how this person views the job after this trial period. Explain your view. Ask for specific suggestions on how the employee will improve.*

______ **c.** *Give an honest and formal evaluation. Listen to the person's ideas. If you see hope, establish goals and guidelines and state a deadline. If goals are not met, demote or discharge. State the rules now.*

______ **d.** *Reveal your apprehensions and the likely consequences of continued failure. Ask for feedback, with the proviso that the person must overcome the deficiency or go.*

	★	★★	★★★	★★★★
RATING	*NO!*	*RISKY*	*BETTER*	*BEST!*

9. *SINKING AT THE DOCK* ANALYSIS

★★

a. Complement the positive; be frank about the negative; offer training or help.

Before offering training or help, wait for the person's response to your comments about shortfalls. If this person were a *trainee* new hire, you could offer more training. But if you hired the person for a specific task (especially a high-tech task or a task requiring vast experience), and the person falls short, there has been some misrepresentation somewhere—either in the new hire's credentials or in your description of the requirements.

You'd be "shocked and angry" if you bargained for a capable, experienced person and ended up with a trainee. If you're paying for experience and ability, and you don't get it, don't offer to train it in. Don't accept slow results. If a hotshot is what you really need, hire one.

★★★

b. Solicit this person's views. Explain yours. Ask for specific suggestions on how the person will improve.

Much better. Open with a review of the job's written requirements (the job description). Ask the person to rate how he or she is doing on each major item. Give your views in the shortfall areas. Be frank if some of the areas cannot be improved on by good intentions or casual effort. If the investment of time and money required to get the person up to speed would be prohibitive, state this now, and discharge the employee during probation. That is what probation is for.

★★★★

c. Give an honest, formal evaluation. Listen. If there is hope, establish goals and guidelines. State deadline. If they are not met, demote or discharge.

Great. Set up a recruitment system that features a short trial period, a formal review, a resetting of goals and deadlines. Demote or discharge if the goals are not met. This is understood from the start, by both sides.

 ***d.* State your apprehensions, the consequences; get feedback. Issue an ultimatum: overcome the deficiency or go.**

Yes. Your fears may be that the person cannot overcome the deficiency even with goodwill, in which case the ultimatum is: Go. Or you may agree that the deficiency can be overcome—in which case, reply *c* gives you the method to follow: new goals, deadlines, final review.

Comment: Because different companies have such different standards for jobs with similar titles, the disaster described here can and does happen despite reasonable recruiting methods. It may seem cruel to offload an employee who fails during probation, but there are many jobs which simply cannot be learned-on-the-job without causing risk and expense to customers and the public.

10. PRUNING PEOPLE

I've been ordered to weed out my "deadwood." Now I wish I'd done sterner reviews on my weaker people; they'll protest they deserve to stay.

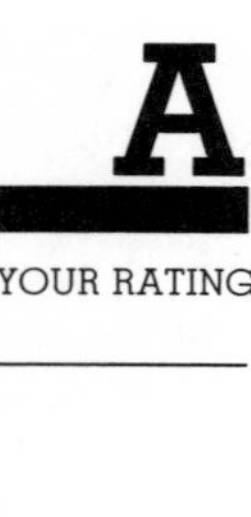

AUDIENCE RESPONSES

YOUR RATING

________ **a.** *Employees must be told, "You just barely met our expectations. Others excelled. When the crunch comes, you go."*

________ **b.** *Drag your feet on weeding out deadwood. Sometimes management changes its mind or eases the orders.*

________ **c.** *Start out by separating your obvious deadheads. Some of the other fringe workers will get the message and leave of their own accord. You may not have to prune so hard.*

________ **d.** *Look around the organization for a haven for some of your people. If pruning is going on everywhere, some of* your *deadheads may be better than some of* theirs.

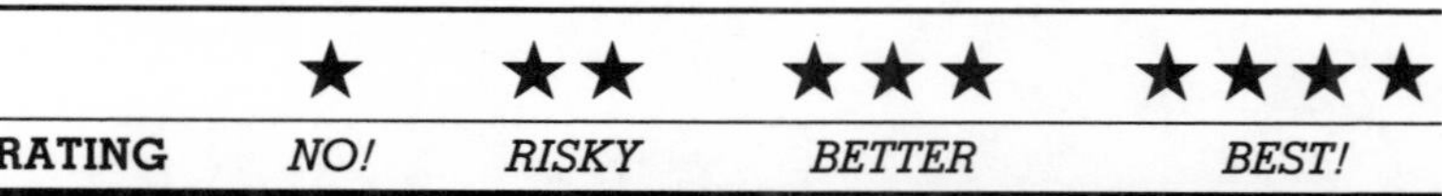

★★ **a. Tell them they barely met our needs. Others excelled.**

Your written reviews had better back this up. If you were accustomed to giving people scores of "8 out of 10" simply to "get the reviews over with," you'll have a hard time making the "mediocrity" label stick now. You may have to focus on the fact that the "layoff" is an *economic* necessity and you must regretfully let people go, even though they are "good." If you failed to make the quality issue clear before, it's really too late now. Get honest when you review your survivors.

★★ **b. Drag your feet. Management may change its mind.**

No. Why salvage deadwood workers when management has given you a "heaven-sent" mandate to prune them out. If you drag your feet in your department, while heads of other departments do their duty, you'll be called on the carpet by management later on. Your people, saved by your footdragging for a while longer, will find you were only prolonging the agony.

★★★ **c. Prune your obvious deadheads. Other "fringe" performers may go, leaving you with fewer hard choices.**

If management's plan allows for pruning in stages, this method would make sense, and do the least damage to the morale of those deserving to stay. Don't expect the most stubborn nonperformers to make things easy. Far from volunteering, they'll hold on tight, knowing you can't give them good references in their job hunt.

Reassure your best people that they are secure in their jobs. Everyone gets the jitters when pruning begins. Layoffs don't go smoothly even when handled well. They threaten everyone's security and cause emotional outbursts by some of the victims and their friends. Seek your boss's advice on the finer points and lean on the discreet advice of mentors at this time.

d. Look around for a haven for some of your people who are better performers than some of theirs.

Good if your company can do it. There are a lot of back-room deals made at these times. Some of your strong performers can move laterally or vertically into another department where they can be valuable. But in many large and government organizations, each department must bite the bullet and separate certain numbers of "heads" without seeking remedies anywhere. Find out the rules before seeking any deals; you may be attacked by your peer managers if you make a wrong move at this extremely sensitive time. What is much better is an "umbrella plan" administered impartially by Human Resources to redeploy people during a "reduction in force" for the benefit of the individual and the organization. Otherwise, a 10 percent cut in all departments may result in losing many fine people from strong departments while losing real deadheads from others.

In the kind of meritocracy many government bosses dream of, the best people would stay and the weakest would go, based on their performance pattern, not on a straight head count per department. Obviously, the organization would benefit by having a total work force of only the "fittest." But issues of longevity, salary rates, and fairness—especially if taken up by adversarial unions or workers' rights groups—still militate against meritocracy systems.

Comment: Whatever system your organization uses to cope with the painful issue of "pruning deadwood," you still need an honest, consistent, written performance evaluation system to aid you in making honorable decisions. Even if you don't have to justify them to employees, you have to justify them to yourself.

11. *FEAR OF FIRING*

I fear the task of separating a vocal and embittered employee. It may bring a lawsuit and upset everyone else in the department.

AUDIENCE RESPONSES

YOUR RATING

_________ **a.** *Seek the counsel of your personnel people and proceed carefully according to their instructions. Let your boss in on the process too.*

_________ **b.** *The employee's attitude is not the issue. His or her performance is. If you have disciplined legally and documented fully, you can go ahead with the next step. Failure to do so would be unfair to all the other employees who toe the line. It would set bad legal precedence for tolerating bad performers.*

_________ **c.** *Proceed. Just pick your timing carefully. Do the deed after hours or at closing time. Instruct the employee to leave the premises and not return. You can do this with care and kindness, to save the employee's face.*

_________ **d.** *Consult your corporate attorney and follow his or her advice meticulously.*

	★	★★	★★★	★★★★
RATING	*NO!*	*RISKY*	*BETTER*	*BEST!*

★★★★ **a. Seek and follow the advice of Personnel. Inform your boss.**

Yes. A vocal, embittered, litigious employee is a hard person to fire. Proceed carefully, but proceed.

★★★★ **b. You must prove performance, not attitude. If you prepared your case, proceed, or pay the penalties of tolerating bad performance.**

Dead right. But consult Personnel and your boss just the same, assuring them your documentation and discipline procedure is being followed to the letter.

c Time it carefully. Do it after hours or at closing time. Instruct the employee to leave and not return. Be kind.

There are risks to this popular method. After-hours firings are for felons who should never darken your door again. But being banished suddenly is harsh punishment for an employee who may only be incompetent. Remember the quality of respect more than ever when you must do the ultimate deed to an employee. If this vocal, embittered employee is a middle manager or higher, there may be entitlement to outplacement service and office space and time for the job hunt (despite the bad manners you dislike). While you need to ensure strict privacy for the conversation in any case—and may want the employee to have a discreet getaway path to hide distress—the employee may need to come back to the company, to reconcile, to adjust, to talk about the separation payments, benefits, other issues.

If you state unequivocally that the decision to let the employee go is final, that it is based on performance factors, that the employees' skills and abilities do not fit the job's requirements, that you greatly regret having to announce this decision, that's the way to start.

State your company's policy about separation pay and benefits, about any transition services you offer. Give the employee time to settle down after hearing this news. Offer to bring in a personnel professional if the employee wants to "test this reality" or explore the benefits side. Invite the employee to voice a reaction and discuss his or her needs now. Ask what the person's own preference would be in handling the closing days or hours.

If the employee is agitated and wants to just "get out of here," allow that and state that you can talk on the phone to arrange clearing up of details when the employee has been able to adjust and make some decisions.

d. Consult your corporate attorney; follow the advice given.

Consider it carefully. Don't necessarily follow it meticulously. Your attorney does not make policy for your company. Legal advice is designed to protect you, but you must still follow your conscience. In larger companies, your personnel people *and* your attorney will give advice. Protect confidentiality as you go.

P A R T

FOUR

FINE TUNING: THE FORMAL REVIEW—MAKE SURE IT'S MUTUAL

For a good performance review, development review, disciplinary review, or raise/promotion review, you must have two parties, armed with preparation, data, and mutual respect.

Here are a few "musts" contributed by my audience members to help you plan your next review whether you are the giver or receiver of an appraisal. Let's look at the giver first:

WHEN YOU GIVE A REVIEW

Preparation

1. Give the person a week or two's notice; give him a copy of the job description and blank forms like the ones you'll use, so he can prepare a personal assessment. Remind the employee that his opinions will be of great importance, that this is a two-way conversation. Ask him to bring along project lists or performance highlights for your attention. What percentage of the final "score" will such highlights be worth? Tell the person.

2. Mention one or two (not more) areas where you'd like to see improvement or progress. Ask the person to think about suggestions for achieving such progress.

3. Invite the employee to prepare a short list (not more than three items) concerning his needs that you could help fulfill: training, access, help, authorizations, technical advice, and the like.

4. Assure the person that in the preparation as well as in the interview, you will devote no more than 25 percent of the time to the past: the lion's share of the joint session will be on the present and future. This helps set the tone for acceptance and nondefensive working toward goals.

The Meeting

1. Make sure your calls are held and ensure an hour's privacy.

2. Greet the employee warmly. State that the interview is designed to recognize achievement, uncover needs, make a plan to get these needs met, set new goals, and certify the person's position on his career ladder.

3. Lay out your forms, and ask the employee to do the same so they can be compared. State that the floor is the employee's rather than yours. You want to hear the person's view of his situation and will respond or ask questions as you need to.

4. To assure that you do not dominate, remember to put questions rather than make statements, for example

   "Which problem do you think is more important?"
   "What do you think we ought to do?"
   "What's the next step, in your view?

5. Wherever the employee has rated himself *below* your scores, ask what he thinks is needed to make your score a reality? Unless he can prove a deficiency, grant him the higher score.

6. Wherever the employee has rated himself *above* your score, assure him that most people do rate themselves higher than the norm. Explain what deficiencies you want improved to let him earn that score, and set a new goal for next time.

7. Avoid criticism. Instead, *ask* for improvements, enhancements, or solutions to problems you see. Don't use any sentence with such words as

   "You should have . . . ."
   "Why did you . . ?"
   "If you could only have . . . ."
   "Why didn't you . . . ?"
   "Too bad you couldn't have . . . "

   Instead, focus on such sentences as

   "Can you see any alternative methods for this?"
   "What kinds of solutions are you researching now?"
   "The result I'm looking for now is . . . , any ideas?"

8. Monitor your involvement. If you are speaking more than half the time, slow down. Let the employee develop his ideas more fully. Pace yourself with such expressions as

   "Yes, I see. What else are you thinking?"

   Then be silent and supportive and wait for an answer.

9. The employee will want to express emotions and opinions. Perhaps some won't be comfortable for you. Don't jump in quickly with a response or argument. Instead, let the message sink in. If an idea is new to you, say so, and state that you'd like to give it serious thought later, and get back to the person.

10. If the employee expresses anger or frustration about some policy of the company or action of yours, *accept* the feelings. Don't say "I understand" unless you are sure that you do. Instead, invite the person to help you understand. Offer solutions where you can, and offer to think of some more if you need to.

The Conclusion

1. When the employee has made his points, go over your version of the forms, side by side with his, and adjust the final version. Show the point scores you apply to each type of achievement. Let the employee see how scores are calculated. (You must use whatever format your company requires, of course, but most are based on numerical scales, point aggregates, or something of the kind, as well as supporting essays or text.)

2. Agree on a final score. Set a new scoring target for the next period, and pinpoint the areas of improvement/progress most likely to produce the next score.

3. Settle on one or two steps to be taken by both sides to achieve this next set of goals. Make your agreement *graphic* if you can, so both parties understand fully *what* and *how much* is to be done.

4. For complex or difficult new goals, set specific benchmarks and follow-up dates so the performer can get support or advice if needed. This reminds the person that you reward effort toward goals, as well as full achievement of them.

5. Go over a written or graphic summary of the person's position on his agreed career ladder. The closing part of most evaluation forms concerns promotability: directions and timetables. Don't keep them secret.

6. Thank the person for his cooperation in making the review effective. Let him have a copy of the working notes since they constitute an agreement. A typed final copy can follow.

Special-Purpose Reviews: Having built a foundation on the kind of development review just described, you will, once a year or so, conduct special reviews for discipline, problem solving, or pay raises and promotions. Here are a few pointers on concluding each:

1. If you've given a disciplinary or negative review, be clear and graphic about the consequences for continued failures and the steps just "contracted" either to remedy the situation or to demote, to suspend or to separate the person. These items should be clear and graphic even on the working papers. (See the next section on "Firing.")
2. If this was a pay raise or promotion interview, the money figure or the agreed new position should be prominently noted on your working papers. That's a contract. Be sure there is no discrepancy (certainly not a downward move) in the final typed version. (I've talked to many people who've been quoted a figure or starting date at a review only to find it discounted or delayed later. Your sheepish disclaimers about what they decided "upstairs" will do nothing to restore trust. You must be prepared to *commit* in a pay review or promotion review; don't enter into it unprepared.)

WHEN YOU RECEIVE A REVIEW

Preparation

1. Keep a private "Me File" in which you drop simple notes whenever you reach a milestone, beat a deadline, do a major favor, receive honors, achieve goals. This not only cheers you up, but it gives you items from which to select a short list of "highlights" for use prior to performance reviews. Select just a few of the creamier items and list them for your boss well ahead of review time. This helps the boss take a proportional look at your year (rather than just recent days) and may help her ask for more if this review will involve your rewards or promotability.
2. When notified of your impending review, gather and study your source documents: your position description, your project lists, your data sheets showing production, financial, sales, or other results for the period.

3. From these, list on a single sheet of paper your main *contributions* to the department or organization since last review.

4. On a separate single sheet, list the main problems/obstacles you faced and the steps you've taken to overcome them. If you're still in trouble with these, list the areas where you may need your boss's help, and make specific requests. Make sure these requests comply with company policy.

5. Fill out a blank copy of the standard performance review sheet your boss will use during the review. (If, for some strange reason, your company does not provide you with this, go to the trouble of getting one. Some people use "white-out" on last year's copy as a desperate measure because their company policy does not provide for "self-review." But unless you take the time to think through every item just as your boss will, you may be taken by surprise and have to swallow your review whole.)

   Calculate the "scores" you think you have achieved. Try to figure out where the boss's scores will differ. Focus on what is still possible, and think of ways to improve those scores when the boss is likely to come in low.

6. Prepare for your own defensive reactions. They are natural, but they lead to tension in the review. If the boss criticizes something you've done, *don't defend*. Instead ask, "Which risks incurred by my action concern you most? I am willing to work to reduce your risks, always." That is a nondefensive approach that will gain you more information on the boss's fears regarding your "weak areas."

7. If you foresee a gap between your scores and your boss's on some items, be prepared with ideas for improvement, or examples of the principles you follow when performing those items. The boss may be able to show you preferred principles to follow.

The Meeting

1. When the boss greets you, say you are glad of the chance to work on your performance with the boss.

2. Be ready to compare your documents and scores with those the boss has prepared. If the boss expresses willingness for you to lead the discussion, go ahead. If the boss wants to take command, hold your documents to one side and listen carefully. Ideally, the boss will want to compare both sets of papers. But if you know the boss does not operate this way, hold your materials until the boss is finished.

3. Because you have done your homework, you will have diagnosed the problems in your performance which the boss may cite. Be ready to offer *solutions* and to ask for specific help and support in improving performance results. Even if the boss is untrained in reviewing and keeps "going back" over past behaviors, you can respond about the present and the future. This will reduce any feelings of powerlessness and frustration that negative comments would normally cause.

4. If the boss asks you why you did such-and-such, you can cite the principle you tend to follow in such cases (bring the discussion to the present) and then ask the boss what risks she wants covered when such an incident arises again. Express willingness to cover these risks. Say what you will do differently, not what you will become.

5. Be prepared to talk about half the time. If the boss is on the ball, she will ask for your ideas about solving problems and improving productivity. Be ready.

The Conclusion

1. Using your "homework" and the points that arise in the meeting, be prepared now to ask for what you need from the boss to meet her requirements. What authorizations, help, training, experience do you need?

2. Make your offers: What changes are you willing to make in your behavior to meet the boss's needs for the next period?

3. Set up your new targets in clear detail. Be sure you know how success will be measured: How will you know that you have hit the targets?

4. If you foresee any problems along the way, set up some checkpoints or benchmarks for specific dates or project milestones, when you can return to report or get help.

5. Before the meeting ends, ask the boss to outline your progress on your career ladder and to pronounce on your readiness for promotion. When and how high will your next step likely be?

Special-Purpose Reviews: For Discipline, for Pay Raises

1. If the review is *disciplinary*, you really must reduce the amount of time you have to spend taking abuse. Be prepared to acknowledge

quickly any damage you have done and to focus on steps you will take now to overcome those disadvantages the company may have suffered. This is no time to defend the "why" of your past actions, but to propose the "how" of your new solutions.

If you want to restore your former good name and enhance your promotability, say what actions you will take to meet the company's requirements now. Thank your reviewer for giving you the opportunity to turn your career around. Say it, mean it, and move past old stumbling blocks.

2. In preparing for a *pay review*, you will have given your boss a short list of your accomplishments as recommended earlier. By all means, give the boss some idea of the pay hike you would like, at the early time. If you can do so briefly, show the boss how this *investment* in your future effectiveness will pay off. You are not asking for rewards for what you've already done. You're asking for an investment in what you will do—and your excellent past performance signifies your ability to make good on that.

   Know your numbers. If turning down your pay request, your boss may comment on your pay raise as setting or breaking precedent or may cite poor profits, business downturns, the "going rate" locally. You'd better know your numbers and offer data that will rekindle your boss's generosity of spirit and honesty of heart. Just make it easy for the boss to get you your raise. Don't expect the boss to do the research.

Subordinate Action is Crucial: In business, almost everyone is subordinate to someone. Since the subordinate has the most to gain from performance reviews, it benefits the subordinate to study independently to become a stronger partner in the evaluation process. The Latham and Wexley book already mentioned gives great detail on job analysis and behavior descriptions. In addition, you may want to study George Morrisey's *Performance Appraisals for Business and Industry*, and *Performance Appraisal in the Public Sector* (both Addison-Wesley, 1983) as well as Richard F. Olson's *Performance Appraisal* (John Wiley, 1981.) You'll build confidence and skill at handling reviews for yourself and those you lead.

TWO CHECKLISTS: HOW TO FIRE, HOW TO GET FIRED

People I meet on airplanes and at seminars seem quite willing to discuss "firings" they have been through. You can get fancier if you like, but here are the basic minimums most of them admit are essential:

HOW TO FIRE WITH CIVILITY

1. Don't let a firing come as a shock. From your previous warnings in written reviews, your "victim" should see it coming.
2. Use compassion and courtesy. Despite warnings, this person has chosen denial. Now economics *and* pride will suffer. Avoid firing at Christmas, one's birthday, or during family crises like births, deaths, divorces. Wait just a bit. The price in morale will otherwise be paid by your whole work group, not just the person fired.
3. Assure the person you have thought over all the options carefully and that you regret having to take this step. If the decision is economic (a major reduction in force), say so and admit you are really sorry. If the decision is based on poor performance, remind the person of the warnings given at previous reviews and say that the person's abilities simply do not match the job's requirements. State that the decision is final. If the person loses composure, offer to give them a few moments alone. Say you will return shortly.
4. Pick a midweek day and a time when privacy will be assured. In my youth, people used to fire people the last thing Friday night, so they could disappear from the face of the earth. If you do that today, others suspect the fired person of larcency or fraud. In addition, the fired person is suddenly cut off, with no choice about how and when to disappear. With midweek timing, the person may elect

to finish out the week, talk things over with you some more, get data about severance, engage in exit interviews, get help with outplacement. Or he may choose to leave forthwith. Only when the person is a felon, or threatens violence, does he get escorted off the premises by security guards (or worse).

5. In some companies, Personnel takes over at this point and covers the person's separation benefits. In smaller companies, the boss must do it. Be prepared with all the answers in such cases. The fired person will be very anxious about security within minutes of being told the shocking news. (In many companies, fired employees of a certain rank get "outplacement" help—a desk and phone, counseling, and real assistance in finding new employment. This kind of benefit restores self-worth and keeps everyone calm. It often aids greatly in the transition period while the person's job gets covered, too.)

HOW TO GET FIRED GRACEFULLY

1. Use your head. When you've had two bad reviews and cannot think how to salvage the third, you should be job hunting in earnest. Resign gracefully, stating that you've had a wonderful offer elsewhere. Most likely, your workmates will throw an exit party for you. Your boss will give a nice speech. On the other hand, you may work in a company where performance reviews are rare. Your failure to please may only have been hinted at, so you could be shocked when your boss calls you in for a firing. Even with warnings, it won't be easy.

2. If you are shocked and feel like crying or putting your fist through the wall, take a deep breath (in through the nose) and count to four. Breathe out at the same slow pace. Say your favorite prayer or mantra until you feel calm. If you cannot regain control, say to your "executioner", "This comes as a shock. Excuse me for a moment." Then exit briefly. Stay out until you feel calm enough to resume the interview.

3. If there have been no performance reviews to forewarn you of your impending dismissal, you have the right to ask

   "Is this decision irrevocable?"

   "What specific behavior of mine makes this decision necessary?"

   "What elements of my job description am I failing to fulfill?

Or what risks would the company face by keeping me in this position?"

Your boss should be in a position to answer these questions, and this may give you valuable data to use in your next job search.

4. Ask when and with whom you may go over your severance benefits—health insurance, outplacement, counseling. State that you would like to know about your entitlements. Ask *when* the company would like you to vacate, and let them know your own preferences if they seem open. If you are in middle management or higher, they will usually be prepared for you to negotiate the best terms for your departure.

   At senior levels, you will doubtless have negotiated a gold or platinum parachute, and you may wish to consult your attorney to make friendly and civilized arrangements to get you all you are entitled to.

5. Particularly if your boss is ill-tempered or bad-mannered (or if *you* are this way yourself), you'll be tempted to throw a tantrum, let them have a piece of your mind, threaten to go to the press, remind them how they'll suffer without you. Do none of these things. If you see the end coming, rehearse the most civilized and calming departure ceremony you can. Firing is stressful enough without adding the draining experience of an angry outburst to your burdens.

   Remember that you want to emerge with your self-worth, with your ability to make choices on your own behalf, with the goodwill of many onlookers and bystanders who may become references for you.

   When you stay calm, you can *choose.* A firing *is* a new beginning. But no one can convince you of that but you.

HOW POWERFUL MANAGERS STAY PROMOTABLE

SESSION
EIGHT

HOW POWERFUL MANAGERS STAY PROMOTABLE

INTRODUCTION

What have you noticed about those great bosses in your background? The ones you'd have followed across the Gobi without a canteen? When I think of the bosses I've worked for, and great CEOs I meet at certain of my client companies, I notice three traits they have in common:

1. *They control competing priorities* with apparent ease, handling the high risks with aplomb and getting the lower-risk but necessary details handled without struggle or fanfare by competent administrative staffers.

2. *They lead by invention*, always coming up with practical new tools, shortcuts, and solutions to problems. They read, talk with others, and come into work at least once a week with "Here's an idea..." or "What if we tried...". They sketch out their ideas graphically, so others can piggyback and make the ideas their own.

3. *They display a consistent and coherent set of values* that subordinates can recognize and rely on. People working with such a boss say such things as

   "You always know where you are with him."

"She's strong, but she's kept her sense of humor. We trust her."

"Yeah. Good boss. Very straight-ahead. Smart. Fair."

People relax and do their best when they know their boss is competent, clear, inventive, and essentially virtuous. The best of our bosses are "naturals"—they possess their virtues unself-consciously; they don't push or persuade you to follow.

You may be saying, "Surely I have these virtues too." Are they coming across to others?

The cases in this session demonstrate how some managers succeed or fail when *control*, *invention,* and *values* are tested. You'll also see how techniques can improve your ability to telegraph your strengths to others.

PART ONE

CONTROLLING COMPETING PRIORITIES

What do you do when several bosses make competing demands on your time—and when all their projects are both legitimate and compelling? Most managers try to satisfy everyone, letting their daily "maintenance" work pile up and hoping they can play catch-up some day soon. Trouble is—senior managers know that if you want something done, you give it to a busy person—so they give you even more projects and your backlogs worsen.

The people you'll meet now have fallen into the overwork trap. They're handling heavy work loads but are also drowning in the routines that underpin them. With overcommitment come service errors, product defects, personnel grievances—all of which must be stemmed before they do permanent harm—all of which must be faced, hour upon wearying hour. Some of these managers have been hammering at the rockpile so long, they have lost their zest. They are "holding down their jobs," not chasing their careers. They push, rather than lead, their tired employees. They avoid customer/client contacts, seeing each new encounter as a possible confrontation.

They avoid opening negotiations with their bosses. They insist that budget and staff limits are firm and that change is impossible.

This session is a collection of questions from people who *just can't*, any more. But the answers are from people who still *can*. You may find their solutions a tonic.

1. PLAGUED BY INTERRUPTIONS

Legitimate interruptions plague my day. I can't master the disciplines of time management.

AUDIENCE RESPONSES

YOUR RATING

_________ **a.** *Before doing anything, decide whether the task is really yours. Should it be shunted/delegated?*

_________ **b.** *Make goal lists. Use a "daytiming" book to block time for these goals by day/week/month.*

_________ **c.** *Plan day-tight compartments and schedule problems into them in a preset order.*

_________ **d.** *Keep a log of how you are spending your time. Then control calls and interruptions.*

	★	★★	★★★	★★★★
RATING	*NO!*	*RISKY*	*BETTER*	*BEST!*

a. Decide if the task is yours: shunt/delegate.
Right. When interruptions are chronic, get back to basics. Which tasks are central to your mission? Which interruptions are central/worthwhile? Schedule them!

Shunt some interruptions. Not every matter should be brought to you. Which capable assistants could handle them? Map out your strategy on paper: Announce which subordinates visitors should see. Make the handover. Use wall signs as reminders.

b. Block out your goals into set times of day/week/month.
Yes. Some goals require months of work to complete; you are taking "bites" day by day until the task is done. Use a daytimer book or monthly calendar spreadsheet to map out these ongoing work load sessions in color so you can see what you are doing. Be strict about keeping these "progress times" uninterrupted.

c. Plan day-tight compartments; schedule problems into them in preset order.
Yes. Without being rigid, reserve chunks of time for decisions/conferring/action. Schedule the vital task into the best time (not necessarily the earliest time) to do it well. Schedule its slot first—even though it may be a late-day slot—and let nothing interrupt you during that slot. In this way, your most vital tasks get protection. Caution: Use up no more than five or six hours per day in this slotting process. You need another hour or two for legitimate interrupters who are encouraged to come only at these open times.

d. Keep a log of how you spend your time; then control calls and interruptions.
Be careful. Assure that your log is highly selective; look at only a few significant things. The practice of logging *everything* is wasteful. If you work-a-little, log-a-little, the

log emerges randomly, just like the interruptions, and becomes a nuisance to analyze. Instead, just head up a column for each major interruption you expect to happen. Then jot-a-dot in the appropriate column when the interruption occurs. These are the ones you want to see and stem.

Armed with *dot chart* data gathered over two weeks, you can show "offending" interrupters their own row of dots—evidence. You can then arrange to see them for a similar amount of time each day or week, but channel their visits to fit better into your program. You can offer better and more thorough *service* to visitors who see you during "channel time" when you have tools and data ready for them.

Comment: To piggyback on responses *b* and *c*, regarding *blocks* of concentrated time, some companies use *quiet hour* as a tool for increasing productivity. While it does not work well when blanketed over an entire organization, small clusters of people can use quiet hour to great advantage. Imagine quiet hour to control phone interruptions. Here's an example:

Try Quiet Hour Coverage: Any five-person group can improve phone productivity by up to 16 hours per week by using a simple tool: Quiet Hour Coverage. Here's how it would work. First, the group determines which hour of each day is *quietest* on the phone. Because the traffic will be low, one member of the team can cover the rest for that single hour. You may have drawn Monday, the quietest hour being eleven to noon, say. For that hour, you cover the whole team—handling as many phone problems as you can—promising callback for any problem you cannot handle. During that hour, the other four members of the team push on with uninterrupted work. Tomorrow, another member covers you and the rest of the team in tomorrow's quietest hour. Other members rotate the plan throughout the week.

Because time studies show that *one uninterrupted hour is as productive as four normal hours,* you will be glad to donate one hour on your duty day, since you will get back four hours (equivalent to sixteen hours) during the rest of the week.

Go further: try Phone-Free Day! If you like the sound of quiet hour for phone relief, you might want to go further for a really massive productivity boost. Ask a select group of your people to test it: a Phone-Free Day.

When a particularly successful product started booming for a Dun & Bradstreet Company, five telemarketers tried this experiment. Each marketer would be "out" — not available on the phone—one day per week. The other four marketers would cover this person, each handling this person's phone calls for two hours of the day "out." During this "out" day, the lucky marketer would do fulfillment work on all that she had sold by phone the previous week. Each marketer was willing to handle a hectic two-hour period each day—to get a full day per week later, free of phone traffic.

In this way, the five marketers increased their output by 40 percent, without increasing fatigue. Their error rate dived downward, they felt more organized about their work, and their absenteeism/lateness record (already excellent) got even better. Using the rule one hour uninterrupted is as good as four normal hours, they opted to tolerate eight high-traffic hours per week to buy eight uninterrupted hours per week (the equivalent of thirty-two hours of productivity. Their net gain: twenty-four hours per week.

For solo operators, use Time Strips Some people cannot find a team of fellows to help with quiet hour cover. In such a case you might try signaling for quiet using a technique called *Time Strip*. Take a strip of acetate, one inch wide by eight inches high. List fifteen-minute segments of your workday down the margin of the strip in indelible pen. Then, use washable markers to block in simple color bars that announce whether you're available or not to callers during that segment of time. You can wash off and reuse the strip daily.

Red: Important work in progress. Don't disturb.
Green: Stop in briefly for questions and answers.
Blue: In conference.
Black: "Clinic time" on announced subject.
Brown: Returning calls.

Since many managers settle on the same time of day for returning calls or conducting clinics, these might be blocked in permanently, making your optional times so few, you could fill them in in only a couple of seconds each day. Post them. Your staffers soon learn where to look: green or black for available periods. Otherwise, they stay away. For a senior manager, this is minimum protection; you need and deserve it. For mid- and supervisory levels, you may have to do some extra "selling" and testing before the idea sticks. Go to it. The time you save will definitely be your own.

2. NO BUDGET FOR NEEDED HELP

Too many problems, no place to disappear for a breather in my public service post. I ask for help; they claim "no money."

A

AUDIENCE RESPONSES

YOUR RATING

________ **a.** *Delegate all possible work to staff.*

________ **b.** *Working two to three hours on weekends helps me clear the decks for a smoother week to come.*

________ **c.** *Make sure all that time is productive.*

________ **d.** *You have to concentrate on high-value priorities, do what low-priority stuff you can until time runs out.*

	★	★★	★★★	★★★★
RATING	*NO!*	*RISKY*	*BETTER*	*BEST!*

2. NO BUDGET FOR NEEDED HELP ANALYSIS

a. Delegate all possible work to staff.

Yes. Get all possible work done at the lowest level and cost per hour where it can be done effectively. Never say, "I wouldn't ask my staff to do anything I wouldn't do myself." The task might be too costly when done at *your* hourly rate. Say, "I *would* ask my staff to do all the work they can do effectively at their level." Read on for ways to get staffers on board when budgets are tight.

b. Work two to three hours on weekend to clear the decks.

Although all of us will work countless hours of weekend and evening time in a career, I do not think we should make this a permanent expectation. Some people with families, full-time, challenging jobs, and dedication to community or political goals should really take a full break on weekends and get the mental rest and physical exercise that allows for *next* week's accomplishments at work. Building the habit of working a few hours per weekend can soon "bleed" into a few more and a few more hours until the job takes over your life. Donate nights and weekends only during peak project times when the results are clearly and dramatically worth it.

c. Make sure all your time is productive.

That's impossible. Everyone must spend some time socializing, walking around, resting. No one works at top productivity all the time: you'd be exhausted. But, do schedule *blocks of time for your highest payoff work*, and make sure that *that* time is productive. No interruptions. Pick a time when your energy is high. Have your tools in order before you start. Reserve such time for work that qualifies as *the right work*, at the *right level*, with *higher impact* than anything else you could be doing now.

d. Concentrate on high-value priorities; do low-priority work until time runs out.

Yes to the first part. But work to rid yourself of low-priority work. Is it worth doing at your rate of pay when money is tight?

Comment: You may need low-cost ways to get help. Here are a few offered by seminar attendees:

1. *Recruit high school students* (some at *no cost* because they are in funded programs at school). They do clerical work, go-fer work, clean-up, and maintenance and are also wonderful at computing. Work through your high school guidance counselor to find top-quality kids.
2. *Recruit retirees*, especially recent retirees from your own business. They know the ropes and can move mountains in only three to five hours per week.
3. *College and graduate students can help* in their specialty (drafting, engineering, research, law), and many do it for close to the minimum hourly wage because they want experience or data for a thesis.
4. *Residents of the local nursing home may be available* to do envelope stuffing and other quantity tasks quickly, cleanly, proudly, and on short notice.
5. *Call your local chapter, Association of Retarded Citizens or your regional Center for the Developmentally Disabled.* Find out about using their excellent people for *precision work* of a repetitive nature, on your premises or at sheltered workshops.
6. If you are a nonprofit agency, *contact your local voluntary action center* to get help with temporary overloads.
7. If you're looking for a high degree of commitment, *think of disabled workers* who have overcome problems of preparing for employment, transportation, and rejection by the uninformed. If you want determination guaranteed, look here. Con-

tact your state, city, or county *Commission for the Blind*, or *Department of Handicapped Affairs*, or *Disabled Veterans*. Contact your local university employment division and express interest in "physically challenged workers" (as Ted Kennedy, Jr., calls them). Contact the *National Training Institute for the Deaf* (located at *Rochester Institute of Technology*). Their high-tech graduates are famous for *performance*, not hearing loss.

Most small- and medium-sized companies have not explored creatively for competent help, especially part-time help.

3. CRISIS HOPPING

My priority system isn't working. One crisis overrules another; one boss overrides another. I'm always in the wrong, whatever I do.

AUDIENCE REACTION

YOUR RATING

_______ a. *I think about my managers' major interests and the company's overall objective. Then I address these projects* first.

_______ b. *Know what your bosses expect, what they consider most important. Allocate time accordingly.*

_______ c. *Assess your agreed areas of responsibility in terms of what matters most to your* immediate *boss.*

_______ d. *Keep track of these crises and switches in priorities. Get a ruling before proceeding.*

	★	★★	★★★	★★★★
RATING	*NO!*	*RISKY*	*BETTER*	*BEST!*

★★★ *a.* **Address your managers' major interests and company objectives first.**

I agree, provided that "first" means "first in effectiveness," not necessarily first in sequence. Always tackle the most vital tasks *at the best time of day or week* to ensure their getting done well. Then fit other lesser (but still important) tasks into the remaining time, when your energy or level of attention may be lower.

★★★★ *b.* **Know what your bosses expect; allocate time accordingly.**

Yes. If this is not clear, make it easier for your bosses to make it clear. Draw up a list or chart that they can red pencil—don't expect them to take time clarifying everything from scratch each day or week.

★★★ *c.* **Assess your agreed areas of responsibility in terms of what matters to your immediate boss.**

This presumes that one of your several bosses can approve your performance without reference to the others. If that were true, you could show your *immediate* boss the whole set of lists red penciled by your several bosses and ask for a ruling on conflicting items. If your immediate boss is unwilling to rule on this, you'll have to bargain with each boss separately for relief from conflicting items. Without the charts, you cannot bargain rationally.

★★★★ *d.* **Keep track of crises and switches; get a ruling before proceeding.**

While you would not bother your bosses for every single switch (you can figure out many for yourself), you would certainly want to show a pattern of switching and get a ruling precedent.

Comment: Here's a tool for *tracking crisis hopping*. It works because it is so selective.

1. Keep a very select "To Do" list each day. Just list the *top three* tasks for the day.

2. If a crisis is so worthwhile that it "bumps" one of your top three tasks, note this in a vivid color.
3. Collect only those "To Do" lists with the vivid color. In a month or so, you have a collection worth showing your boss, because
   a. The tasks listed in black and white are *the* worthiest in your day, the best tasks on your job description.
   b. Vividly colored items prove a trend of worthier tasks that keep arising. They indicate that you're doing even better work than you're being paid for. What are they worth to your boss and department?

In short, not all crises are blameworthy. Some crises are trailblazers into your company's next breakthrough.

4. ADMINISTRATION AS AFTERTHOUGHT

In our small private partnership, we're all doers, technicians. We drop the ball on paperwork, details. No one's an administrator.

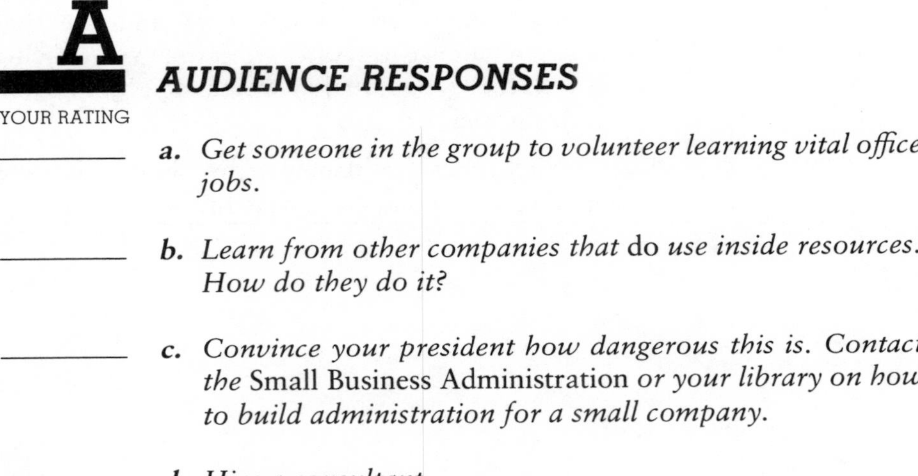

AUDIENCE RESPONSES

YOUR RATING

________ **a.** *Get someone in the group to volunteer learning vital office jobs.*

________ **b.** *Learn from other companies that* do *use inside resources. How do they do it?*

________ **c.** *Convince your president how dangerous this is. Contact the* Small Business Administration *or your library on how to build administration for a small company.*

________ **d.** *Hire a consultant.*

	★	★★	★★★	★★★★
RATING	*NO!*	*RISKY*	*BETTER*	*BEST!*

4. *ADMINISTRATION AS AFTERTHOUGHT* ANALYSIS

★★ **a. Have someone volunteer to learn administration.**
Although you should *all* read up on it, you're probably too busy in your separate roles to give it the time it needs. You're not too small for administration; you're too big to leave it uncovered now. Get each member of the team to list or "dot chart" the administrative slippages in a typical week. Then, decide how a part-time administrator could take over these. Recruit one. Probably none of you fits that bill now that your volume is growing.

★★★★ **b. Learn from other companies that do have resources.**
Absolutely. Small companies are at great risk from isolation. Often, there is no other company just like yours in your town. But remember, there are other small companies in your vicinity, *not* competitors, who would help if asked. Ask your accountant, your banker, your attorney to put you in touch with other simpatico people who can help you keep a sense of proportion and supply you with options on this and many other subjects.

★★★★ **c. Contact the Small Business Administration.**
Definitely. They provide business and management counseling as well as funding and financial advice. A phone call (see federal government listings at the back of your phone book) will often give you a dozen "leads" that you can then pursue. In your town, there may be regular monthly networking meetings of small business owners, under the SBA aegis, which will help you to break out of your isolation.

You might also want to contact the Center for Family Business, directed by Leon Danco, Cleveland, Ohio, for help with the emotion-laden problems of passing on your business to sons or daughters and with problems of command when your employees are blood relatives. Once you discover you are not alone with your problems, you begin to see options that had never occurred to you before.

Finally, you might contact S.C.O.R.E. (Service Corps

of Retired Executives) who conduct classes for small businesses on subjects you might have missed in your background. They are good contacts, too, for other resources.

☐ ★ *d.* **Hire a consultant.**

No. Hire a good professional career secretary! There is no faster or better route to getting your administration under control. A secretary with a *CPS* (Certified Professional Secretary) qualification can handle every administrative aspect of a small business with flying colors.

To locate a *professional* secretary, contact Professional Secretaries International (Kansas City, Missouri) and ask to contact the president of your local city chapter. They'll refer you. Then let your local chapter president know you are looking for a CPS holder to take over administration in your company. Take it from there. A CPS holder will not only handle your business administration, but will help with legal, accounting, data processing, and human resources decisions as well. Pay her!

PART

TWO

INVENTIVE LEADERSHIP

Outstanding leaders seem to build self-reliance in those who follow them, thus reducing the time they must spend supervising and buying more time to invent new opportunities for the whole group. They seem to *trust*, *empower*, and even *inspire* top performance from their employees and are able to upgrade output even from problem employees.

You don't need a violin accompaniment to explore exactly how these managers demonstrate trust, empowerment, and inspiration:

1. *THEY TRUST.* They seem to trust the sincerity of their people, even in adverse circumstances. Not out of naivete, but out of self-caring. As Hugh Prather puts it, they are able to accept that "everyone is innocent."[1] They treat errors and shortcomings as honest deficiencies, not malicious attacks.

   You could make such a decision consciously each day, to give yourself peace of mind, and to conserve your energies for constructive work. To assess your own trust quotient, ask yourself:

   How do I *show* my team that I trust them? (Cite some recent examples.)

   How do my staff members show they trust me? (Cite some recent examples.)

2. *THEY EMPOWER.* Inventive leaders help staff members to acknowledge their own particular strengths, to overtop the requirements of the job description. While they don't label or limit anyone, they do acknowledge to the workers which one is "our technical wizard," which person is "a born diplomat," who is "a strong negotiator." They cite examples when giving praise/thanks and encourage people to take the internal consultant's role in problem

[1]Hugh Prather, NOTES ON HOW TO LIVE IN THE WORLD . . . AND STILL BE HAPPY (Garden City, N.Y.: Doubleday & Co., Inc., 1986), p. 242.

solving. They also take great care to make their subordinates' authority known to those above and around whose cooperation will be needed in the boss's absence. If they empower someone officially, they tell others, even if those powers are temporary. How does your record stand up in this vital area?

3. *THEY INSPIRE.* For the inventive leader, this is no miracle, no maudlin aspiration. It happens every day. Hasn't it happened to you? Your face flushes, your eyes brighten, your pulse quickens when you spot a genuine opportunity and communicate it vividly to your associates and staff. Your mind immediately runs to the possibilities, and your excitement expands. People don't have to wonder if you really care about this project: they can *see* it. And you can see and hear the response of those who start to share your commitment. It's not magic, but it is contagious.

The questions that follow are not about routine leadership. They are about inspiring and leading those problem populations that take real skill to manage: marginal workers, burnout cases, cynics. While they are a small proportion of your total population at work, they take an inordinate amount of care to manage and cannot be offloaded with impunity. Inventive leaders know how to get a performance, even from problem groups.

The questioners are baffled, but inventive audience members give some good solutions. See if you agree.

5. *HOPE FOR MARGINAL WORKERS*

What real hope can I offer to marginal and minimum wage people. They can see the uncrossable gap between themselves and the high-flyers here.

AUDIENCE RESPONSES

YOUR RATING

_______ **a.** *Give lots of praise and help each person feel important.*

_______ **b.** *Introduce a profit-sharing plan.*

_______ **c.** *Show them the educational and performance steps leading to promotions; show the valuable experiences they can gain in your organization.*

_______ **d.** *Ask their predecessors who "made it" to help encourage them.*

_______ **e.** *Give them what control you can. Allow them to handle their own schedules, their own procedures. Give them a taste for self-management so that those with potential start making it.*

	★	★★	★★★	★★★★
RATING	*NO!*	*RISKY*	*BETTER*	*BEST!*

5. *HOPE FOR MARGINAL WORKERS* ANALYSIS

★★★

***a.* Give lots of praise; help each to feel important.**
Praise must be sincere and timely and tied to specific performance factors, or it will be seen as patronizing by the one you praise. Don't presume that your lowest-rung workers envy or relate to the goals of your flyers.

★★

***b.* Introduce a profit-sharing plan.**
If the plan rewards only *individual* contributions, your marginal people may get such a small share, they hardly notice it. If they are part of a group award, they may do better, but incur the resentment of the high-flyers whose "group score" is dragged down. Profit-sharing plans have attractions, but not when the workers in it are light-years apart in ability. There are other ways.

★★★★

***c.* Give them educational/experiential chances to climb.**
Now you're talking. Perhaps you were "marginal" once yourself while still a student or neophyte. But you rose, through experience and training. You can offer this to your staffers, and some will cross the gap. Other marginal employees are more patient and dogged than you imagine, in pursuit of goals that excite *them*, even though those goals might not excite your "flyers." There is always hope, always a new chance. Create and light a path.

★★★★

***d.* Ask their predecessors who "made it" to encourage them.**
Sure. Pick predecessors who won't patronize but will coach. Then cheer them on.

★★★

***e.* Give them more control of their own schedules and procedures. Let them taste self-management**
Make sure that this freedom is safe (i.e., based on procedures that increase chances of success and reduce

chances of error). Don't presume that inexperienced people want total freedom; many of us relish clear rules and standards of performance so we build confidence and sureness as we go. When teaching minimum wage people, give them good learning tools (visual and checklist-style tools) to aid memory and help them avoid repetitive questions.

6. *END OF THE ROADERS*

Some of my people are topped out young. This is the end of their career ladder.

A

AUDIENCE RESPONSES

YOUR RATING

________ **a.** *Encourage self-education to widen personal horizons and create self-esteem.*

________ **b.** *Involve them in new target projects that might advance your whole department. Give them sabbaticals; put them to work in community service as a PR gesture. Don't ignore the obvious: Could they be useful if transferred or cross-trained?*

________ **c.** *Emphasize the virtues of their current position. Not everyone wants to advance.*

________ **d.** *Ask them their longer-term career plans? What do they envision for the next five or ten years? This process should be required by your company's performance review system. Support any constructive plans they have.*

	★	★★	★★★	★★★★
RATING	*NO!*	*RISKY*	*BETTER*	*BEST!*

★

***a.* Encourage self-education to widen personal horizons and create more self-esteem.**

Why? So they'll be happy in early retirement? If these people are topped out young, suggest *paid* education in a new set of *skills* your company can *use*. They already understand the politics and background; they've already put in some good years. Don't put them out to pasture with "arts and crafts." Rebuild and use their skills.

★★★

***b.* Give them new projects that advance the whole department. Short term, think about transfers.**

Sure. Don't let spare talent and energy lie around. Put it to work. Have your "topped out" folks pursue new projects from the ground up. Have you always said, "If only we could do this?" Put them on it. What procedures need debugging? Put them on it. Who needs training? Put them on it. What needs researching? Put them on it. Ask *them* what they'd do if management said, "We don't want to lose you, we want to use you, before you top out." Listen. Save these people in whom you've already invested so much.

★★

***c.* Emphasize the virtues of the current position. Not everyone wants to advance.**

True. But how many topped-out people will you need as their technology grows familiar and the steps get consolidated and taken over by computers? Some can stay as they are. Others will have to grow or go.

★★★★

***d.* Ask them their career plans. Make it part of your performance review process.**

Absolutely. Topping out should not come as a sudden surprise to victim or boss. It should be anticipated and avoided months and years before it can happen. What my suspicious mind notices is that many companies are actually cynical in their policies about older, more experienced workers. These workers are

Often expensive per hour.

Replaceable by younger less expensive workers.

Tempting to "dump" or "early retire" before they start drawing full retirement and other benefits.

This is not so much a supervisory matter as a corporate policy issue, but your people will come to you first when they start maturing or topping out. You'd do well to probe your company's policies early before you have to fight out injustices case by case. To catch up on the ways various companies have dealt with this issue, read *Managing Human Assets* by Michael Beer, Bert Spector, et al. (The Free Press, 1984). Check your local library for current articles on retraining and early retirement—at opposite ends of this spectrum.

Comment: If your company is too small to provide career counseling for midcareer managers, suggest that people try their local YMCA/YWCA or a nonprofit organization called *Catalyst*. Both specialize in midcareer counseling for people who need to make a change but cannot see options. They often "find themselves" and start contributing again right at your company.

7. CHRONIC CYNICS

My whole group (professionals and technicians) is cynical about motivation. Any peptalk is "corny," any criticism is "punitive."

AUDIENCE RESPONSES

YOUR RATING

_________ **a.** *They don't trust you or the company. Be open and direct. Explain your reasons for needing their full cooperation. No hearts and flowers.*

_________ **b.** *Say what you feel and what you want. Ask others to be equally blunt since that is their preference.*

_________ **c.** *What is* your *motivation? Are you trying to manipulate with peptalks? Are you trying to instill guilt with your criticisms? Is this conflict coming from you or them? Perhaps they feel themselves "inner directed" and do not welcome* any *pushing from a boss. Perhaps they don't need it. Try a different tack.*

_________ **d.** *Focus them on goals; require written action plans. Make it a* numbers *game since they don't like words.*

	★	★★	★★★	★★★★
RATING	*NO!*	*RISKY*	*BETTER*	*BEST!*

7. CHRONIC CYNICS ANALYSIS

★★ **a. They don't trust you or the company. Be open and direct. Explain your reasons.**

Not a substantial cure. You can change your style from hearts and flowers to open and direct and only confuse them further. If they don't respond well to peptalks or criticism, of course, cut out both. But you're not the one who needs to talk. *They are.*

★★★★ **b. Say what you feel and what you want. Ask them to be equally blunt.**

Yes. Be prepared for some embarrassment when you hear blunt truths. But begin!

★★★ **c. Look to your own motivation. Is this question about you or them? Perhaps they are motivated already and don't need yours.**

Worth a half-hour's meditation. While we say that all human beings are already motivated in certain ways by adulthood, and cannot have motivation "planted" from outside, some studies find this to be even truer of professional and technical people. They are swayed by their technology and their power over it, not by their relationships with a boss.

When they *want* you, they'll *call* you!

★★★ **d. Focus them on goals and written action plans. They may prefer a numbers game.**

Certainly try a fresh tack; move away from the hearts and flowers approach that failed. You may assume that technicians prefer numbers to words, but many are quite at home with both. The simpler approach is to dump *any* communication ploy that fails and use the next logical *different* approach.

For already motivated people, numerical and graphic signals—charted plans with milestones and deadlines—are more welcome than are vague "do it for the Gipper" admonishments.

My favorite endorsement for graphics with motivated workers came in the wonderful book *Leaders* by Warren Bennis and Burt Nanus. They tell how the taciturn genius Bill Moog leads his controls company. When they asked Moog if his "quietness" was a drawback for his employees, he replied,

> Seems to me that when I feel strongly about something, people know it. I'm not sure how or why. I do draw pictures from time to time and send these out, or else I build a model. When we decentralized a couple of years ago, I sent around a mock-up of the way I wanted our organization to look. Drew it on graph paper . . . people seemed to get it. Made the move from one kind of organization to another—including some physical moves—without losing a day's productivity.[1]

Going graphic won't make you a genius. But if you already are one, it will help ordinary mortals to do your bidding.

Comment:

Try some inventive leadership with your cynics. A leadership technique called *Graffiti*. To get your group moving in a new situation, divide them into opposing camps and assign each a topic. For example:

> What's Great About Our Work Overload?
> What's Terrible About It?

Each camp is given a flip chart or blackboard on which its members will list (*with you out of the room*) every emotion, reaction, feeling, and consequence they can think of concerning their assigned topic. They do this in silence, but their ideas are further triggered as they see their colleagues' ideas coming out on the board. The teams must come up with a large number of entries in a short time.

You return in ten minutes. Then you and the entire group begin to analyze the two boards. Together, you

[1]Quoted by permission of William C. Moog, president, Moog, Inc.

1. Accept and validate every single emotion, good and bad, listed on the two boards.
2. Accept that these overloads *do* produce some good feelings and consequences, as well as threats.
3. Come up with ideas to reduce the bad feelings and harmful consequences of being overworked.
4. Test these "remedies" against company policy and group requirements until the group has a proposal that top management might accept—and that will give relief to the group.

Because the group can work on Graffiti anonymously, with you absent, they tend to tell the truth. They express their negative emotions without fear of reprisal.

The big surprise comes, though, from the "positive" boards because, often, the group is amazed to discover how cohesive and strong their teamwork has become. While they weren't looking.

I've tried this Graffiti exercise in many companies. At one computer manufacturer, the company had "decided" that workers were overtired and would be relieved if the monthly progress report requirement were dropped. But a Graffiti exercise, conducted just in time, showed that fourteen out of twenty participants saw the monthly report as a way they could brag about their pride in performance. Their "What's Awful" list gave management a totally different view on how to cut unnecessary effort, while leaving the Monthly Report in place.

8. *MASTERING MEETING MANIA*

Every day's calendar is littered with meetings, many not meaningful to me, but all compulsory.

AUDIENCE RESPONSES

YOUR RATING

________ **a.** *Take other work along. Your appearance at these meetings may be politically required.*

________ **b.** *Send the subordinate you deem to be an expert on the subject either to "audit" or to contribute and commit your department.*

________ **c.** *If you are senior enough, request the agenda and send a written "bid" ahead of time. Request minutes if you want to follow up.*

________ **d.** *When enough managers submit written or numerical evaluations on this meeting mania situation, a policy meeting will doubtless be held to get the meeting situation in control. Ha!*

	★	★★	★★★	★★★★
RATING	*NO!*	*RISKY*	*BETTER*	*BEST!*

★ **a. Take other work along. Just appear, for politics' sake.**
Many managers do this. It insults whoever is speaking. If meeting arrangers would set up an agenda and stick to the times, your company could install a policy called "floating attendance" where executives could show up only for *their portion* of a larger meeting, to hear the relevant data, vote, and depart. Consider this. Their commitment can be short and courteous.

b. Send a subordinate expert to listen or vote.
An excellent practice. In large hierarchical organizations, you'll have to "sell" this to top management and really *trust* your subordinates. But inventive leaders can.

c. Request an agenda; send your ideas ahead; request minutes to follow up.
A low-cost way for powerful people to participate.

d. Track the waste; call for a policy change.
As suggested earlier in this chapter, keep a "dot track" record headed as follows:

> *Meetings:* a. Needed to be there . . . b. Waste of time . . . c. Should have sent subordinate . . .

Count the dots collected in each category in a month. Submit your findings, and ask colleagues to do so.

Comment: At least when you call a meeting yourself, you can ensure that others will not count it a waste of *their* time. Follow this procedure: start practicing with weekly staff meetings:

1. Always send an agenda in advance. For emergency meetings, put your agenda up on the blackboard/flip chart first.

2. *Time* each item on the agenda. Stick to these limits. It helps people concentrate.

3. Note on your flip chart the outcome or decision on each item. When people see outcomes up on the wall, they have the *action minutes* in front of them.

4. Responsible or concerned parties should copy these *action minutes* into their own notes; no typed postmeeting minutes are required. If people disagree, they must speak up now or prepare to "hold their peace" after the meeting.

5. For regular staff meetings, do not upgrade leftover items from previous meetings. Instead, each item, old or new, must fight its way to the top of the list according to its importance or impact, not its age. This teaches people to order by impact, not by urgency or age of an item.

6. If an agenda item keeps sinking to a low spot on your staff meeting agenda, assign it to a subcommittee for research or action; get it off your main agenda.

7. Poll the members of your regular staff meetings for agenda items they want to propose for the next meeting. Note these "on the wall" for all to see. You can get agreement with the group as to which future meeting will consider these items.

8. Never censor a suggested item, but you can assign it to a subgroup if it requires further research or work-up before coming under group scrutiny.

9. Be sure to inform senior management, in writing, of recommendations or positive results achieved in your meetings. Your meeting must gain commitment, not only from members but from management, too.

10. Finally, consider rotating the chairmanship duties among your staffers. It provides training and encourages greater commitment.

Carry these habits over, even to your informal meetings. When someone wanders into your office for an informal meeting, grab an index card, jot down what subjects your visitor wants to cover and how much time should be spent on each. Two or three notations on a card can constitute an agenda. Stick to it. When the card is done, so is the meeting.

PART

THREE

DISPLAYING COHERENT VALUES

How do you radiate your sense of values? Your excitement about your company's work and progress? Your sense of justice and fair play? What signals do you use to announce your commitment to

Productivity?

Inventiveness?

Excellence?

Perseverence?

Openness?

How do you show your admiration and thanks when your team turns in a top performance? What word would people use to describe the *climate* you've created as a leader in your department or company? Is it *fun* to work for you? How?

HOW'S YOUR FINESSE UNDER FIRE?

How do you handle failure? disappointment? danger? Your subordinates watch you very carefully when things start going wrong. Even if you're a "yeller"—so long as you are consistent—people know what to expect; your troops may be able to stay effective during a crisis. It's the unpredictable boss—the person with severe mood swings—who cannot lead coherently during the ups and downs of a business week.

If you suffer from mood swings, see a doctor and check your chemical intake: alcohol, coffee, cigarettes, and sugar. Then review your "coping skills" and start making some changes in the direction of consistency.

A powerful manager uses "wins" to build team confidence. But that manager also uses "losses" to build team resourcefulness. A smart manager never discounts the learning value of a loss. I know one brilliant manager who makes that her first question during a disaster: "What am I able to learn from this?" She writes it down in a yellow pad, and *answers it*!

If you take risks, you are bound to err on occasion. These errors give you and your team practice in three vital areas:

1. Fixing errors quickly and quietly: *damage control.*
2. Making net gains despite temporary losses: *bottom line.*
3. Seeking help when you dare not fly solo: *alliance building.*

A successful turnaround can build confidence and self-worth even better than a straight win. Getting help from adjoining departments and managers shows your team that you have made friends and created obligations that you can call in when you need them. No one wants to work for an isolated boss who hides adversity.

DOES YOUR CONFIDENCE CALM PEOPLE?

Recently, I stood in a hallway with a group of people. Their boss walked by, and they looked me in the eye and said—admiringly—"he's a cool customer." This manager has convinced his troops that he can spot and evade the traps and snares that await around every political corner in their organization.

Yes, your people watch how you handle yourself in those subtle contests for power in your organization. They watch how deftly you parry with critics, how you move through political maelstroms, how you sidestep scandals, how you score in contests for power, without denting your integrity.

The questioners you'll meet next aren't "cool customers" yet, but some of their respondents are. See if you would agree with their advice.

9. HANDLING CRITICISM COOLLY

How can I handle critics with dignity when they tackle me in meetings or other groups?

AUDIENCE RESPONSES

YOUR RATING

_________ **a.** *Be fully prepared for meetings. Find the soft spots in your proposals and be ready with options. Have a smart friend play devil's advocate before you face the bad guys.*

_________ **b.** *Listen. Your critics may have good points. Consider the "what" and respond to it, even though you abhor the "how" of the criticism.*

_________ **c.** *Believe in your own worth as a person; then accept that others have a right to their opinions. Make your proposals easy to accept, concrete, nonthreatening.*

_________ **d.** *Having been warned, arrange to meet your potential critics* before *the meeting. Work things out then. If faced with sudden anger/hostility in a meeting, diffuse the heat by inviting the attacker to state clearly: "What it is he needs." (This gets him off the subject of* you.*)*

	★	★★	★★★	★★★★
RATING	*NO!*	*RISKY*	*BETTER*	*BEST!*

Four stars to all four answers combined. Congratulations: All respondents avoided sarcasm, defensiveness. Instead, they propose preparation, openness to others' comments, self-caring, and focusing the attacker's attention on what's still possible.

Comment: To respond to private criticism brought by your boss—when you realize you must show a new commitment to renew your boss's trust:

- Be sure to let your executive know that you've adjusted after a criticism and are grateful for constructive advice. Put it in writing.
- Don't reiterate your "shortcoming" which caused the critique. Instead, cite the positive pointer you were given and show how you will use it. This eases your own pain, puts the past behind you, shows your new commitment, and reduces any discomfort your critic felt when taking you to task.

Here's how your memo might read: "Thanks for taking time yesterday to help me with good advice. Here's how I plan to carry out your suggestions:

Starting immediately I will . . .

To follow up, I will . . .

I will keep you informed of results by (date).

Thanks for your interest in my programs."

10. CAN YOU BE BOSS AND FRIEND?

How can I manage to remain an authority figure and still have close relationships with my subordinates?

AUDIENCE RESPONSES

YOUR RATING

_________ **a.** *Give up wanting close relationships with subordinates. If you try to be close, you'll lose your ability to perform your supervisory responsibilities. "It's lonely at the top" just as they say.*

_________ **b.** *It is impossible to remain an authority figure and have close relationships at the same time. If you risk having these relationships, you must be able to communicate and get the respect of the employee at the same time.*

_________ **c.** *You can't! You will find that you must remain on a higher plane when in management. Otherwise, you run into trouble with subordinates who want you to be more friend than supervisor.*

_________ **d.** *Nice goal but not always possible. Better to develop your close friendships outside of work.*

	★	★★	★★★	★★★★
RATING	*NO!*	*RISKY*	*BETTER*	*BEST!*

10. CAN YOU BE BOSS AND FRIEND? ANALYSIS

★ ***a.* Give up wanting close relationships. It's lonely at the top.**

Nonsense. It will be lonely from bottom to top if you adopt this idea. If brought in from outside, you might choose a remote stance from the start. Even then, you will find yourself drawn into natural friendships with subordinates whose characters you come to esteem.

On the other hand, when you're promoted from within (something that will happen much more often), you can hardly dump a person who was a friend only yesterday, as soon as you move up. Relax. Allow the pressure of your new responsibilities to alter, gently, the *pattern* of your friendly contacts without undermining their value. Your new job will demand more thinking/deciding time. Many lunch hours will be occupied with new contacts among your new peers. You'll regret the loss of opportunities to mingle with your old buddies; don't be afraid to tell them so.

For those close friends who used to meet you after work, continue this if you can. But openly discuss new pressures on discretion and fairness. You musn't be seen to flaunt your friendship in front of other subordinates. You, the boss, will have to be fair and detached when handing out assignments. Even with good friends, one simple rule must be clearly stated from the start. In a dispute, you—as the responsible party—must make the final decision, even though you take advice and opinion from any or all of your team members.

★ ***b.* It's impossible for authorities to be close friends. If you risk it, you must communicate for respect.**

No, to the first statement. ★★★ Yes, to the second. If you practice effective communication and avoid playing favorites on assignments, critiques, promotions, raises, if you invite people to air their legitimate worries, and keep a climate where joy and thanks, as well as doubts and objections, are welcome, you can retain and nurture your friendships. Many successful businesses are built on friendships that weather the storms of business/political life. What it takes is maturity and openness.

c. **You can't. Subordinates will want you to be more friend than supervisor.**
Surprise, surprise. You may find that your subordinates actually want you to be more supervisor than friend. Make no assumptions. Instead, make a new agreement and revise as you go.

★★★

d. **This not always possible. Better develop friends outside of work.**
Correct. Not *always* possible, but quite often, it is. Still, while I rhapsodize about friendships made at work, I agree that you need (and doubtless enjoy) friendships from your private life. They help you to maintain your equilibrium when—from time to time—everyone at work would like your head on a plate—and the feeling is mutual!

Nickerson's Recommendations

For a four-star answer, start with *d*, and then accept that for you, friendships are always *possible* across the boss/subordinate line, whenever shared interests and personalities attract. Don't give yourself unnecessary tension by setting rigid limits on friendships.

Comment: Friendship is a bonus, not the primary mission of your career pursuit. As your interests come into tight focus in midlife, you will concentrate intensely on achieving certain goals, and you will develop some deep, warm, and lasting friendships with people who join you in your vital pursuits. You will come to appreciate one another, warts and all, as you fight and win business battles together.

I look around me at friendships made decades ago which flourish across continents and oceans. Teams of boss/secretary, president/VP, supervisor/workers built important relationships and then went to the trouble of nurturing them to maturity, despite temporary setbacks and disappointments . . . and other people's mischief. Trying to *avoid* friendships, simply because of power differentials, will put an unnecessary chill on your life. Take the risk; the warmth is worth it.

11. TAKING SIDES IN A SCANDAL

How do I handle people who corner me during a political scandal and grill me for an opinion on the latest corporate stupidity?

AUDIENCE RESPONSES

YOUR RATING

________ **a.** *Ignore it. Put your head down and do the best job you can. Be careful; you'll be quoted.*

________ **b.** *Put up with it. Slander is still the favorite pastime of many. You cannot outlaw it. All organizations relish these juicy political scandals.*

________ **c.** *Depends on the situation. In some cases, cooperate with the complainer. In some, be friendly, benign, detached. Ignore others, or simply reverse the question.*

	★	★★	★★★	★★★★
RATING	*NO!*	*RISKY*	*BETTER*	*BEST!*

★★ ***a.*** **Put your head down; you'll be quoted.**
Ignoring or evading may not work. Suppose the questioner is your boss? A powerful person looking for support? A sincere questioner using you as a sounding board? You'd owe such a person a reply. You have many choices. You can give a sincere opinion. You can say honestly that you have no solution to offer that you could guarantee. Or you could answer a question with another question such as, "You seem deeply concerned about this. Have you thought of some solutions to propose?" Then let the person talk, and reply at a minimum. In this way, you avoid damning anyone, or taking sides—yet, you allow the other person to ventilate. If you are afraid that your nods and grunts will be taken as assent, you can close the conversation by saying, "I see it's a complex question. I don't feel able to take sides with the information at hand. But good luck . . ."

b. **Put up with it. Slander is a favorite pastime.**
This attitude may help you cope, but it does not help you respond in the situation. You must still find and express some responses, verbal or nonverbal.

c. It depends; cooperate, detach, ignore, or reverse the question.
Here's the right answer. Let's flesh out some details:

Cooperate: You may agree with the "griller" and have some solutions you want to explore. Do so.

Detach: You may feel that the problem is not your specialty or your business. In such a case you could reply, "I prefer not to comment since I have no expertise to contribute to a solution. Perhaps you could take your problem to Dept X." (In this way, you won't seem uncaring, but you will merely acknowledge that you aren't qualified to comment.)

Ignore: In instances where the questioner is merely idle and has no power over your fortunes, it really is all right to say "Beats me" . . . or "I wasn't aware of any problem . . ." and just keep on with what you were doing.

Reverse: Again—with idlers or sincere grillers, you can safely reverse by saying, "I have no immediate reaction. Did you want me to know your views on this?" Anything the questioner now says is clearly at his or her own risk. If you use a "benign and detached"—never sarcastic tone as *c* suggests you'll be okay.

Comment: Here's a tool for use when faced by a risky question: Whether your reply is declarative or interrogatory, make sure it concerns the future—that is, what we should do next. Never go back to the past in your replies or remarks; otherwise, you may sink to blaming or criticizing. Instead, go forward. Both your words and body language should reach forward to the future, never backward to the past, when you are faced by an embarrassing question or a grilling.

12. SELF-SACRIFICE VERSUS SELF-INTEREST

My people are "out for number one." How can I show our employees that the needs of the organization outweigh any personal considerations?

AUDIENCE RESPONSES

YOUR RATING

________ **a.** *You can't. It's not true.*

________ **b.** *Show how meeting the organization's goals may enhance their personal needs. Show how certain self-seeking behaviors may damage the organization and, eventually, the employee.*

________ **c.** *Build a sense of ownership and pride in their attaining corporate goals. Share more information. They can't embrace what they don't know about.*

________ **d.** *Has your company earned loyalty and sacrifice from its employees? Does it give training and promotion? Is your company faithful to customers with quality products and services. If people see shortfalls in company performance, they feel no obligation to keep up the hypocrisy.*

	★	★★	★★★	★★★★
RATING	*NO!*	*RISKY*	*BETTER*	*BEST!*

12. *SELF-SACRIFICE VERSUS SELF-INTEREST* ANALYSIS

★★★★ **a. You can't show people that the organization comes first. It doesn't.**

Correct. Although you could not make this stick in the military. In wartime, the army's needs come first: Your life is expendable. But private corporations cannot operate that way. As Maslow and Herzberg showed, the employee's needs for physical safety and job security are neither trivial nor optional. They come *before* and as a *condition* of dedicated performance.

Even when physical and security needs are adequately met, people may exercise their choice to quit or malinger if they are dissatisfied with social and achievement opportunities at your organization. You cannot show a free employee how your organization's need comes before theirs. They must decide this for themselves, case by case and day by day. Luckily, with good companies and proud employees, this decision is usually made in your favor.

★★★ **b. Show how meeting your needs may enhance theirs. Show how failure may damage theirs.**

You'd better be specific and convincing. In a typical case, long-term career damage seems remote to an employee bent on taking a day off to go fishing, just when you need him. Your employee is committed to "calling in sick." Your philosophy won't outvote the sunshine and fishing rod.

★★★★ **c. Build a sense of ownership and pride in attaining corporate goals.**

Contests, credit and thanks, celebrations, tangible rewards, excitement, publicity . . . all can help to build "ownership" and pride in employees—at least in the majority. (Tolerate the small proportion of workers who are as numb to your goals and rewards as they are to the rest of the universe. They'll go along for the ride, while the best of your people steer and accelerate!)

d. **Has your company earned loyalty and sacrifice? Is it faithful to employees, customers. Or is hypocrisy rampant?**

Good questions. If normally good people start "looking out for number one," you can bet there's a threat to their security. People are quite sane to protect themselves when they face physical or security threats. At such times, your company must avoid silence, delay or prevarication. Ironically, companies often "clam up" when a genuine threat appears—just when they should be most open and communicative. They fear making promises they cannot keep or "coming clean" when they've made a mistake. But employees lose heart when they witness hypocrisy. While giving a good example won't necessarily make your employees "good," giving a bad example is very likely to make them falter.

FINE TUNING: PACING YOURSELF FOR THE LONG CLIMB

Staying promotable means staying awake—consistently alert, ready to chase opportunities and solve problems. Promotable managers may get tired, but they seldom look it. How do you develop and sustain the energy an ambitious manager needs to stay promotable?

WHERE PROMOTABLES GET THEIR ENERGY

1. ***Conviction:*** The promotable managers I meet are in absolutely no doubt about what they want. They are not ambiguous about moving up. They are certain they have the mental and technical equipment to trail blaze and the right, almost God-given, to lead others on that trail.
2. ***Connectedness:*** They are independent minded, but politically aware and interested in what others are doing—especially powerful others. They swap information for information, help for help; they build alliances and mutual debts with people whose values they share or whose help they need; they "get along," without "going along." They approve of "politics" as a necessary lubricant between powerful forces running fast, side by side.
3. ***Clarity:*** They know what constitutes "their own business," and they neither interfere nor volunteer for duty with other people's quagmires.
4. ***Creativity:*** Promotable people relish problem solving. They find it fun to invent, innovate, and play "what if" with people from

several disciplines and viewpoints. They love an argument if the explosion produces new combinations of opinion for synergy. They're never satisfied; they like to push for something beyond the obvious. They tinker, until they get a result worth exploiting.

5. ***Commitment:*** Promotable managers are dogged in the pursuit of their objectives. They can concentrate mind and energy for long periods to get a result. They don't watch the clock; they are absorbed in the hunt and intent on achieving victory. Their compulsion is by choice.

Without these traits, you may eke out your early promotions and reach a moderate level of management, but you won't be in the running for the long climb.

Still, conviction, connectedness, creativity, clarity, and commitment are not rarities. You may well have more than your share of all of them. In that case, you need only some fine tuning to help you maintain and restore energy whenever you meet the roadblocks and disappointments that dog all good risk takers.

HOW TO DEVELOP STAYING POWER

- *Maintain visibility.* Conduct and contribute to meetings where your expertise can be helpful. Prepare good punchy presentations and make them available to people who need them. Help your enterprise celebrate it's high points. Emblazon victories on the wall.
- *Discriminate among tasks.* There will always be someone wanting to dump busywork on a "do-it-now" department like yours. Help them see *where* it can get done quickly and cheaply, but be careful that it's not left with you. Stick to your own knitting, be sympathetic or admiring about other people's.
- *Develop broad interests.* While you concentrate and contribute well in your area of specialty, explore the accomplishments of other departments and mix with those people genially. You may need them some day. It's better if they know you first.
- *Enhance your image.* Look, speak, and dress the part of the job you want, not the job you've got. Don't ignore status symbols: Use them.
- *Track and translate your results.* Make your victories meaningful to others. If you achieve a technical breakthrough, for example, find out what percentage sales increase it promises, and say so to the sales people. Know what cost reduction it portends, and say so to the comptroller.

- *Coordinate your personal and professional lives.* As much as you can, *balance* your work and home life so you are not attempting a "big push" at home simultaneously with a "big push" at work. Coordinate with your family, and give them quality time when things slow down, by design, at the corporation. *Ask* for R&R time when senior management is feeling grateful for current triumphs. If you don't ask, you won't get.
- *Display an attitude of gratitude.* The next dark time you burn the midnight oil and ask yourself, "Why did I ever get into this?" grab a sheet of paper and start listing the parts of your job that make you feel competent, in control, contributory to the good of humankind, happy, sane, glorious. You'll come up with quite a list. You'll get through the gloom of the current drudgery, and back on track.

You may want to add a few of your own self-propelling tools at this point. Then read the rigorous list of "Musts for Promotability" that follows.

CHECKLIST: TEN MUSTS FOR PROMOTABILITY

1. Plan each year's work against clear, quantified objectives. Be sure that your goals tie directly to senior management objectives and that they are seen as *central/crucial* to the enterprise. Discuss and agree the list with your boss.
2. See that more than half your time is spent on planning/priority setting/development issues: new products, markets, services, cost saving ideas. Shoot for 20 percent *new* meaningful programs or projects each year. Otherwise, you can become a "fixture" department and lose momentum.
3. Delegate work. Develop, cross-train, and coordinate your people's efforts. Avoid any post where you do the same repetitive work as your people for significant periods. Such "pseudomanagerial" assignments will hold you back.
4. Actively prepare your budget requests and cost-control programs. No matter how nonfinancial your background, you must stay on top of the dollars. Top management does, and this *knowledge is power* in negotiations.
5. Create a demand, internally, for your department's service or expertise. Constantly seek to increase the group's contribution by working smarter. Advertise: Celebrate your group's achievements.
6. Negotiate. Assert what you need to get more value out of each workday. Don't stint on budget for equipment, people, or space that will help you excel. Make it attractive and low risk for your executive level to approve your request.
7. Make your boss look good, particularly new bosses or appointees who may need to learn the local ropes from you. Graciousness now will pay off when the boss comes into full power.

8. Build alliances; exchange help and information with fellow managers. Being "on the team" is vital for your reputation and will keep you "in the know" when change is imminent.

9. Extend yourself. Join the leading professional group in your industry. Being well known to suppliers, competitors, and industry leaders heightens your reputation back home.

10. Revitalize. Don't drudge endlessly, neglecting weekends and vacations. Never move straight from one exhausting project to the next. You need energy and alertness to stay promotable. If you're buoyant in this job, you've got a chance at a better one: You STAY PROMOTABLE.

For further information on
Pat Nickerson's seminars and books, contact:

Pat Nickerson
FOUR STAR MANAGEMENT WORKSHOPS
386 East H. Street, Suite 209
Chula Vista, CA 92010.
(619) 691-8820

A

B

C

D

E

F

G

H

I

J

K

L